D1602905

WITHDRAWN

International Conflict Resolution

International Conflict Resolution

The U.S.-USSR and Middle East Cases

Louis Kriesberg

Yale University Press   New Haven and London

Published with assistance from the Louis Stern Memorial Fund.

Library of Congress Cataloging-in-Publication Data
Kriesberg, Louis
International conflict resolution : the U.S.–USSR and
Middle East cases / Louis Kriesberg.
p. cm.
Includes bibliographical references and index.
ISBN 0-300-05175-1
1. Pacific settlement of international disputes.
2. Diplomatic negotiations in international disputes.
3. Conflict management.   4. United States—Foreign
relations—Soviet Union.   5. Soviet Union—Foreign
relations—United States.   6. Israel-Arab
conflicts.   I. Title.
JX4473.K75   1992
341.5'2—dc20   91-30305 CIP

Designed by Sonia Scanlon
Set in Times Roman type by
Keystone Typesetting, Inc., Orwigsburg, Pennsylvania.
Printed in the United States of America by
Edwards Brothers, Ann Arbor, Michigan.

The paper in this book meets the guidelines for permanence
and durability of the Committee on Production Guidelines
for Book Longevity of the Council on Library Resources.

10 9 8 7 6 5 4 3 2 1

To the many persons who, with little
recognition, have worked with their
counterparts in adversary nations to create
solutions to conflicts or have worked with
compatriots to promote peace and
reconciliation with adversaries.

Contents

Abbreviations

ABM   antiballistic missile
ACC   Arab Cooperation Council
ASAT   antisatellite [weapons]
CAT   conventional arms transfer
CCD   [UN] Conference of the Committee on Disarmament
       (formerly ENDC)
CCP   Conciliation Commission for Palestine
CFE   Conventional Armed Forces in Europe
CIES   Council for International Exchange of Scholars
COPDAB Conflict and Peace Data Bank
CPSU   Communist Party of the Soviet Union
CSCE   Conference on Security and Cooperation in Europe
CTB   comprehensive test ban
ENDC   Eighteen-Nation Disarmament Committee (changed
       to CCD, September 1969)
GCD   general and complete disarmament
GRIT   Graduated Reciprocation in Tension-Reduction
ICBM   intercontinental ballistic missiles
ICFTU International Confederation of Free Trade Unions
IGY   International Geophysical Year
INF   Intermediate-range Nuclear Forces
IREX   International Research and Exchanges Board
ISA   International Sociological Association
MBFR   Mutual Balanced Force Reduction
MIRVs Multiple Indepently Targetable Re-entry Vehicles
NAS   National Academy of Sciences
NATO   North Atlantic Treaty Organization
NORC   National Opinion Research Center
NPT   Non-Proliferation Treaty
NRDC   Natural Resources Defense Council
OAS   Organization of American States
OPEC   Organization of Petroleum Exporting Countries

PDFLP	Popular Democratic Front for the Liberation of Palestine
PFLP	Popular Front for the Liberation of Palestine
PLO	Palestine Liberation Organization
PNC	Palestine National Council
PNE	peaceful nuclear explosions
PRC	People's Republic of China
PTBT	Partial Test Ban Treaty
SALT	Strategic Arms Limitation Talks
SANE	(National Committee for a) Sane Nuclear Policy
SCC	Standing Consultative Commission
SDI	Strategic Defense Initiative
SIPRI	Stockholm International Peace Research Institute
START	Strategic Arms Reduction Talks
TTB	threshold test ban
TTBT	Threshold Test Ban Treaty
UAE	United Arab Emirates
UNDC	United Nations Disarmament Commission
UNEF	United Nations Emergency Force
USIA	United States Information Agency
VOA	Voice of America
WTO	Warsaw Treaty Organization

Preface

This book has been long in the making. Several years ago, recognizing that the role of persuasion and of positive sanctions in waging international conflicts had not been given much attention, I began to investigate how such inducements were actually employed in specific conflicts. I soon began to focus on de-escalation efforts and achievements as the likely occasions to use them. Most research on international conflict has concentrated on crises and the outbreak of wars, as if they would provide lessons about avoiding war and making peace; but relatively little research has been focused on de-escalation and peacemaking. I entered this neglected field by examining major de-escalation attempts in the conflicts between Israel and its neighbors and between the United States and the Soviet Union.

After a few years of research and writing on selected instances of de-escalation, I saw the need for a comprehensive treatment of the phenomenon. My work on the project was affected by the rapid developments in the theory and practice of conflict resolution and by the evolving U.S.–USSR and Middle East conflicts.

As the writing of the book was well under way, the transformation in the Soviet Union and in East–West relations became dramatically apparent. That transformation confirmed many of the ideas advanced in this book. There is good evidence supporting the conflict resolution approach and its contributions to explaining the end of the cold war and the failure, until now, to achieve transforming resolutions to the conflicts between Israel and its Arab neighbors.

The analysis presented in this book helps to explain the course of other international conflicts not examined here. It therefore has implications for international conflict resolution theory and for policies to be pursued by persons seeking to advance peace.

I am indebted to a multitude of persons for their contributions to the writing and production of this book. They have provided information and insight about the issues examined here and guidance about how to communicate my findings and interpretations to readers.

Many people kindly met with me for interviews, and several of them are cited in the Notes for the book. In addition, the writing has benefited by conversations and encounters with friends, colleagues, and members of various partisan groups. Among the very many persons whose information and insight contributed to this work are: Richard Ablin and Batya Ablin, Vladimir G. Andreenkov, Yaacov Bar-Siman-Tov, Robert H. Baraz, Elise Boulding, Mark A. Heller, Saad Eddin Ibrahim, Dafna and Dove Izraeli, Egbert Jahn, Elihu Katz, Herbert Kelman, Viktor Kremenyuk, Daniel A. Kriesberg, Joseph A. Kriesberg, Lois A. Kriesberg, Martin Kriesberg, James Laue, Milton Leitenberg, Saul H. Mendlovitz, John Nagle, Terrell A. Northrup, Yosef Olmert, Jeffrey Z. Rubin, Harold Saunders, Edward Said, Carolyn M. Stephenson, Salim Tamari, Stephen Tiedtke, I. William Zartman, and Yuri A. Zamoshkin.

The research on which the book is based was aided by support from the Syracuse University Senate Research Fund. In addition, a grant from the John O. and Catherine T. MacArthur Foundation supported a pilot study on the assessment of positive inducements in international conflicts. The William and Flora Hewlett Foundation has provided basic funding for the Program on the Analysis and Resolution of Conflicts (PARC), based in Syracuse University's Maxwell School of Citizenship and Public Affairs. PARC has provided me with a stimulating and supportive environment for my work. Several graduate students have helped in gathering data or in doing other work that contributed to this book, notably Lisa Boro, Douglas Challenger, Susan French, and Ross A. Klein.

I am indebted to my colleagues in the Syracuse Area Middle East Dialogue group (SAMED) for helping me to understand how people from presumed adversary groups feel as well as think and how they might resolve their differences. SAMED, with equal numbers of Americans of Jewish, Palestinian, and "other" identities, has been meeting since 1981.

Several people read chapters of the manuscript, and I am grateful for their comments and suggestions; they include: Nish Jamgotch, Christopher R. Mitchell, Martin Patchen, Thomas Princen, Stuart J. Thorson, and the anonymous reviewers of the manuscript.

I wish to thank Irving Kriesberg for his thorough editing of the manuscript and for his helpful critiques of my writing style. Anica Sturdivant not only helped in redoing drafts of the book, but ably prepared the map and some of the graphics in the book. I also want to express my appreciation to Gladys Topkis of Yale University Press, who encouraged me to complete the book in a fashion that would make it attractive and accessible, and to Lorraine Alexson who skillfully did the final editing.

1

The Quest for Peace

onflicts in world affairs, as in other arenas of social life, are frequent and often persistent. Yet particular international conflicts *do* end, sometimes with mutually beneficial settlements and sometimes with enduring and mutually acceptable accommodations. Although nearly everyone wants peace, most people seek other goals as well: many strive for individual and collective freedom or for justice; many want equality; some even insist upon recognition of their superiority or acceptance of their view of what constitutes *the* true religion or ideology. Our quest, therefore, is to understand how to build peace without jeopardizing other important values.

In this book I consider two major sets of conflicts over more than forty years—one resulting in growing accommodations, the other leading to partial settlements among some adversaries but increasing animosity among others. The first, the U.S.-USSR conflict, now offers the prospect of enhanced peaceful relations; the second, the Arab-Israeli conflict, seems to be far from resolution despite intense wars and peacemaking efforts. I examine the record of many efforts to reduce international tension and to move toward peace in these two cases. In comparing alternative ideas about peacemaking, I seek to account for the relative success and failure of those efforts.

Analyzing past efforts can help us to improve future attempts only if we draw the correct lessons and apply them effectively.[1] In the West, for example, the lesson drawn from the failure to maintain peace and prevent World War II was that appeasement does not pay. That oversimplified lesson guided and misguided much of U.S. conduct toward the Soviet Union after the war. With greater insight into the reasons for past successes and failures, we are less likely to neglect opportunities for de-escalation and less likely to pursue mistaken efforts at peacemaking.

In social life, conflicts are inherent; they occur within and among organizations, communities, social classes, and countries. But they are too often managed in ways that harm the conflicting parties. Here, peace within or among countries refers not to the absence of conflict but to the process of handling conflicts so that they do not escalate into large-scale violence.[2] Peacemaking includes developing relations among adversaries that are not threatening and entail mutual dependence, thereby raising the cost of conflict escalation. Peacemaking also includes the development of shared rules and procedures for settling disputes.

Countries that are physically, economically, and socially isolated from one other can easily avoid war; for parties that cannot avoid relations, however, preventing war is more complicated. It might be possible for adversaries to have recurrent confrontations and yet stop each crisis from erupting into war through skilled diplomacy; even confrontations are made unlikely by becoming so highly integrated that war would be nearly inconceivable, as is the case, for example, between the United States and Canada.

A struggle persists when the adversaries cannot agree on the terms of settlement; each party says it wants peace, but only on terms that are unacceptable to its opponents. Thus, an escalation of the conflict may necessarily precede a transition to de-escalation, as it did after the Iraqi invasion of Kuwait (see Epilogue). Concluding an international agreement, therefore, is not enough; the terms of settlement do matter.

There are groups that romanticize fighting, dying, and killing as noble efforts to advance various goals—among them a just peace. There are people who accept violence, even war, as a regrettable necessity, while others reject all or particular means of violence, even when the end is peace. The U.S. National Council of Catholic Bishops, for example, has put on record that it does "not perceive any situation in which the deliberate initiation of nuclear war, on however restricted a scale, can be morally justified. Non-nuclear attacks by another state must be resisted by other than nuclear means."[3]

Given the varying conceptions and priorities of peace, deciding how to de-escalate a conflict is not simple. Although people have killed others and have died themselves to bring about peace, warfare has frequently failed to produce peace and has become increasingly devastating. Others have sought to placate an adversary as a means of securing peace, a route that has also sometimes failed.

We need to be as realistic about resolving international conflicts as we are about making war, considering immediate and long-term consequences. Such realism requires having a strategy. Being tough is a posture, not a strategy, and the same is true of being conciliatory. We should consider what mixtures of toughness and conciliation are needed for which purposes in different circumstances. We also need to consider what combination of parties and issues in particular situations contribute to effective de-escalation and peacemaking.

Peacemaking includes a wide range of actions, from ending a war to building integrated relations. My focus here is the course of these efforts to lessen tension and settle particular disputes in constructing the building blocks of integration.[4] President John F. Kennedy's June 1963 speech at American University makes this point: "I am not referring to the absolute, infinite concept of universal peace and good will of which some fantasists and fanatics dream. . . . Let us focus instead on a more practical, more attainable peace, based not on a sudden revolution in human nature but on a gradual evolution in human institutions—on a series of concrete actions and effective agreements which are in the interest of all concerned. . . . For peace is a process, a way of solving problems."[5]

To move from intense conflict to enduring peaceful relations, from a constant threat of war to a relationship in which war is improbable, requires many de-escalation steps. Although that journey might be thought to begin with the total defeat of one party, defeat is never total and victory never permanent. Even approximations are rare in international affairs. Thus, years after the fiercest warfare and the unconditional surrender of Nazi Germany, signs posted in East Berlin read, "Hitlers come and go, but the

German people remain.—J. Stalin." Although governments fall, nations persist and erstwhile adversaries must work out mutually acceptable terms one step at a time. This is clearly the case for the conflicts examined here. None of the parties involved is able to impose a final settlement.

Phases of De-escalation

One obvious, effective way to lessen the likelihood of violence in international affairs is to reduce the antagonism between adversaries—a long-term process. That process can be examined in four phases: initiating de-escalation, undertaking negotiations, reaching agreements, and sustaining agreements.

The first phase centers on two questions: Why does hostility between adversaries begin to diminish when it does? and, When are initiatives taken to reduce antagonism? The answers to these questions will suggest when the time is right to undertake peacemaking initiatives. But initiatives may be dismissed as propaganda, ignored, or even exploited. In the second phase, we need to know what leads to sufficient reciprocation for negotiations to be undertaken. Not all negotiations result in agreements, however. In the case of the U.S.-USSR conflict, negotiations on the reduction of conventional NATO and Warsaw Pact military forces in Europe were begun in 1975 but were not concluded until unilateral actions in 1989 transformed the Warsaw Pact. Understanding why some negotiations—the third phase—fail to conclude in agreements will help us to develop negotiation strategies that result in satisfactory agreements. Agreements may not be implemented or may not endure. They may even lead to renewed antagonism if expectations are raised and then frustrated or if one or more of the parties come to regard the agreements as unfair or believe they have been violated. Thus several U.S.-USSR treaties were concluded during the early 1970s, the period of relaxed tension known as détente. To some U.S. critics of détente, its decline in the late 1970s was the result of its flaws.[6] The agreements of détente, they allege, placed the United States at a disadvantage that the Soviets exploited. Considering when and how agreements are sustained—the fourth phase—should suggest when it is preferable not to reach an agreement as well as what strategy can lead to an agreement that is likely to be beneficial in the long run.

Figure 1 illustrates that these four phases do not constitute the only possible sequence of de-escalation. Conflicts may de-escalate implicitly, either unilaterally or jointly. Most initiatives result not in explicit negotiations but in escalation, continuation of the status quo, or tacit bargaining. Similarly, many negotiations conclude not in an explicit accord but in an

Figure 1   De-escalation Steps

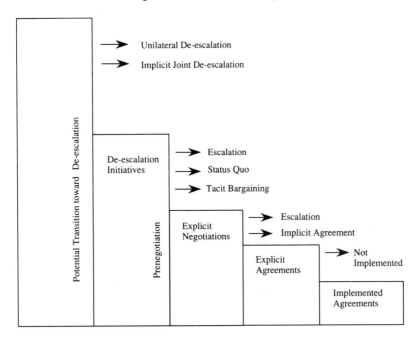

implicit agreement or escalation. Finally, some agreements may be signed but not implemented or sustained.

Theoretical Approaches

In trying to answer the questions posed here, I draw a great deal from the relatively new conflict resolution approach. I compare the major older approaches to the study of international relations and then consider how they supplement conflict resolution ideas.

The many theoretical perspectives that have been applied to international affairs, fall into three broad categories: statism, populism, and pluralism. These general approaches make different assumptions about the way the world is structured and how major players perform; they also often implicitly assign high priority to different values and the ideas they provide about the de-escalation of international conflicts are sometimes contradictory.

Statism   The traditional statist, state-centric, or realist perspective is the dominant international relations approach. The analysts who developed statism and those who apply it are particularly interested in understanding war and crisis. They view the state as a unitary entity that operates according to a clearly ranked set of values and interests (or utilities), choosing policies rationally in terms of relative costs and benefits. As articulated by Hans Morgenthau in the 1950s, statism also tends to be conventional, tough-minded, and power centered.[7] Its adherents argue that their own leaders in a struggle must be tough in order to convince an aggressive adversary to settle a conflict on reasonable terms. De-escalation emerges from a balance of power or from the overwhelming superiority of one party. The statist approach has dominated interpretations of international relations, and its description of the world is often used by government officials to justify their actions. Believing in statism and acting according to its terms help to make it a reality.

Critics of the statist approach correctly observe that it implies the belief that peace is based only upon military strength—a position C. Wright Mills called "crackpot realism."[8] Critics also justifiably note that in the statist view, the concepts of peace and military security are highly associated if not identical.

Populism Populism has two major variations: idealism and interpersonalism. The idealist version emphasizes the role of values and the views of the masses as well as of elite groups. In the period between the two world wars, it was an influential approach, its adherents advocating policies for peace based on national self-determination, open diplomacy, international institutions, and collective security rather than a search for a balance of power.[9] Today, it still emphasizes the morality of means as well as ends and the socially constructed nature of international conflicts and their transformation through changes in thinking.

Adherents of idealism criticize other perspectives for accepting existing practices and social conventions as givens rather than offering alternatives. They argue that by acting on their assumptions people produce a world consistent with their beliefs; if they acted on other assumptions, they would create another world.[10] Some stress reconciliation among adversaries and the avoidance of threats and violence. According to this view, conciliation will generate trust and the discovery of mutually beneficial outcomes to conflicts. De-escalation, they believe, requires conciliatory initiatives rather than coercive threats. It means taking account of the interests of major adversaries and seeking a way for their interests to be (at least partially) served. Although this method has scarcely been tried by government officials and seems risky, populists argue that conventional approaches have often failed and carry more risk in the nuclear age.

Populists emphasize rules that constrain conduct as people learn new norms and identities, the initiation of peace efforts, and a search for mutual accommodation, noting how conflicts can be redefined or reframed so that they become amenable to settlement or even resolution. Often, they direct attention to missed opportunities for peacemaking.

The idealist approach is close to the relatively new interpersonal perspective, which holds that personal factors, interpersonal interaction, social movements, and general subjective orientations affect both the outbreak and avoidance of wars.[11] Aspects of this approach have long been emphasized by psychologists and social psychologists. Recently feminists such as Betty Reardon, Diana Russell, and Carol Cohn have made a special contribution to this point of view by noting that in nearly all cultures men are socialized to be aggressive and that this is often elaborated into a militancy that supports a war system.[12]

Interpersonalists usually define peace very broadly. Interpersonal and community violence are often linked to international violence, to be overcome by greater empathy among adversaries. Security, then, means not only the security of the state but of all men, women, and children in every country.

Finally, they stress the role of popular forces, often in the form of social movements. Peace movements and other large-scale, sometimes transnational, social movements generate forces that change government policies and even topple regimes.

The populist approach provides a basis for a critical stance toward an unsatisfactory reality and yields insights for change. Sometimes, however, its adherents seem to be asserting that if people would only think and behave properly, conflict could be resolved. Often they underestimate the reality of competing interests and the role of coercion.

Pluralism   The third approach, pluralism, was developed to explain day-to-day international conduct and foreign policy making. Two major variations are usefully distinguished: the globalist and "multiple-actor" versions. The globalist or world-systems perspective focuses on economic development and socioeconomic inequalities in the world as a whole.[13] Analysts such as Wallerstein, Cardoso, and Magdoff have sought to explain the rise of capitalism as a world system and the ways in which dominant economic countries maintain their dominance. The perspective considers global inequalities and underlying conflicts, especially among major developed capitalist (core) countries and peripheral, developing countries that are economically dependent on the core countries. Underlying conflict is viewed as the basis for overt conflicts, particularly among peoples from underdeveloped countries and among rival core countries. This approach aids in understanding de-escalation moves by providing insight into the context and long-term trends of particular international conflicts.

Many analysts of the contemporary world system go well beyond global economic interdependence to stress the proliferation of transnational organizations, nongovernmental and governmental, such as the United Nations. Peace is based on high levels of integration and mutual dependence and must rely on the effective working of international organizations.

The multiple-actor version of pluralism emphasizes that world participants are not only states or transnational organizations but also subnational groups that interact through many processes besides coercive conflict.[14] This approach views foreign policy as the product of bureaucratic politics and routines; it assumes that a government's preferences are not fixed but are the product of contending domestic and international actors. Since there are many relevant actors, noncoercive as well as coercive inducements are important in international relations. Persuasion and offers of benefits are crucial as each actor strives to rally supporters and divide opponents.

In this view, peace cannot be reached in a final, stable set of conditions. It is rather an accommodation among many in shifting coalitions based on power, values, and interests. Adherents of the pluralist approach tend to be relativistic, assuming that no one actor has legitimate absolute claims while its opponent lacks them. This is consistent with the search for common security—that is, security that does not create insecurity for an adversary.

Conflict Resolution The newly emerging conflict resolution perspective—also referred to as conflict mitigation, conflict management, and dispute settlement—has particular relevance for peacemaking. I use the term conflict resolution in a broad, inclusive sense as it is generally used, incorporating the other terms. The important intellectual sources of this approach include game theory (based in mathematics and economics), the analysis of interaction (based in social psychology and sociology), and the analysis of organizations and interorganizational relations (based in political science and sociology).

Dispute settlement and conflict management have been practiced for many years in many settings. In U.S. industrial labor relations, for example, they are relatively well institutionalized in government and private conciliation and mediation programs. In recent years, conflict resolution activities have expanded into the areas of community conflicts, intraorganizational disputes, and conflicts over the environment. For example, neighborhood dispute-settlement centers have been established throughout the United States to mediate negotiated settlements of interpersonal disputes as alternatives to an adversarial judicial system.[15]

The conflict resolution approach as applied to international conflict draws from this diverse field and also from the pluralist and populist perspectives. In this approach, each international conflict can be regarded as moving through a series of stages. Furthermore, every conflict is inter-locked with others in many ways, each being embedded in a larger scale conflict (in time or social space) or encompassing several smaller scale disputes.[16] Thus, the U.S.-USSR conflict has been viewed as part of an ongoing struggle between socialist and imperialist camps or between the free world and Communist totalitarianism. It has also been variously seen as a dispute over Soviet troops in Afghanistan and as a conflict having a course of development over more than forty years. It might also be seen as a dispute between the Reagan administration and Gorbachev's over the development and deployment of a strategic defense system. The emergence, escalation, de-escalation, and termination of a fight depend on how the protagonists view themselves and each other and the issues that divide them.

The conflict resolution or conflict mitigation approach also presumes that conflicts are never wholly zero-sum; that is, one party need not gain only at the expense of the other. Consequently, there is the possibility of discover-ing options for an integrative outcome whereby all adversaries gain much of what they need or want. Many adherents of this approach assume that all adversaries have interests that should be taken into account in resolving a dispute.

This perspective suggests specific methods to inhibit conflict escalation, prevent crises, advance negotiations, and reach agreements that are advan-tageous for both adversaries. Many of these methods are effectively used by persons acting as mediators.

Like pluralism, conflict resolution views social conflict as inherent to social life. Conflict management requires constant attention to prevent the escalation of conflict into intense violence. Ultimate harmony is not attain-able, but a peace that limits conflict escalation and avoids violence is possible. Such peace is reliably based on true integration among potential adversaries and established rules for mediating conflicts.

Analysts such as John Burton stress the importance of resolving underly-ing problems, not merely settling conflicts.[17] Other analysts regard such resolution as the rare outcome of a very long process. To them a settlement is usually the most that can be achieved, and it may be a step toward fundamental resolution. Even when a struggle has ended, other disputes are likely to erupt.

In this book the conflict resolution approach is used as the framework for analyzing the de-escalation of international conflicts. It allows us to learn from other conflicts and to recognize problematic elements. For example, although in international fights it might be assumed that the protagonists are unchanging, experience has proved otherwise—witness the shifting adversaries in Middle East conflicts. Conflict resolution, enriched by ideas from other approaches, can help to construct strategies for peacemaking that are focused on primary goals and alternative means of achieving them. Effective peacemaking depends on making practical goal choices and using appropriate means to achieve those goals, mindful of the interests of adversaries. Like the statist approach, conflict resolution assumes that peacemaking must allow for the use of coercion. As the other perspectives maintain, however, coercion alone cannot achieve de-escalation and may provoke further escalation.

Populism adds insights about how conflicts are shaped and reshaped by the perceptions of adversaries, which are often culturally generated. People create rituals to give meaning to their lives and struggles: "The ritual process is a central element in the social dialectics of conflict and conflict resolution among nations."[18]

Of course, many analysts now draw from the conflict resolution approach as well as from several international relations perspectives when they examine particular issues, such as the effectiveness of deterrence. The value of comparing and integrating several approaches is also evident in the attention to new topics. For example, recently analysts have examined the development of normative regimes guiding conduct in particular domains, as in the control of arms.[19] Research is also being conducted on the reciprocity in both confrontational and conciliatory interactions between countries, and whether reciprocity results in cooperative relations.[20]

Implications of the Conflict Resolution Approach

In conflict resolution, three aspects of international conflict have major implications for peacemaking steps: the number of parties, the diversity of issues, and the use of noncoercive inducements. In other words, international conflicts involve many actors and issues and can be waged using positive sanctions and persuasion as well as coercion. The implications of these general features of conflict for international peacemaking are not fully recognized.[21]

First, every international conflict involves several adversaries and allies; none is a neatly bounded, homogeneous unit. Every person has multiple identities and loyalties, variously including religion, language, ethnicity, an occupation, an ideology, an employer, and a country. Groups divided according to one of these factors may be united by another. Which identity is salient varies over time and by circumstance. Thus, for Muslims living in Egypt, the salience of being Egyptian or Arab or Muslim varies depending on who is seen to be the primary enemy or which identity is aroused by elite groups. In addition, each protagonist obviously seeks allies and mobilizes supporters while trying to break up the coalitions of its adversaries. Each party usually comprises many subparties while itself being part of a larger entity.

Second, since every conflict involves many parties, it also involves many issues.[22] Even if a conflict involves only two adversaries, several issues will always be in dispute. The multiplicity of parties and issues means that every international conflict is inevitably intertwined with many others,[23] which may escalate or de-escalate, depending on their relation to other conflicts and their changing predominance. Thus, a conflict that one government wages against another is only one of many conflicts in which it is engaged. It is likely to be involved in several concurrent struggles against domestic challengers and other foreign enemies. Those other conflicts may influence officials to de-escalate the focal conflict according to resource limitations. In other circumstances, a conflict may cause government leaders to escalate the focal conflict in order to divert popular attention.

The focal conflict of one foreign government may be embedded in a larger conflict between two allies, where differences of interest and value may coincide and be superimposed, hampering a settlement of any one of them—as when a U.S.-USSR dispute over support for rival political groups fighting for control of an African country is seen as part of a world historical struggle between socialism and imperialism *and* over military bases.

Two antagonistic governments in a focal conflict may be allied against a common enemy and find that they are engaged in another conflict that crosscuts the focal one. Such crosscutting battles reduce the intensity of the focal conflict.

That conflicts are also serially linked over time has paradoxical implications. Sometimes a protagonist in an ongoing adversarial relationship knows it will have to struggle again and again. In that case, it may be willing to settle for less, anticipating a better outcome in the next encounter. This is most likely to occur in a relatively institutionalized conflict with many disputes, as in union-management collective bargaining. In a relatively noninstitutionalized conflict, however, the sequential nature of fighting means that one fight sets a precedent for the next. For example, Americans in their relations with the Soviets often have regarded each situation as a domino in a series. Winning one fight is important because the fall of one domino will bring down the others and do great damage to U.S. interests.[24]

The multiplicity of parties and issues means that no international conflict is ever zero-sum: The outcome of a conflict need not be the defeat of one side and the victory of another. A win-win solution is conceivable and frequently possible through trade-offs that form the basis for a settlement that gives every party what it most needs.

Finally, having multiple conflicts means that a major conflict may become less salient when a new one becomes more prominent—allowing de-escalation of the former. A change in conflict salience is an important element in understanding conflict de-escalation and escalation.[25]

A third condition arising from recent developments in the world system, intergovernmental interaction, and domestic conditions is the increased importance in international affairs of noncoercive inducements, that is, of persuasion and positive sanctions.[26]

Persuasion refers to the use of symbolic communication to influence others to change their perception of a conflict.[27] One party tries to convince an adversary that what it seeks should be granted, without threats of coercion or promises of rewards. This may entail an appeal to the adversary to empathize with its position. For example, on 21 May 1981, General Secretary Leonid Brezhnev wrote President Ronald Reagan:

> Try, Mr. President to see what is going on through our eyes. Attempts are being made to revitalize the U.S.-made military and political alliances; new bases are being added to those which already exist thousands of kilometers away from the U.S.A. and are aimed against our country; the American military presence abroad, in general, is being increased and expanded; large areas of the world are being declared spheres of "vital interest" to the U.S.A.[28]

In addition to asking an adversary to exchange roles, persuasive arguments may appeal to shared interests, such as avoiding war or taking a stand against a common threat. Appeals are also made to shared values, such as freedom and justice.

Positive sanctions include the granting or promising of rewards.[29] They are usually offered on a contingency basis but are sometimes given unilaterally in expectation of appropriate reciprocation.

Noncoercive inducements are less likely to lead to escalation than would coercion, which can successfully intimidate an adversary but is often reciprocated, causing the conflict to intensify. Noncoercive inducements are likely to be important in de-escalating a conflict and may be critical in initiating a reduction in hostility and in negotiating an agreement settling a dispute.

Contexts and Strategies of De-escalation

In accounting for effective peacemaking, these ideas can be assessed only by applying them in specific historical contexts to actual peacemaking efforts. Three contextual realms are important: the global system, domestic conditions, and intersocietal interactions.

The global system includes the physical and social systems of state and nonstate participants and elements that obstruct as well as foster peacemaking efforts. Specific international conditions affect the impact of various de-escalation moves. For example, when the cold war has been intense, the UN Security Council has been limited in de-escalating conflicts in the Middle East.

Domestic conditions may stimulate or impede de-escalation efforts. For example, de-escalation is fostered when major groups of one society do not support a confrontational policy against an adversary either in wartime or during periods of more limited hostility.

Domestic factors in the form of interest groups, public opinion, or social movement organizations not only directly affect their governments' foreign policy but may also affect an adversary's government. They provide a possible audience or constituency to which an adversary government may appeal, as the Soviet government has in peace campaigns during the cold war.

Interactions between societies are conducted in many ways in addition to publicly conveyed official messages, such as speeches at UN General Assembly meetings. Officials also convey messages in confidence and may take actions that are expected to convey information so that subsequent responses are in the form of tacit bargaining. In addition, governments may institute domestic policies that an adversary desires and so initiate de escalation moves. Furthermore, many nongovernment actors conduct a wide variety of relations across political borders, for example, as informal intermediaries, as colleagues in the arts or sciences, or as commercial traders.

In this book, I consider strategies for nongovernmental groups as well as government officials, focusing on factors that can be modified by individuals and groups engaged in conflict. I concentrate on policy choices that are particularly relevant to interaction and that are affected by domestic conditions. Often, the international system will be assumed to be unchanging.

Other times, I consider how settlements contribute to the transformation of the global system. Questions in three areas of strategic choice are considered: parties, issues, and inducements.

First, which parties in a conflict should be involved in peacemaking efforts? Should mediators participate? Should all relevant parties be involved or only those ready to agree to a settlement? Second, should peripheral or major issues be settled first in de-escalation efforts? Should several issues be linked or each considered in isolation? Third, what mixture of carrots and sticks is effective in bringing an adversary to the negotiating table and to an agreement? Should positive and negative inducements be presented together or in sequence? Should a would-be peacemaker match the level of cooperation or threat to the level of the adversary's actions?[30]

Many arguments about peacemaking efforts are based on differences over the importance of context relative to the strategy and tactics employed. Some observers and protagonists argue that de-escalation occurs when conflict conditions make it necessary. Background circumstances are the result of major social forces, and those factors shape events while the skill, determination, and wisdom of particular leaders have little impact.

Background conditions include domestic circumstances within each major adversary country; the power balance and other aspects of relations among adversaries; and the international context of a particular struggle. Disagreements also exist over the relative importance of different background issues. Some contend that what is critical to peacemaking is the relative power among adversaries; that is, peace is achieved when adversaries have attained essential parity or when one has overwhelming power relative to its enemy.

Others argue that although conditions may impose constraints, applying the right methods is crucial to peacemaking. Methods include techniques of initiating de-escalation or negotiation agreements. Many prescriptions for lessening tension and moving toward peace stress conciliatory initiatives to interrupt conflict escalation or to improve the bargaining process.[31] In this view, such microprocesses are critical, particularly in times of crisis.

Finally, some observers argue that although background circumstances may not determine the course of peacemaking efforts, the application of a particular technique alone cannot bring about de-escalation. Rather, a strategic view is necessary, encompassing the appropriate choice of parties, issues, and inducements for conflicts viewed over the course of their development. In so doing, attention must be given to the relation between background conditions and the appropriateness of alternative strategies in peacemaking.

Simple, universally applicable techniques are not what I present here. Rather, I emphasize strategic considerations that link macro- and micro-processes and factors. I also examine how the historical context and the techniques employed at each stage of de-escalation contribute to answering crucial questions about the process. I have not assumed that the participants involved in de-escalation efforts always employ a consciously selected strategy or a particular set of techniques. We need only interpret retroactively what that strategy turned out to be and what techniques were used.

A strategy of peacemaking must consider what means are effective at various stages of a conflict. That is why this book is organized in terms of four major phases of conflict de-escalation: the preconditions for de-escalation initiatives, starting negotiations, negotiations leading to agreements, and the consequences of agreements.

I take a broader view than that which considers conflict resolution technique as more or less effective under different circumstances. Every party in a struggle has many goals, more than managing how the struggle will be conducted. The nature of a settlement and its consequences must also be considered.

In examining real-world efforts to move toward peace, I also recognize the fluidity of the parties in a conflict. Not only do governments change but states as well, as recent developments in Eastern Europe make evident. More significantly, entities that crosscut states are also relevant participants, and they too change over time. They include multinational corporations and religious organizations, all contributing to the complexity of conflicts and the potential for any particular conflict to become less salient in the eyes of partisans.

2

The U.S.-USSR and Middle East Cases

ow international adversaries seek to lessen disputes and move toward increased accord can be explained only by considering specific conflicts in their historical context. In this chapter, I outline major developments in the global system since 1948 and review the changes in the conflict between the United States and the Soviet Union since the onset of the cold war in 1948 and between Israel and its Arab neighbors after the establishment of the State of Israel in 1948. This time frame allows examination of several de-escalation efforts, showing how they are linked over time, and how government and nongovernment leaders routinely interpret current happenings based on their experience of a conflict.

The U.S.-USSR and Arab-Israel conflicts have often seemed intractable:

irreconcilable issues have persisted, adversaries have continued to impose or threaten great injury to one another, and peacemaking efforts have often failed. Yet both conflicts have also seen notable movements toward peaceful accommodation that have endured for several years, including a peace treaty in 1979 between Israel and Egypt and limited cooperation between Israel and Jordan. The U.S. and Soviet governments both have avoided using direct, large-scale violence against each other, for example, by agreeing at various times to regulate their rivalry in nuclear arms. In the late 1980s, these de-escalation moves culminated in a profound transformation of U.S.-USSR relations.

Historical Context

Conflicts and their amelioration are shaped by the overarching global system, the interactions between major international adversaries, and the domestic conditions of each adversary. Factors and processes in each realm can both obstruct and facilitate de-escalation efforts.

The Global System

The current world system constitutes a major impediment to peacemaking. It is largely a system of countries ruled by governments that claim absolute sovereignty. The system has no effective international law with widely accorded legitimacy or power to command settlements. No single government or coalition of governments dominates all others enough to arbitrate conflicts and make settlements by fiat.

In many ways, we live in an anarchic world, huddling in families, communities, and countries, each with its own institutionalized order. Often, government heads presume to represent the indubitable will of all their people. Generally adopting the statist perspective, they believe they are the sole legitimate wielders of force for their countries and that in a world of sovereign states, they constrain other governments from using force only by counterthreats. As President Anwar el-Sadat of Egypt said on 4 February 1971, referring to Israel, "Due to our knowledge of the enemy, we are fully convinced that he can only be checked by force, and will only retreat under pressure."[1]

Besides the insatiability of mutual threats is the immense inequality that characterizes the world's peoples and constitutes a continuous source of international dispute.[2] Countries differ greatly in material living standards and military power. The less affluent and weaker are likely to seek greater equity; the more affluent and militarily stronger countries will use their resources to maintain or increase their superiority.

National and other loyalties constitute another problem. We are all socialized to be loyal to our country.[3] We generally identify with our compatriots and think of our state as our representative, giving our government the right to demand individual sacrifices for the common good—an important component of the war system. Nevertheless, the claims of government leaders are sometimes challenged because people are also loyal to many other entities. When these entities do not coincide with the state, there is the potential for conflict, as for example, when different states claim to represent the same ethnic group.

A world system of states also means that statehood is the goal of many nonstate actors. Ethnic groups, represented by national liberation organizations, have sought states of their own against the will of existing ruling states. Most wars since the end of World War II have been struggles of national liberation. A major actor is the Palestine Liberation Organization (PLO), which has struggled against another national liberation movement, Zionism.

The world is made up of many more nations than there are states. Few states control territories that locate a single people within those borders and nowhere else.[4] As a result, political boundaries imposed by states cause many international conflicts as ethnic groups seek new borders to correspond to their identities, often violating borders claimed by other ethnic groups.

That the world is highly and progressively integrated is a source of conflict as well as cooperation. Because the actions of governments affect people across borders in trade, environmental matters, investment, tourism, migration, and so on, countries have become increasingly interdependent and vulnerable to external pressures. This was the case, for example, in 1973 when oil was used by the Arab governments to gain the support of the United States and other governments against Israel.

The profound global integration already attained, contrary to statist assumptions, means that nongovernmental organizations and individuals also significantly affect the people of other countries. Thus, the consumer preferences and political ideas of one country may spread to another where they are regarded as subversive, as, for example, has been the case in the Soviet government's response to popular cultural products from the United States.[5]

The technology of violence is a product of world developments and widely shared technological advances. The increased capacity of many actors to engage in extreme violence can lead to a rapid escalation of conflict as in the intense Middle East wars and in selective killing by small groups.

Despite these ominous forces, recent developments in the world system have also significantly facilitated de-escalation and conflict transformation. The post–World War II global system, as stressed by advocates of the pluralist and populist approaches, is marked by the growth of major transnational actors.[6] Some of these are governmental—including global organizations such as the United Nations and its specialized agencies—and significant regional organizations, such as the European Economic Community. Transnational nongovernmental organizations have also increased in number and scale. Many are multinational corporations such as Toyota, IBM, and General Motors. Others are not-for-profit organizations—labor unions and professional, religious, recreational, and ideological associations—such as the International Confederation of Free Trade Unions and the International Sociological Association. These organizations can and sometimes do increase the intensity of conflicts, but they may also facilitate peacemaking.

International governmental organizations provide mediation and institutionalized ways to interrupt conflict escalation. The United Nations and regional organizations such as the Organization of American States have often been effective in limiting the escalation of conflicts.[7] Despite some decline in the effectiveness of the United Nations in settling and isolating international disputes, it continues to be effective in abating them. In the late 1980s, with the end of the cold war, it began to a play major role in settling several regional conflicts. For the two conflicts discussed here, the United Nations has been important. It was crucial in the birth of Israel and important in every subsequent war and numerous peacemaking efforts. Even in the U.S.-USSR conflict, the United Nations was not only an arena, it was the setting for multilateral negotiations, particularly on disarmament.

Nongovernmental international organizations also perform peacemaking functions. For example, the Pugwash movement has had a series of conferences on arms control topics that "played an important role in opening up a channel of communication between the United States and the USSR in the late 1950s and early 1960s."[8] Its core members are natural scientists from the United States, the United Kingdom, the Soviet Union, and other countries. Multinational corporations have featured, not only in fostering conflicts, but in inhibiting their escalation. In the Middle East, the oil companies have influenced the foreign policies of many governments, sometimes furthering mutual dependency and inhibiting conflict escalation. Other multinational corporations have been involved in U.S.-USSR trade relations; for example, companies such as Cargill, Continental, and Louis Dreyfus conducted major U.S. grain sales to the Soviet Union.[9] Modern communication systems mean that events in one part of the world affect people in distant parts of the world. The movement of goods, services, labor, and capital have also become extensive. For example, imports as a percentage of the U.S.

gross national product increased from 3.7 percent in 1950 to 13.1 percent in 1988, while exports rose in the same period from 4.3 percent to 10.9 percent,[10] and the remitted earnings of foreign workers have influenced the economies of Europe, the Middle East, and South Asia.

This interdependence can encourage restraint in escalating a conflict. The fear of rupturing advantageous relations constrains hostility and war making, and the anticipation of positive bonds may lead to de-escalation initiatives.

Finally, and most unrecognized, the emergence of the United States and the Soviet Union as dominant world powers has fostered a world system in which nonmilitary means of struggle are increasingly used. Different as the two powers have been ideologically, both have stressed new international styles: They emphasize the importance of public opinion and the common people; they operate internationally through various nongovernmental transnational organizations, including multinational corporations and political parties.

The Soviets pride themselves on the open diplomacy they introduced with the 1917 revolution, distinguishing themselves from the czar's secret deals with imperialist allies. U.S. leaders also have often asserted their desire for openness. With American participation in World War I, President Wilson denounced secret diplomacy and proclaimed the goal of open covenants openly arrived at. Many U.S. leaders also have made ideological appeals to people everywhere for democracy and have waged an ideological war against Communist totalitarianism. The recent revolutionary changes in the USSR and Eastern Europe are a product, in part, of those appeals. Soviet leaders also have stressed the ideological nature of the struggle between the two social systems that they identified as capitalism and socialism.

Georgi Arbatov, director of the Soviet's Institute for U.S. and Canada Studies, for example, when a member of the Central Committee of the Soviet Communist party, wrote in his book, *The War of Ideas in Contemporary International Relations* (1973), that "there has been an unprecedented growth of the role played by the masses in foreign policy,"[11] and continued "we are witnessing a world-wide collision of the two basic classes of modern society representing the two social systems—the capitalist class and the proletariat, who are locked not only in an economic and political but also an ideological struggle."[12]

Government Interaction

The way governments interact has both positive and negative impacts on the prospects of peacemaking. Government officials seeking to remain in office must placate and appeal to domestic constituencies.[13] In furthering domestic interests, they are likely to challenge and compete with foreign governments. They may contend, for example, for control of the same land or for influence and markets. Their claims may be widely shared and supported by their constituencies, as is the case of Israeli and Palestinian leaders. These circumstances are the bases for realistic conflicts: Contending government heads correctly perceive that they are pursuing incompatible objectives.

In addition, government officials may *mistakenly* believe that a basis for conflict exists; unrealistic perceptions have several possible sources. For example, a player may misinterpret an adversary's defensive efforts as a threat and, assured of its own innocence, prepare to defend itself. Government officials may try to mobilize the people against a foreign adversary to solidify domestic support; they may also seek to thwart a challenge by political rivals that they are soft toward an enemy by taking a hard-line position themselves. Government heads may cater to domestic interest groups pursuing activities that another country views as threatening. For example, expenditures for a new weapon system might result from domestic pressures from a military-industrial complex and be mistakenly viewed by outsiders as an intentional threat.[14]

Actual conflicts always mix realistic and unrealistic elements. A little rivalry can gradually create a vicious cycle of persistent enmity. Once a fight is under way, each side is likely to see itself as the unjustified target of the adversary's threats while its own actions are obviously defensive. If this goes unrecognized by the adversary, it is seen as further evidence of the adversary's evil intentions. As U.S. Secretary of State John Foster Dulles once said, "Khrushchev does not need to be convinced of our good intentions. He knows we are not aggressors and do not threaten the Soviet Union."[15]

What is regarded as realistic ultimately depends on the judgment of a particular analyst. Government leaders may argue (and even believe) that domestic troubles, such as ethnic or class protests, result from a foreign government's subversive efforts; the leaders may use threats to stop presumed intervention. An analyst might concur or disagree, believing that an ethnic or class conflict arises from internal policies. An analyst's interpretation may be based on an examination of changes in adversary relations. When a government changes and a new foreign policy seems more accommodating, the earlier conflict loses some credibility. For example, the rapid transformation of the U.S.-USSR conflict indicates that the cold war consisted of many unrealistic components.

Of course, developments in intergovernmental relations have contributed to de-escalation efforts. Actions against an adversary are always played before a wide audience, including those of both sides of a conflict; government officials often seek a positive image and appear conciliatory and peaceful to such audiences. Thus, public opinion is an incentive to use persuasion and positive sanctions rather than just coercion.

The growth in the size and number of transnational organizations and expanded communication media enable nongovernmental actors to initiate and promote de-escalation efforts. These agents also provide the basis for Track II diplomacy,[16] whereby nonofficial representatives can explore possible de-escalation efforts between adversaries, initiate communication about these efforts, and provide additional channels to support official diplomacy.

Rival governments seeking to maintain or gain influence also engage in both covert and overt operations in order to affect popular opinion and government decisions in other countries. The U.S. and Soviet governments have conducted extensive covert activities, usually through the Central Intelligence Agency and the Committee for State Security (KGB). National and transnational organizations are used more or less openly as agents for influencing other peoples and governments. For example, although the Reagan administration placed great emphasis on military means, it also expanded United States Information Agency (USIA) activities and established the National Endowment for Democracy. The endowment lends support to groups in other countries acting in ways consistent with U.S. foreign policy. Support is channeled through such organizations as the Free Trade Union Institute of the American Federation of Labor and the Congress of Industrial Organizations.[17] Transnational organizations, many domestic voluntary associations, and professional societies foster individual, person-to-person contacts. In the early years of the Reagan administration, such links continued and private initiatives even expanded during renewed official antagonism in American-Soviet relations.

Although governments often rely on armed coercion in dealing with each other—particularly as antagonists—several recent developments tend to limit the effectiveness of armed force. The very increase in the scale of possible violence makes its use increasingly inappropriate for any reasonable political objective. This is certainly true of nuclear war.[18] Even the threat of nonnuclear violence escalating into a nuclear war may inhibit a recourse to violence.

The extraordinary destructiveness of nuclear weapons means that the U.S. and Soviet governments both claim to deploy weapons only to deter one another from using weapons! Even against countries without nuclear weapons, the superpowers have found severe limits to the use of military force to gain their objectives. Armed struggle by U.S. forces did not suffice to maintain American influence in South Vietnam, nor did Soviet military strength enable it to retain influence in Egypt when Sadat requested Soviet military advisers to leave Egypt.

Military force seems more useful for regional powers; but even there, armed force has often failed to achieve significant goals. The Israeli government has not been able to impose a peaceful settlement upon the Palestinians and neighboring Arab states. Similarly, the PLO has not been able either by armed struggle or civil harassment to establish a democratic, secular state in all of Palestine, nor a Palestinian state in a portion of it.

Domestic Conditions

Some domestic conditions generate international conflict escalation while other conditions inhibit it. Domestic conditions can foster conflict in several ways. Within each society some groups support policies that advance their interests and values but that may also harm or appear to threaten people in other countries. Thus, religious and ideological sentiments, advocated for domestic reasons, may be justified by the specter of threat from a foreign adversary and may themselves challenge the adversary. For example, in the United States in the 1950s, the anti-communism of Sen. Joseph McCarthy served particular domestic interests and narrowed the range of possible responses to the Soviet Union.[19] In the USSR, even in the early 1970s, during the years of détente, Soviet leaders stressed the importance of the ideological struggle at home, which restricted détente. Similarly, the military and trade policies that serve domestic interests may unintentionally harm or threaten another country.

Furthermore, the immediate personal concerns of individuals tend to supplant interest in external affairs; with the resulting ignorance, foreigners—particularly adversaries—become undifferentiated stereotypes. They also become easy targets for personal and group anger. Ethnocentric sentiments are widespread, and leaders cannot entirely choose to ignore them. Neighboring peoples often regard each other as natural enemies. As the French writer Anatole France wrote, "He who says neighbor, says enemy." In the Middle East, this conviction seems to have been fulfilled: Syria and Iraq, Iran and Iraq, Egypt and Libya, Jordan and Syria, and Israel and its neighbors all have been enemies for many years.

Governments and the leading institutions in a society may even socialize members of the society to feel that people in other countries are enemies. For example, in many Arab countries the hostility toward Israel and Jews has been expressed in school texts.[20] A grammar exercise theme in a 1965 Egyptian junior high school text reads: "The Arabs do not cease to act for the extermination of Israel." A Syrian junior high school text explains that the Jews live "exiled and despised since by their nature they are vile, greedy and enemies of mankind."

Many domestic conditions are nevertheless conducive to peacemaking. In recent decades, the advocacy of peace has become a popular enterprise. In many countries large-scale peace movements have burst forth and flourished; they comprise a variety of organizations and many supporters of like mind.[21] In some countries, such as the Soviet Union, peace organizations have been directed by government or party officials; but even there, in a period of glasnost, they play an increasingly independent role. Where peace demonstrations are more autonomous, they can help to dampen a government's bellicosity, as they did in Israel during the 1982 war in Lebanon.

Once some de-escalation has occurred, interests are created to maintain and even foster de-escalation. For example, as arms control agreements were reached between the U.S. and Soviet governments, an arms control community developed in each country, including government officials, experts in research institutes, and peace activists.[22]

In many countries, some organizations have a special interest in limiting a conflict with particular countries. These interests may be based on trade concerns or shared ethnicity or feelings about a common enemy. For example, a major source of the popular resistance to U.S. military involvement in World War I and World War II derived from Americans of Irish and German background not wishing to be allied with the British against Germany.[23]

Another domestic development has underlying importance in furthering peacemaking. Governments are increasingly viewed as providers of social welfare. The legitimacy of the state and of the regime depends on how well it provides for the people's well-being. Military expenditure, war preparation, and certainly war making interfere with the provision of social goods and therefore threaten regime stability.[24]

Case Studies

Answers to the questions posed in chapter 1 will be sought by examining de-escalation efforts in the context of the American-Soviet and Arab-Israeli conflicts. These two protracted conflicts have obvious substantive importance. Nearly every scenario about the outbreak of nuclear war has involved one or both of these conflicts. The Arab-Israeli conflict has erupted into ferocious wars several times, and the intensity of the hostility contributes to instability in the Middle East and to terrorism in many parts of the world.

Table 1. Major U.S.-USSR Conflict Escalations, 1948–1983

February 1948	Communists assume power in Czechoslovakia
June 1948	Soviet blockade of West Berlin begins
April 1949	NATO treaty signed
June 1950	North Korea invades South Korea
October 1950	People's Republic of China enters Korean War
November 1956	Hungarian revolt crushed by Soviet military force; Great Britain and France invade Egypt
November 1958	Soviets threaten Berlin blockade
May 1960	U.S. U-2 espionage plane shot down over Soviet territory
August 1961	Berlin Wall erected
October 1962	Cuban missile crisis
August 1964	Congress approves Gulf of Tonkin resolution authorizing U.S. actions in Vietnam.
February 1968	Communists assume power in Czechoslovakia
August 1968	Warsaw Pact armies intervene in Czechoslovakia
April 1970	U.S. sends troops to Cambodia
April 1972	Nixon orders mining of North Vietnam ports and heavy bombing
December 1979	Soviet military forces invade Afghanistan
October 1983	U.S. forces invade Grenada

The American-Soviet conflict has permeated nearly every other conflict in the world, usually exacerbating them. Its de-escalation and transformation must be understood in order to guide future policies aimed at peaceful stability.

Drawing cases from these two major conflicts also has analytic usefulness. The conflicts differ significantly; that variability can help us to generalize and specify our findings. It also enables us to examine the applicability of more ideas than would be possible if only a single conflict were studied.

Until the great transformation in the Soviet Union and Eastern Europe that began at the end of the 1980s, U.S. USSR relations after World War II have also been viewed as a series of crises and confrontations, except for the interruptions of cold war thaws and arms control agreements. The Arab-Israeli conflict is usually described as a series of wars and violent confrontations. The history of peacemaking efforts generally is not reviewed, except to tell the story of the Egyptian-Israeli peace treaty. The peacemaking efforts in both conflicts is the focus here. The wars and crises cannot be ignored, however, and they are listed in tables 1 and 2. Those escalation events themselves often stimulate de-escalation efforts, as is discussed in later chapters.

Table 2. Major Arab-Israeli Conflict Escalations, 1948–1987

May 1948	State of Israeli proclaimed and Arab armies attack
July 1954	Israeli agents in Egypt arrested for sabotage
October 1956	Israeli Sinai campaign; Israel attacks Egypt in Sinai, joined by U.K. and France
June 1967	Six-Day War between Israel and Egypt, Syria, Jordan, and other Arab countries
March 1969	War of Attrition between Israel and Egypt begins with Egyptian shelling across Suez canal
September 1970	Hijacking of four airliners to Jordan leads to Jordanian army driving PLO from Jordan
October 1973	Egyptian and Syrian forces attack Israel
July 1976	Air France plane hijacked to Entebbe, Uganda
June 1982	Israel invades Lebanon in attack on PLO
October 1985	Israelis bomb PLO headquarters in Tunis; Archille Lauro hijacked
December 1987	Uprising on West Bank and Gaza Strip begins

The bases of each conflict and how they differ should be recognized. Different ways of working for peace are likely to be more effective for conflicts with different bases. An example is the Arab-Israeli conflict where the goals sought often threatened the very survival of the major actors.

The United States and the Soviet Union, as superpowers, might seem relatively autonomous, while in some ways Israel and the Arab countries have seemed to be only proxies in a big-power struggle. Indeed, although the degree of autonomy of the smaller countries has varied considerably over time, the parties in regional conflicts have never completely lost autonomy; consequently, the superpowers were not always able to control events. The fact that these conflicts have been linked is in itself important in explaining de-escalation efforts.

Volumes have been written about the real or imagined bases of the U.S.-USSR and Arab-Israeli conflicts.[25] My scope here is to describe the conflicts to indicate the issues and assumptions underlying peacemaking efforts. In later chapters, analyses of de-escalation efforts will either support or disconfirm the interpretations summarized here.

U.S.-USSR Relations

The basic issues in contention in the U.S.-USSR conflict are not self-evident and are not always consonant with popular perception. Even the parties to the conflict have not been consistently identified. Has the struggle been between democracy and totalitarianism, between imperialism and socialism, between the heads of the U.S. and Soviet governments, between NATO and Warsaw Pact countries? For each pair of adversaries, a different set of issues is a possible source of contention. Here, the primary adversaries will usually be taken to be those holding the highest offices in the U.S. government and in the Soviet government and Communist party.

As a matter of fact, the actual constituency of these leaders has varied greatly since the onset of the cold war. In the late 1940s and early 1950s, the Soviet leaders controlled a tight alliance in which ideological, military, and political interests coincided. That cohesion broke down with the split between the USSR and the People's Republic of China (PRC), the growing independence of several Communist parties of Europe, and the somewhat greater autonomy of East European governments.[26]

U.S. government leaders for their part have varied in their emphasis on sometimes being leaders of a military alliance against the Soviet Union, at other times crusaders against communism, or promoters of American economic interests and democratic values. The various emphases have required different sets of coalition partners; in addition, the cohesion of those coalitions has shifted over time.

Even identifying the adversaries does not necessarily define the matters of contention between them. The U.S. and Soviet governments have each said, since the beginning of the cold war, that it seeks only to defend itself from the threat of the other. Accepting such claims at face value, the conflict was unrealistic—just a misunderstanding. But almost certainly, each government's leaders usually had goals that were more ambitious than simply defending what they already possessed.

The United States, in the post–World War II period, has often been characterized as a status quo party, seeking to avert change.[27] But all U.S. governments since the end of the war have sought a change in relations with the Soviet Union. Over the years, the changes desired have varied in magnitude and intensity. In the immediate postwar period, the wish to reduce Soviet domination over the countries of Eastern Europe—and even to roll back Soviet control—was clearly expressed. The incorporation of Estonia, Lithuania, and Latvia into the Soviet Union was not officially recognized by the U.S. government, but there was no active support for their independence. Even in 1990, when declarations of independence in various forms were made, the U.S. government acted with caution and regard for Moscow's concerns.

Social and political conditions within the Soviet Union have also been frequently criticized by American officials. The expansion of human rights for Soviet citizens, as interpreted by the U.S. government, has been a long-standing objective of U.S. government policy.

Many Americans have believed that the Soviet Union, by becoming more like the United States, would become an ally in building a peaceful world. As Secretary of State George Shultz declared on 15 June 1983 before the Senate Foreign Relations Committee, "We take it as part of our obligation to peace to encourage the gradual evolution of the Soviet system toward a more pluralistic political and economic system and above all, to counter Soviet expansionism through sustained and effective political, economic, and military competition."[28]

The United States has been the world's dominant capitalist economy, and American officials have tried to maintain a world system congenial to it. As Secretary of State Alexander Haig said in 1981, "We are fully conscious of our historic role in the defense of freedom wherever it may be. . . . Our objective remains simple and compelling: a world hospitable to our society and our ideals."[29]

Soviet government leaders have also sought changes in the world that others would regard as more than simply defensive. Until the end of the 1980s, they imposed and dominated regimes in Eastern Europe, and they sought world acceptance and legitimation of that domination. They have supported national liberation movements in colonies and revolutionary organizations in newly independent countries. They have aided regimes that pursued foreign policies in opposition to U.S. foreign policy.[30]

In short, there have been objective bases to the conflict between the two powers. The issues in contention largely derived from the rivalry between the two regimes, since the leaders of the U.S. and Soviet governments each sought global influence. Neither government faced immediate or direct threats to its vital interests, such as its territorial integrity or the survival of its socioeconomic system. That is, although each government's leaders may generally have believed in the virtue of their ideology, socioeconomic system, and their eventual worldwide prevalence, neither seemed intent upon acting to impose them in the short run.[31]

But if the rivalries were real, there also existed unrealistic components to the conflict. For example, within each society some groups supported the expansion of military capabilities for domestic reasons at least as much as for foreign policy reasons. Such internally driven forces for military expansion were often seen as threatening by the foreign adversary, and thus a domestic arms dynamic often introduced a source of misunderstanding.[32]

Despite many continuities, the conflict changed significantly over the years. At the end of World War II, the United States had overwhelming economic and military power, but the growing military might of the Soviet Union meant that by the end of the 1960s it had the capability of destroying

American society with nuclear weapons—a capability that the United States had enjoyed against the Soviets since the 1950s. The alliance of Communist party–dominated countries, directed by the Soviets, was split by the end of the 1960s; this was marked by antagonism between the Soviet Union and the People's Republic of China. U.S. dominance of its allies also gradually lessened as the allies gained economic and military strength. These changes altered the parameters of the conflict between U.S. and Soviet government leaders.

The issues in contention between the superpowers were frequently vague and unclear, and they shifted over time. Ideological issues have varied in prominence and when relatively salient fostered conflict escalation. For example, in the early 1980s, the Reagan administration renewed emphasis on the ideological struggle between the free world and communist totalitarianism. When a specific dispute was placed in the context of that larger struggle, its settlement became very difficult.

Of course, some matters of dispute were regarded as relatively pragmatic and nonideological; the content of these varied and sometimes were of major significance. In the early post–World War II years, disputes about the governments and boundaries of European countries were paramount. The U.S. government initially challenged the Soviet domination of Eastern and Central Europe, but no military attempts were made to roll back that domination. Even when uprisings erupted in East Germany in 1953 after Joseph Stalin's death and open revolt broke out in Hungary in 1956, the U.S. government provided no military support against the Soviets.

In the early years of the cold war, Germany was a major arena of contention. The Soviets sought to prevent a rearmament of West Germany and proposed various plans for the reunification of East and West Germany. The Western powers also proposed reunification but always based upon free elections in both countries. No proposal leading to a unified Germany was acceptable to both sides.

It was only in the 1970s, after the Social Democratic party formed the West German government, that the West accepted the postwar boundaries of the Soviet Union and of the Eastern European states. The legality of two German states was acknowledged, and reunification was put off to the distant future—since no one anticipated the early arrival of that future.

American-Soviet rivalry in the Middle East became important as early as the mid-1950s. Rivalry in other parts of the world, including Africa, Asia, and even Latin America, grew in the 1960s and 1970s. Some governments in those regions became supporters of the Soviets and received military and economic assistance; these governments were generally regarded as gains by the Soviets. When a government broke that relationship, as Sadat did in the early 1970s, it was regarded as a Soviet defeat.

Despite the many issues that divided the two countries, there were also common interests. Most obviously, Soviet and U.S. leaders had an interest in avoiding nuclear war or any war that might escalate into a nuclear war. There were other possible complementary benefits, notably in reducing the burden of arms spending, in trade, and in cultural and scientific exchange. There were even benefits the two countries shared as superpowers: by joining together, they could keep others from challenging their dominant roles in the world. With the transformation of the conflict, some of these complementary benefits are now being realized.

Arab-Israeli Relations

In the Arab-Israeli conflict, the actual contending parties are even less clear. Is the struggle between ethnic Jews and Arabs? Between persons of the Jewish and Muslim faiths? Or is it between the Israeli government and the PLO, Israeli Jews and Arab Palestinians, Western imperialism and the Arab nation, the Israeli and Arab governments, or between the Israeli and Egyptian governments? Clearly, separate definitions of these adversaries imply somewhat different struggles with different parameters and different possible resolutions.

This breakdown suggests that peace efforts can be undertaken among many different sets of adversaries. Such variability among adversary-designates should not be forgotten, even though this book necessarily gives most attention to the conflicts between the leaders of the Israeli government and those of the Egyptian and Jordanian governments and the PLO. These are the parties most able to make binding commitments to de-escalation agreements. Of course, the actions of each must be understood in the context of domestic conditions as well as the surrounding global system.

The bases for the several interconnected conflicts in this case have changed since the State of Israel was established in 1948.[33] Initially, the Arab-Israeli conflict appears to have been a struggle over the establishment of a Jewish state itself in any of the lands evacuated by the British. All Arab governments seemed to be united in opposition to the partitioning of Palestine and favored Arab control. Once the 1948 war was over, however, the claims of the Palestinians and the various Arab governments were not the same. For example, Jordan occupied and then annexed the West Bank and East Jerusalem. Although other Arab governments did not recognize that annexation, no one actively opposed it and no Palestinian state was established.

The issues in dispute focused upon Palestinian refugees and their claims

Figure 2   Map of Israel and Neighboring Areas

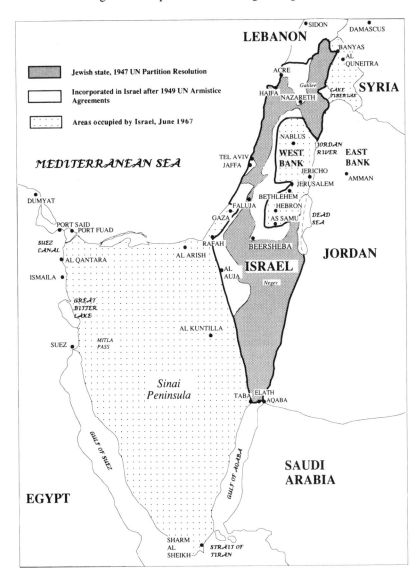

for repatriation and compensation. Another issue was the dispute over Israel's borders, the differences between the 1947 UN partition boundaries and the 1949 armistice lines (see figure 2).

After the 1967 war, Israel occupied the West Bank, the Sinai, the Gaza Strip, and the Golan Heights, and it incorporated East Jerusalem; the basis of the conflict was thus radically changed for all of the major adversaries. Meanwhile, the Palestinians were gradually emerging as independent actors under the leadership of the PLO.[34] The goal of the PLO—to establish a democratic secular state in all sectors of formerly British-mandated Palestine—was regarded by the Israelis as an intention to destroy the State of Israel. But as time has passed, more Palestinians seem reconciled to accepting the goal of a Palestinian state in the West Bank, Gaza, and East Jerusalem, side by side with Israel. Only a small proportion of Palestinians want a federation with Jordan.

Egyptian leaders' goals have always been multiple but with varying priorities. For Gamal Nasser, president of Egypt in the 1950s and 1960s, leadership of the Arab nation, incorporating Palestinians, had a very high priority. For Sadat, narrower Egyptian national interests assumed higher salience, and the restoration of Egyptian sovereignty over the Sinai, lost in 1967, was a primary objective.[35] For King Hussein of Jordan, the maintenance (and perhaps the expansion) of the Hashemite dynasty has been the primary objective.[36] For Syrian leaders, the maintenance of the ruling party as the government and the extension of Syrian dominance in the region have been primary. Across these and other Arab countries, intellectuals, clerics, business owners and managers, military leaders, and other groups share other views of Israel as an adversary. For example, many regard Israel as an extension of historic Western imperialism.

The Israeli government's definition of the conflict has also varied. Initially, a full peace with Arab governments along the cease-fire lines of 1948 would have been regarded as a successful resolution. After the June 1967 war, the unification of Jerusalem as part of Israel was sought as part of a resolution with the Arab states. As the occupation of the West Bank continued, new Israeli governments, led by the Likud party, sought continuing Israeli control of those territories as well. More and more Jews have settled in the annexed territory in and around eastern Jerusalem and throughout the occupied territories, creating a new reality.

After the separate 1979 Egyptian-Israeli peace treaty, the conflict focused increasingly on Palestinian claims. For some Israelis, this meant an intensification of the struggle with the PLO; for the Jordanian government and many Israelis, the search for a settlement involving the Palestinians became urgent. Thus, many Israelis became increasingly concerned over the future of a Jewish state that would have a majority of non-Jews—an inevitable result if demographic trends continued and the West Bank and Gaza Strip were incorporated into Israel.

Clearly, the nature of the conflict has varied considerably over time. For some adversaries the most vital of possible interests were in contention. For most of the time since its establishment, the very existence of the State of Israel seemed to be at stake. Similarly, for the Palestinians, their claim for an independent state was denied first by Jordan and then by Israel. Meanwhile, the goals of some Arab governments were not totally irreconcilable with the goals of some of the Israeli governments; this became evident with the peace treaty between Israel and Egypt.

The adversaries can also be seen to have common interests and potentially complementary benefits. Although these benefits are most often viewed in terms of avoiding the costs of military preparations and deaths from violence, there are also potential economic and social benefits from cooperation.

Comparison of the Conflicts

The two conflicts differ in the character of the parties and the issues of contention. The Arab-Israeli conflict involves many actors in central ways, the configuration is not static, and the adversaries sometimes disagree about who the antagonists are. To some degree, this has been true in the U.S.-USSR conflict as well, but the variability was not as marked nor as readily recognized. In addition, the primary adversaries in the Arab-Israeli conflict are less autonomous than are the primary adversaries of the U.S.-USSR conflict.

The issues themselves are also significantly different in the American-Soviet conflict than in the Arab-Israeli conflict. For many of the adversaries in the Middle East, the most vital interests—survival itself—appear to be immediately and directly at risk. In the U.S.-USSR conflict, although the number of contentious issues is great, none has entailed the same level of challenge to vital interests. The threat of violence, however, has been disproportionately greater: It has extended to a nuclear war that would destroy both societies and much more.

3
Taking Initiatives

O ften, perhaps most of the time, de-escalation occurs because someone *takes the initiative*. That someone may be the head of a government engaged in an international conflict, an official of an international organization, or a private citizen. The initiative may be a proposal for settling a conflict or a unilateral conciliatory action. In this chapter, I discuss why certain parties undertake various initiatives and what the actual initiatives are in the U.S.-USSR and Arab-Israeli conflicts.

Alternative Explanations

Most writing on peacemaking and conflict resolution has focused more on the conduct of negotiations than on the prenegotiation stage.[1] Yet, the

conditions that make an acceptable settlement between adversaries possible
are obviously critical. When the parties to a hitherto intractable conflict
come to believe in settlement, the conflict begins to change into one that can
be at least partly settled.

Effective peacemaking efforts require conducive background circumstances combined with appropriate de-escalation tactics and strategies.
Peacemaking efforts must therefore be grounded on an appraisal of major
background factors, including those that no single actor, no matter how
powerful, can change unilaterally. An effective strategy includes modifying
conditions; since all actors are not equally capable, the options in peacemaking efforts vary according to the actors. Factors contributing to a shift
toward de-escalation may arise from domestic conditions, international
affairs, and the relations between adversaries.

Which background circumstance is especially significant can be a matter
of dispute. The conflict resolution approach, for example, gives particular
attention to the shifting relations between adversaries. Populists, however,
might argue that domestic pressures, especially peace movements, induce
de-escalation efforts.[2] Other adherents of this approach assert that the
international context is important and that intermediaries play the critical
role in a transition to de-escalation. Pluralists would make a similar argument.

Analysts taking a statist approach emphasize coercive power in international conflict, stressing that the power relationship between adversaries is
most relevant in explaining the timing of accommodative initiatives.[3] De-
escalation efforts, therefore, are likely when adversaries are either roughly
equal in power or overwhelmingly unequal and when they believe they
cannot alter the balance of power.

Domestic Conditions

Domestic pressures may propel a government to undertake de-escalation
initiatives. The pressures may take the form of mass-based support to
reduce confrontation with an adversary or a protest against a specific
policy.[4] They may also be indirect, as when demands for improved living
conditions pressure political leaders to consider settling an international
dispute. According to the populist approach, domestic pressures are conducive to peacemaking because they presage a change in values about issues in
contention; they signify a popular shift in priorities. For statists, however,
such domestic pressures weaken resolve and whet the enemy's appetite.
Under these circumstances, de-escalation may be delayed as the adversary
tries to take advantage of internal dissension and raises its demands.

From the conflict resolution and pluralist perspectives, whether or not domestic pressures foster de-escalation depends on many other circumstances—especially the nature of the regime, the alternatives its leaders believe they have, and the kind of challenge rival elites pose. Regime leaders are often hard-liners, believing it necessary to be assertive and threatening.[5] The effects of domestic pressures also depend on the response expected from adversary countries and on other conflicts facing the government.

A conflict becomes institutionalized when vested interests develop in continuing the struggle or maintaining a high level of antagonism. Consequently, de-escalation moves may be resisted, for example, because of bureaucratic inertia or a commitment to ideological consistency. A change in leadership often makes new de-escalation initiatives possible, as it did when the rigidities of Stalinism gave way.

Populists believe that domestic ideologies and the way a society views itself and its adversary will affect the likelihood that de-escalation initiatives will take place. Certainly, viewing oneself as peace-loving and one's adversary as cruel and unresponsive to anything but threats reduces the chances of peacemaking efforts occurring. The very form of an initiative is also similarly shaped. Thus, the U.S. emphasis on social and cultural exchanges with the Soviet Union as a de-escalation initiative reflected the view of Americans that they were in a free society and that Soviet society was closed. Opening up the Soviet Union was regarded as a way of bringing about peace and even victory; the Soviets, however, have often regarded such efforts as subversive attempts to undermine their system.

International Context

In the international context, two conditions are particularly significant for peacemaking: the relative importance of the several conflicts in which each adversary is engaged and the action of intermediaries.

When crosscutting or concurrent conflicts increase in importance, the focal conflict is likely to decline in importance and hence invite de-escalation. Thus, the growing tension in the 1960s between the Soviet Union and China was an incentive for the United States to make accommodative overtures to each nation. If, however, conflicts are superimposed on each other, a rise in the salience of one conflict can be extended to another. Thus, the 1967 Arab-Israeli war intensified the U.S.-USSR conflict, since at the time the Egyptians were supported by the Soviets and the Israelis by the United States.

Emphasizing the multiplicity of parties in a conflict directs attention to the role of allies and other coalition partners. A particular conflict may seem especially threatening to the allies, and they may pressure their coalition leader to de-escalate the conflict. U.S. allies in Europe have often taken such a position. But in trying to end a war, some allies have believed vital interests to be at stake and have resisted a de-escalation that might endanger those interests. This was true when the U.S. government sought to negotiate an end to the Korean and Vietnam wars satisfactory to its protégé governments.

Intermediaries are an important part of the international context and can stimulate de-escalation initiatives.[6] Once adversaries are locked into an institutionalized conflict relationship, movement away from it requires—or is at least greatly facilitated by—the intervention of mediators. They may be members of international governmental or nongovernmental organizations, national organizations, or even private persons from countries not directly involved in the conflict. The existence of international organizations such as the United Nations and of the many parties whose interests would be harmed by a war provides both the capability and incentive for intervention, which frequently becomes the instrument for de-escalation.

The statist perspective, however, suggests that intermediaries are not likely to play an important role unless the power balance among adversaries is already conducive to de-escalation or unless they are powerful enough to impose a settlement. From the conflict resolution and other perspectives, however, intervention can help produce the conditions needed for de-escalation efforts to begin, particularly if the intermediary is trustworthy and alters the perception of the dispute. Sometimes adversaries will offer de-escalation initiatives or appear to accept those of an intermediary only to please the intermediary, laying the ground for deception.

From the conflict resolution and pluralist perspectives, intermediaries are always part of the larger context of a conflict; the success of intervention depends upon the role they play in that conflict. Intermediaries can and often do enhance the parity of adversaries, which may contribute to peacemaking efforts. Sometimes, however, their support of one side enhances the odds for future victory but impedes immediate de-escalation efforts.

The multiplicity of actors and issues suggests that sometimes initiatives are taken in order to rally support from a diverse constituency or to divide an opposing coalition, which increases the likelihood that initiatives will be undertaken only for appearance' sake.

Adversary Relations

Two major aspects of the relationship between the adversaries themselves are important: the relative power of the adversaries and the degree to which they accept each other as legitimate antagonists.

The idea that the power relations of adversaries determines de-escalation moves is often cited,[7] but more than one kind of power relationship may lead to de-escalation. According to one view, the parties must be approximately equal in power for de-escalation to be initiated. Once parity is attained and neither side believes it can dominate the other in the immediate future, the conflict may be de-escalated and kept at an acceptably low level. This model has frequently been named in crediting the decline in labor-management violence and the development of collective bargaining in industrial societies.[8] Similarly, Soviet officials have argued that détente developed in the early 1970s because the "correlation of forces" had shifted so that the United States was no longer able to dominate the world militarily and because realists in the United States recognized this fact.[9]

This explanation also fits the statist approach. Peace is the mutual acceptance of the status quo, which occurs when the parties have abandoned hope of improving current conditions. For a previously dominant power, that abandonment is likely to be grudging and reluctant, while for the emerging power there is likely to be a sense of triumph. Because "peace," will therefore be different for different parties, misunderstandings about the settlement are likely to arise.

Another path to de-escalation is compulsion.[10] Militant leaders argue that the other side understands only force, that the enemy will come to the bargaining table only when it otherwise faces defeat. And government leaders will often assure their constituency that it is necessary to bargain from a position of strength. For example, as plans to install U.S. cruise missiles and Pershing II rockets in Western Europe moved ahead in 1981, Gen. Bernard W. Rogers, NATO's supreme commander, argued that the installation would enable the United States to negotiate constraints on theater nuclear weapons from a "position of resolution and strength, the only things the Soviets understand."[11]

A less aggressive stance than a show of force is that of "standing firm." As Secretary of State Dulles observed after the 1955 Austrian State Treaty was signed, the Russian withdrawal of its occupation forces from Austria was "one of those breaks that come if you keep on steadily, steadily keeping the pressure on."[12]

Conflict mitigation and populist advocates argue that explanations stressing coercion are inadequate or misguided. They emphasize that power is an ambiguous dynamic, that power equality is illusory, and that the balance will change. These are subjective matters affected by the intensity with which each party desires its goals and the time frame used; power exists relative to goals, to the strength of an adversary's force, and to its determination.

The adequacy of power is not separable from the goal. After all, it takes little power to get someone to do what he or she would do anyway. For example, perhaps the "correlation of forces" of the early 1970s was such that the U.S. government acknowledged the Soviets to be a superpower. But if the Soviets thought this meant they could play the same major economic and political role they played as a military actor, they soon discovered that their power was insufficient.

Another factor in an adversarial relationship is that both parties must accord the other legitimacy in the struggle. This may entail an abandonment of certain claims, acknowledging that some goals are lost, for example, the aim of destruction or subjugation of an enemy. Mutual respect for the values and interests of an adversary, or at least an acceptance of the legitimacy of the other's existence and a tolerance of its values and interests, must underlie peacemaking efforts.

Often, conflicting parties make clear that they await that acceptance from an adversary. For example, the Israeli government has consistently argued that it cannot negotiate with parties that do not acknowledge its legitimacy. The insistence upon face-to-face, direct negotiations with Arab governments is an assertion of the importance of legitimacy. Similarly, the PLO has insisted upon recognition as the sole legitimate representative of Palestinians and of the right of self-determination before negotiations can begin.[13]

In conflict resolution, preparing to de-escalate involves discovering a particular set of subadversaries to select a subset of contentious issues for which the level of mutual acceptance and balance of power is appropriate.[14] This approach combines attention to coercive strength and to the adversaries' conception of one other and the conflict and matches them with specific issue choices. In the Middle East, for example, there have been many attempts by both mediators and officials of an adversary party to find a set of negotiating partners and an appropriate set of issues to negotiate. The frequent failure to find a successful combination of parties and issues might make this approach unrealistic, evidencing a need for a fundamental shift in the balance of power or mutual acceptance before initiating de-escalation efforts.

The statist approach also acknowledges the importance of mutual acceptance but stresses that it derives from a recognition that coercive power is balanced. Mutual acceptance, however, can be derived from other conditions as well. Populists, for example, suggest that shared values can lead people in enemy countries to recognize each other's humanity and suffering. The pluralist approach adds another suggestion, that positive bonds gradually increase as claims decline.

Acknowledgment of one another's legitimacy is often related to a shared view of the nature of the conflict. Conflicts are often intractable because adversaries do not agree on their disagreement.[15] One party may resist what it regards as an ideological invasion, while the other believes the resisting party to be seeking better terms for an economic relationship. Such misunderstandings handicap de-escalation efforts, for example, in conflicts between the U.S. government and some third world countries. When a shared view of the issues in contention emerges, the parties can envision a mutually acceptable outcome.

In addition to relative power and a recognition of legitimacy, special circumstances may affect the possibility of undertaking peacemaking initiatives. Domestic conditions, a change in leadership, economic difficulties, or a mobilized peace movement in one society may be viewed by an adversary as an opportunity to de-escalate a conflict. But for some leaders, it may also provide an opportunity to raise new demands to improve the settlement.

The various arguments that stress specific preconditions for de-escalation efforts are not mutually exclusive. Domestic and international factors and adversary relations can reinforce each other in providing the bases for peacemaking initiatives. One especially important, related process is the decline in the salience of a particular fight. Since every conflict is interlocked with many others, a particular conflict can decline in importance when another becomes more prominent.[16] For example, as the struggle between China and the Soviet Union escalated in the 1960s, Chinese leaders came to view the United States as Enemy Number Two rather than Enemy Number One.

Cases of Initiatives

Reviewing actual de-escalation initiatives can help to assess the relevance of various preconditions, even though certain preconditions may have been present for one party and not for another. Consequently, it is to be expected that one party may undertake a peace initiative that is not reciprocated.

Identifying Initiatives

De-escalation initiatives are precursors to possible agreements. They include an invitation from an adversary to talk about an issue, a detailed proposal for an agreement, and perhaps a proposed means for carrying out de-escalation. Just *when* a de-escalation initiative is being offered is not always clear. Government officials often state their terms for a conflict settlement, but are these peace initiatives or are they quietly asserted demands? Whether an action is a true peace initiative might be decided by uncovering the intentions of the initiators, accepting the adversary's judgment, deciding independently, or by simply taking the initiator's word. Each alternative, however, has its problems.[17]

Uncovering the intentions of a government is nearly always impossible, for at least four reasons. First, a government consists of many individuals and groups, and not all have identical intentions. Second, government officials are not always unequivocal about their intentions. Third, gaining access to relevant data for clarification is often difficult. Finally, intentions change as circumstances change and as an adversary responds to initiatives.

Following the judgment of the adversary also has serious problems: A publicly stated perception of an initiative may be a subterfuge; relying on it means that the initiators' enemies have determined the reality of a peace initiative. Making an objective assessment requires having widely accepted standards—unlikely in major international conflicts; we are left with the research analysts devising their own standards. Finally, the initiators' own characterization is likely to be self-serving.

Often initiatives are purported to be aimed at de-escalation, but the initiator and many observers will expect them to be rejected. For example, at the 1955 Geneva Foreign Ministers Conference, the United States, France, and the United Kingdom proposed to the Soviets a seventeen-point program to expand exchanges, including: "All censorship should be progressively eliminated. The obstacles which hamper the flow of full factual information and varied comment between the peoples of the West and those of the Soviet Union should be removed. . . . The systematic jamming of broadcasts of news and information is a practice to be deplored."[18] Foreign Minister Vyacheslav Molotov rejected the proposal as an interference in internal Soviet affairs. The motives of the Americans may indeed be questioned when we read the UN National Security Council statement of policy (NSC 5607) underlying the proposal. It begins with the assertion that "the basic strategy of the United States vis-à-vis the Soviet bloc is: a. To promote within Soviet Russia evolution toward a regime which will abandon predatory policies . . . and which will increasingly rest upon the consent of the governed rather than upon despotic police power."[19]

Sometimes, conversely, a government takes an action that might seem aimed at de-escalation but is not officially presented as such, government officials claiming that an action was taken for domestic or other reasons. For example, Carter publicly explained that he had canceled the B-1 bomber program in 1977 because it was wasteful and because more effective weapons were being developed.[20] The best solution here is to accept the purpose of an action to be as stated publicly by the initiator. This is readily accessible and also provides a basis for assessing the adversary's response. Sometimes one can judge an action to constitute an initiative from the politics of the parties involved.

Tables 3 and 4 list major de-escalation initiatives in the American-Soviet and Arab-Israeli conflicts chronologically since 1948. To select the initiatives in the major conflicts, I searched U.S., Soviet, Israeli, and Arab accounts of the post-1947 history of both conflicts. These sources include memoirs, textbooks, yearbooks, journals, and contemporary newspaper stories. Some actions were not mentioned by all relevant sources but involved major institutions or the highest officials of adversary governments and were cited by at least one party to the conflict; they could be included with little doubt.[21]

One difficulty in selecting initiatives was that some were part of an extended campaign conducted over a long period; other initiatives related to a single matter of contention and took varying forms; while still others were isolated actions. For campaigns with many initiatives, only one or two of the first ones appear. If they were reciprocated and negotiations followed, later initiatives are treated as part of earlier actions; if negotiations did not follow, subsequent initiatives are included if they were more than reiterations of earlier ones. They do not include actions that are predominantly coercive, for example, making or threatening war to force an adversary to accept predetermined terms of settlement. Although such actions may actually help to create the preconditions for de-escalation initiatives, they are not properly de-escalation efforts.

Initiatives may be undertaken by officials from one of the primary adversaries or by one of their allies and may belong to another country or to an international organization. Private individuals from one or more of the adversary parties frequently attempt to resolve a conflict by making suggestions and acting as mediators. Persons from countries not immediately involved in the conflict may also make such efforts; they are included in the tables only if they are government officials or leaders of major transnational actors.

Varieties of Initiatives

A de-escalation action may consist of a speech or a letter in which an effort to communicate a proposal is made. The communication may be made through an intermediary (a government official or private individual) or directly, as in an exchange of letters or discussions through normal diplomatic channels, including formal meetings such as conferences. Or, the action may be a unilateral gesture, a conciliatory move accompanying or separate from a peacemaking proposal.

Table 3. Chronology of Major U.S.-USSR De-escalation Initiatives,
1948–1989

1948–1957

1948

May: Joseph Stalin replies to open letter of Henry Wallace, approving his program as a basis for agreement.

1949

January: Stalin says he is prepared to meet Truman to discuss a world pact, but not in the United States; Truman announces he would be glad to welcome Stalin in Washington, D.C.
January: Stalin responds to question by correspondent about ending Berlin blockade and omits reference to extension of West German currency reform to West Berlin.
April: World Peace Council established in Paris with Soviet encouragement, followed within the year by the Stockholm Peace Appeal.

1950

November: USSR proposes a meeting of Big Four foreign ministers to negotiate a peace treaty for Germany (unified and demilitarized).

1951

June: Soviet ambassador Jacob Malik, Soviet delegate to the United Nations, suggests negotiation of cease-fire in Korea.
June: U.S. Congress adopts resolution welcoming all honorable efforts to resolve differences with the Soviet government.

1952

March: Soviets send a note to the Western powers proposing negotiations on a peace treaty for Germany (reunited and neutral).

1953

March: Soviet Premier Georgi Malenkov announces that there is no U.S.-USSR dispute that cannot be decided by peaceful means, lifts roadblocks around West Berlin; and Chinese accept voluntary repatriation of prisoners of war in Korea.
April: Churchill expresses desire for a Big Four summit; Eisenhower calls for Soviet deeds to prove sincerity.
December: Dwight Eisenhower, at UN General Assembly, proposes "atoms for peace"—diverting fissionable material for peaceful purposes—to the United Nations.

1954

January–February: A conference of Big Four foreign ministers opens in Berlin on German and Austrian treaties; Vyacheslav Molotov proposes a conference on security in Europe and that East and West Germany establish a provisional government.
April: At Geneva conference, France, U.K., PRC, and the USSR meet to discuss armistice in Indochina; Soviets offer to join NATO.
June: French and British representatives submit to the five-power subcommittee (Canada, France, U.K., U.S., and USSR) of the UN Disarmament Commission (UNDC) a comprehensive plan to reduce nuclear and conventional arms in stages.

June: Prime Minister Churchill proposes a U.K.-USSR summit meeting to Foreign Minister Molotov.

1955

March: Soviets propose nuclear weapon test ban.

April: The Austrian chancellor visits Moscow, and agreement is reached on the neutralization of Austria.

May: USSR announces reduction of armed forces by 1,200,000 men.

May: U.S., U.K., and France send notes to USSR proposing Big Four foreign-ministers meeting.

June: Molotov calls for a world economic conference to develop international trade.

June: USSR announces liquidation of Soviet military base in Finland.

July: At Big Four summit meeting in Geneva; Eisenhower proposes "Open Skies" and Bulganin proposes twenty-six-nation European security treaty to replace NATO and Warsaw Pact.

October: Conference of Big Four foreign ministers opens in Geneva; U.K. and U.S. propose seventeen-point program to remove barriers to exchange; discussions of European security and disarmament.

1956

February: Khrushchev at Twentieth Party Congress presents doctrine of peaceful coexistence; in secret, attacks Stalin.

March: U.S. proposes that both the U.S. and the USSR cease production of fissionable materials.

1957

October: U.S.-USSR negotiations on cultural, educational, and scientific exchanges begin.

October: Polish Foreign Minister Adam Rapacki proposes denuclearized zone in Central Europe.

December: Premier Nicolay Bulganin formally writes proposing an East–West summit.

1958–1967

1958

March: Soviets suspend nuclear weapons testing.

April: Eisenhower invites Soviets to participate in meetings of the twelve countries having done scientific work in Antarctica during the International Geophysical Year about the future of Antarctica.

August: Eisenhower proposes trilateral negotiations on a verifiable test ban;
    Khrushchev calls for end of four-power occupation of Berlin.

October: United States and sixteen UN members cosponsor a UN resolution to suspend nuclear weapon testing and urge agreement for a ban, under effective international control; United States stops testing nuclear weapons.

1959

August: Soviet Union pledges not to resume nuclear testing if Western powers do not resume testing.

September: Khrushchev meets with Eisenhower at Camp David; they discuss Berlin, disarmament, nuclear test ban, and trade and credit.

1961

June: At summit with President Kennedy in Vienna, Khrushchev insists on agreement on peace treaty with Germany, otherwise USSR will sign a separate treaty; they also discuss Laos and nuclear testing.

September: John J. McCloy (U.S.) and Valerian A. Zorin (USSR) talks lead to Joint Statement of Agreed Principles for Disarmament Negotiations.

December: At the UN General Assembly, Irish propose to foreclose options for additional countries to have nuclear weapons; Sweden proposes voluntary self-organization of a nuclear-free club.

1962

March: UN Eighteen-Nation Committee on Disarmament convenes.

October: Soviets agree to withdraw missiles from Cuba.

1963

June: Kennedy speech at American University.

July: Averell Harriman (U.S.) and Lord Hailsman (U.K.) meet with Khrushchev and Andrey Gromyko (USSR) in Moscow to negotiate PTBT; Khrushchev proposes East–West nonaggression pact; Harriman proposes non-proliferation treaty.

September: Bilateral U.S.-USSR negotiations begin on consular rights and practices.

October: Kennedy authorizes sale of surplus wheat to USSR.

October: U.S. and USSR support UN resolution calling on all states to refrain from placing in orbit any objects carrying nuclear weapons.

December: Upon invitation from the Soviets, Najeeb E. Halaby (head of U.S. Federal Aeronautics Administration) visits Moscow; instructed by Lyndon Johnson to work for a civil aviation agreement with the Soviets.

1964

January: Khrushchev sends a message to Johnson proposing an agreement to settle territorial disputes by peaceful means; Johnson announces in State of the Union address a cutback of 25 percent in the production of fissionable material for nuclear weapons.

April: Johnson announces further cutbacks in the production of enriched uranium and that the USSR is also reducing its production of fissionable material.

May: Johnson gives speech at the dedication of the George C. Marshall Library, Virginia Military Institute, expressing his desire to build bridges of trade, travel, and humanitarian assistance across the gulf that separates Eastern and Western Europe.

1965

February: Johnson appoints Special Committee on U.S. Trade Relations with Eastern European Countries and the Soviet Union.

1966

January: In his State of the Union speech, Johnson announces that he intends to introduce a bill to remove special tariff barriers to East–West trade (subsequently introduced in May).

September: Gromyko, in talks with Dean Rusk, indicates that the Soviets accept conditions on the Western European nuclear role compatible with the non-proliferation treaty.

October: Johnson, in a major speech, indicates acceptance of Polish–German border and reduced priority for German reunification and initiates several trade and other cooperative actions.

December: U.S. ambassador to the USSR confidentially proposes bilateral talks on limiting ABMS.

1967

January: The Soviets accept an offer to negotiate on ABM and propose that talks cover offensive missile systems as well.

January: Johnson removes additional commodities from the strategic control list and widens authority of Export-Import Bank to help finance export sales to Eastern Europe.

June: Johnson and Aleksy Kosygin meet at Glassboro, N.J.; Kosygin proposes Israeli withdrawal from Sinai and U.S. withdrawal of combat forces from Vietnam; Johnson urges ABM and SALT agreements.

August: Delegate from Malta to UN General Assembly calls for preservation of ocean floor for peaceful purposes.

1968–1977
1968

June: U.S. signals readiness to discuss force reductions in Europe.

July: U.S. and USSR announce agreement to hold talks on the limitation and reduction of strategic nuclear weapons and of ABM's.

August: British delegation at Geneva Disarmament Commission proposes moving to a prohibition of microbiological methods of warfare.

November: Johnson suggests, through diplomatic channels, a summit meeting with the Soviets.

1969

February: Anatolyn F. Dobrynin broaches the idea of a summit meeting with President Nixon.

March: Warsaw Pact meeting proposes a European security conference; Soviets propose demilitarizing seabed.

May: May Day celebration in Moscow, for first time since end of World War II, it does not include a military parade.

July: In speech to the Supreme Soviet, Gromyko calls for closer American-Soviet relations.

October: Secret U.S.-USSR talks on Middle East peace.

November: Nixon renounces use of all methods of bacteriological warfare.

December: UN General Assembly affirms customary law prohibiting chemical and biological warfare.

1970

January: Dobrynin suggests summit meeting.

March: Status of Berlin negotiations by American, French, and British ambassadors to West Germany and Soviet ambassador to East Germany.

1971

May: Brezhnev expresses interest in force reductions in Central Europe and invites negotiations.

June: Nixon rescinds 1963 requirement that 50 percent of American grain sold to Soviet Union move in U.S. ships.

September: USSR proposes U.S.-USSR sponsorship of a comprehensive settlement of Arab-Israeli conflict.

November: U.S. trade delegation visits Moscow.

1972

January: Dobrynin suggests that a declaration of principles be issued at forthcoming summit.

February: Dobrynin advises Kissinger that Soviets are ready to reopen talks to settle U.S. lend-lease claims.

April: Soviets propose U.S.-USSR sponsorship of comprehensive settlement of Arab-Israeli conflict; Soviets propose U.S.-Soviet treaty renouncing the use of nuclear weapons against each other.

May: Nixon and Brezhnev meet at a summit in Moscow and conclude ABM, SALT I, and other agreements.

November: Conference on Security and Cooperation in Europe (CSCE) opens in Helsinki.

1973

January: Exploratory talks on Mutual and Balanced Force Reduction (MBFR) begin in Vienna.

June: Brezhnev and Nixon meet at summit in Washington, reach agreements on SALT II principles; discuss bilateral cooperation and CSCE.

December: Geneva Peace Conference on Middle East is held, cochaired by U.S. and USSR.

By year's end, 34,733 Jews emigrate from the USSR, a new annual high.

1974

June: Nixon and Brezhnev begin summit in Moscow; Brezhnev urges comprehensive test ban (CTB); together they negotiate a 150-kiloton threshold test ban (TTB).

October: Conclusion of long-term U.S.-USSR grain agreement.

November: Ford and Brezhnev meet in Vladivostok; discuss terms for SALT II.

1975

September: Negotiations for a long-term grain sale agreement between U.S. and the USSR, following U.S. moratorium on grain sales.

1976

July: Ford meets with Brezhnev in Helsinki in conjunction with CSCE; they discuss SALT II and Middle East.

1977

January: Carter publicly urges comprehensive test ban; writes Brezhnev that his goal is to improve relations, reach a quick SALT accord, agreement on a CTB, and MBFR; and to have an early summit.

March: U.S. raises and obtains Soviet agreement to antisatellite (ASAT) arms control talks.

March: Cyrus Vance, in Moscow, presents Carter's comprehensive SALT proposal: a large reduction in strategic weapons compared to Vladivostok understanding.

June: CTB talks open, with U.K., U.S., and USSR representation.

June: Carter cancels B-1 bomber.

September: CSCE follow-up meeting in Belgrade opens; East proposes mutual undertaking against first use of nuclear weapons.

October: Joint U.S.-USSR statement on Geneva conference on the Middle East.

November: Brezhnev announces moratorium on peaceful nuclear explosions.

December: Talks to limit conventional arms transfer (CAT) open.

1978–1989
1978

April: Carter defers production of enhanced radiation weapons.

1979

June: Carter and Brezhnev meet at Vienna—discuss human rights, U.S.-China rapprochement, and SALT III.

October: Brezhnev announces unilateral withdrawal of twenty thousand Soviet military personnel from East Germany; proposes theater nuclear-force negotiations separate from MBFR.

December: NATO approves two-track plan to deploy Pershing II and cruise missiles in Europe and to negotiate limitations of long-range theater nuclear weapons.

By year's end, 51,333 Jews emigrate from the USSR, a new annual high, following a decline after 1973.

1980

November: Soviet and American delegations meet in Geneva to open negotiating track of NATO two-track plan.

1981

April: Reagan lifts fifteen-month-old embargo on grain sales to USSR.

May: Reagan indicates intention of U.S. to begin negotiations with USSR on European nuclear forces within the SALT framework by the end of the year.

November: Reagan presents zero-option proposal for intermediate-range nuclear forces (INF) in Europe.

November: Brezhnev, in Bonn, offers unilateral reduction of "hundreds" of medium-range missiles and proposes new version of long-standing Soviet proposal.

1982

May: Reagan unveils START proposal, with deep cuts in intercontinental ballistic missiles (ICBM's).

June: Gromyko declares before UN General Assembly's special disarmament session that USSR would not be the first country to use nuclear weapons in war; massive demonstrations in New York to freeze nuclear arms.

July: U.S. negotiator Paul H. Nitze and Soviet negotiator Yuli Kvitsinsky, in a "walk in the woods," reach compromise on INF.

1983

March: Reagan describes vision of the Strategic Defense Initiative (SDI).

August: USSR and U.S. agree to negotiate new cultural and scientific exchange agreements.

August: Soviets call for eliminating ASAT systems.

1984

January: George Shultz and Gromyko meet in Stockholm.

April: U.S. proposes to forty-nation Disarmament Conference in Geneva a comprehensive treaty banning chemical weapons.

May: U.S. House of Representatives denies funds for production of chemical weapons.

1985

March: Vice President George Bush, at Chernenko funeral, conveys Reagan's interest in summit meeting.

April: Soviets announce a moratorium on further deployment of SS20's.

July: Gorbachev announces a unilateral moratorium on nuclear-weapons testing.

December: Gorbachev offers to allow U.S. inspection of Soviet nuclear facilities.

December: Regarding MBFR, NATO proposes to defer Western demand for prior data agreement on Eastern forces.

1986

January: Gorbachev proposes banning all nuclear weapons by the year 2000.

September: Soviets release U.S. correspondent Nicholas S. Daniloff; accused Soviet spy Gennadi F. Zakharov exchanged for group of Soviet dissidents.

December: Reagan administration trade officials report plan to remove most controls on exports of oil and gas equipment and technology to the USSR.

1987

February: Gorbachev proposes agreement to eliminate intermediate-range nuclear missiles in Europe, abandoning link with SDI.

April: Gorbachev announces USSR has stopped production of chemical weapons.

May: Soviets end jamming of "Voice of America."

1988

December: At UN General Assembly, Gorbachev pledges to reduce Soviet military forces unilaterally by five hundred thousand by 1991 and assume defensive posture.

1989

January: Soviets begin final withdrawal from Afghanistan.

May: Gorbachev states Soviets will reduce nuclear arsenal in Eastern Europe and proposes both NATO and Warsaw Pact cutback of 1 million troops.

May: Bush proposes specific ceilings on weaponry and combat forces of NATO and Warsaw Pact.

July: In address to Council of Europe, Gorbachev asserts that any attempt to restrict the sovereignty of states is inadmissible.

November: East Germany opens borders, including Berlin Wall.

Table 4. Chronology of Major Arab-Israeli De-escalation Initiatives,
1948–1989

1948–1957
1948
May: UN General Assembly appoints Count Folke Bernadotte as mediator for Palestine.
September: Bernadotte proposes plan, is assassinated, and Ralph Bunche is appointed mediator.
December: UN creates the Conciliation Commission for Palestine (CCP); members are governments of France, Turkey, and the United States.
Winter of 1948/49: King Abdullah of Jordan begins secret negotiations with Israeli government about peace.

1949
January: Israeli and Egyptian delegations meet in Rhodes for armistice negotiations chaired by Bunche.
April–May: Lausanne conference initiated by CCP; Arab and Israeli delegations negotiate regarding Palestinian refugees and Israeli borders.
August: CCP establishes mixed committee on blocked bank accounts; arranges talks between Israelis and Egyptians.

1950
April: UN Trusteeship Council approves statute for the internationalization of Jerusalem.
May: U.S., U.K., and France issue Tripartite Declaration, limiting arms sales to and opposing use of force in the Middle East.

1951
September: Paris conference begins with representatives of Arab and Israeli governments. CCP presents comprehensive outline for settlement.

1952
August: Israel extends "friendship" to new heads of Egypt, offering benefits if peace negotiated.
December: Israel submits to General Assembly "Blue Print for Peace in the Middle East."

1953
March: Israel and Egypt begin series of indirect meetings.
August: Nasser states that Egypt needs peace to solve internal problems and suggests that U.S. government mediate.
October: Eisenhower appoints Eric Johnston to help establish a regional water development project based on the Jordan River.

1954
August: Israel makes several small conciliatory moves regarding refugees and land links.

1955
April: Egyptian ambassador to the United States approaches American Quakers to explore formulas for settlement between Israelis and Arabs; Elmore Jackson undertakes mission.

August: Secretary of State John Foster Dulles proposes active U.S. role to help resolve specific problems in Middle East.

November: Eden announces that United Kingdom would give a guarantee to Israeli and Arab states if they settle boundaries.

1956

November: General Assembly calls for cease-fire in Egypt, withdrawal of foreign troops, restoration of freedom of navigation. (Follows invasion of Egypt by Israeli, British, and French forces.)

Moshe Sharett, visiting the U.S., informs Dulles of Israeli readiness to make concessions as a contribution to a peace settlement.

1957

January: Eisenhower announces new U.S. policy in the Middle East, proposing economic aid to foster national independence (Eisenhower Doctrine).

February: Canadian External Affairs Minister Lester B. Pearson proposes to the UN General Assembly, among other points, that the UN Emergency Force be deployed along Egyptian-Israeli armistice demarcation lines.

June: Ben Gurion announces Israel's acceptance of Eisenhower Doctrine in the Knesset.

October: Australian Prime Minister Robert G. Menzies suggests six points as basis for Middle East settlement and proposes establishment of international advisory body to offer advice on economic problems of countries in the Middle East.

1958–67
1958

June: UN Secretary General Dag Hammarskjöld visits Middle East for talks on Israel-Jordan tension.

November: Israeli Ambassador Abba Eban renews Israel's readiness to compensate Arab refugees before a peace settlement.

1959

June: Hammarskjöld presents General Assembly with a plan for the integration of Palestinians in the economic life of the Middle East.

October: Egyptian representative tells the United Nations that Israel will be permitted to use Suez canal after Palestinian refugee problem is settled.

1961

May: Upon U.S. initiative, CCP decides to use a "special representative" on the refugee question; in August, Joseph E. Johnson is named Special Representative.

1962

October: Johnson proposes a plan for Palestinian refugees to be allowed to choose between a return to Palestine or compensation.

1963

September: King Hussein of Jordan initiates secret talks with Israel.

November: UN General Assembly's Special Committee on Palestine approves a U.S.-suggested resolution that CCP continue its efforts to enable Palestinian refugees to return to Palestine or be compensated.

1964

January: Arab summit conference in Cairo discusses Jordan River diversion, establishment of a joint military command and establishment of Palestine Liberation Organization (PLO).

1965

April: President of Tunisia Habib Bourguiba calls for a settlement of the Arab-Israeli dispute on the basis of the UN Partition Resolution.

May: Israeli Prime Minister Levi Eshkol proposes a peace settlement based upon 1949 armistice agreements and direct negotiations between Israel and the countries that signed agreements.

Fall: King Hussein meets secretly with Golda Meir in London.

1966

May: Eshkol calls for limitations on regional arms buildup.

1967

June: UN Security Council calls for cease-fire as Israeli forces advance against Egyptian, Syrian, and Jordanian forces.

President Johnson outlines five-point peace plan.

Soviet Premier Kosygin calls for Israeli withdrawal from territories occupied in the June war.

August: President Tito of Yugoslavia proposes plan including Israeli withdrawal from all occupied areas, indemnification of Palestinian refugees, bipower guarantee of Israeli borders, and Arab declaration of end of belligerence.

November: Security Council adopts resolution 242; Gunnar Jarring appointed special representative of the UN secretary general.

1968–77
1968

October: Foreign Minister Eban offers nine-point peace plan at UN General Assembly.

1969

April: American, French, British, and Soviet representatives meet to discuss Middle East situation.

Hussein, in Washington, indicating that he is speaking also for Nasser, proposes solution of Arab-Israeli conflict, including recognition of the rights of all states to live within secure and recognized boundaries and requiring the withdrawal of Israeli forces from all territories occupied in the June 1967 war.

October: Secret U.S.-USSR talks on Middle East peace.

Israel proposes home rule for the West Bank, retaining responsibility for security.

December: Secretary of State William P. Rogers announces peace plan based on an Israeli withdrawal in exchange for peace treaty with Arabs.

1970

March: Hussein meets secretly with Israeli officials.

June: Rogers discloses U.S. initiative to end War of Attrition along Suez canal for ninety days; Jarring resumes mission.

November: UN General Assembly calls for ninety-day extension of cease-fire and resumption of Jarring talks.

1971

February: Israel and Egypt accept in principle the idea of an interim agreement for reopening of the Suez canal.

Anwar Sadat informs Jarring that Egypt is willing to envisage peace arrangements with Israel under certain conditions.

Israel informs Jarring that it is ready to negotiate peace with Arab states but cannot give prior commitment regarding borders.

May: Rogers visits the Middle East for talks on interim agreement.

September: USSR proposes U.S.-USSR sponsorship of a comprehensive settlement of the Arab-Israeli conflict.

1972

March: Hussein announces a plan to make Jordan a federal state.

April: USSR proposes U.S.-USSR sponsorship of a comprehensive settlement of Arab-Israeli conflict.

1973

October: U.S. and USSR propose to the UN Security Council a cease-fire resolution to end the fighting between Israeli forces and Egyptian and Syrian forces.

November: Israel and Egypt negotiate an agreement to stabilize the cease-fire.

December: Geneva peace conference on Middle East is held.

1974

January: Henry Kissinger shuttles to negotiate an Israeli-Egyptian separation of forces agreement (Sinai I).

Kissinger begins to mediate an Israeli-Syrian disengagement on the Golan Heights.

Summer: Kissinger tries to negotiate an Israeli-Jordanian disengagement.

October: The UN General Assembly invites the PLO to participate in deliberations on Palestine.

Arab leaders meeting in Rabat declare the PLO to be the sole legitimate representative of the Palestinian people.

1975

March: Kissinger undertakes to negotiate a second Egyptian-Israeli disengagement (Sinai II).

1976

April: Local elections held in Israeli occupied territories; pro-PLO candidates win.

December: The UN General Assembly passes resolutions calling for the reconvening of the Geneva conference on the Middle East by 1 March 1977, a Palestinian state, and PLO participation in the conference.

1977

January: Carter initiates consultations with Israeli and Arab leaders about holding a Geneva conference on the Middle East, to be cochaired by the U.S. and Soviet governments.

August: Israeli Foreign Minister Dayan meets secretly with King Hussein in London to discuss possible peace initiatives and peace settlements.

September: Dayan meets secretly with Doctor Hassan Tuhami, representing Sadat, to discuss a possible peace settlement.

October: As a prelude to the Geneva conference, U.S. and Soviet governments issue a joint statement, declaring that a comprehensive settlement of the Arab-Israeli conflict would be based on, among other things, an Israeli withdrawal from those territories occupied in the 1967 war and ensuring the legitimate rights of Palestinians.

November: Sadat announces to Egyptian parliament that he is ready to address the Knesset; Prime Minister Menachem Begin invites him and he goes.

December: Sadat invites Arab states, Israel, the United States, and the United Nations to a meeting to prepare for the Geneva conference; the Arab states do not attend.

Sadat and Begin meet in Ismailia, each brings peace proposals.

1978–1989
1978
July: At the suggestion of the United States, Egyptian, Israeli, and American delegations, headed by foreign ministers, meet at Leeds Castle, U.K., to discuss proposals.

September: Upon President Carter's invitation, Egyptian, Israeli, and American delegations, led by heads of government, meet at Camp David, Maryland.

1979
March: Autonomy talks conducted by Egyptian and Israeli delegations.

1981
April: Secretary of State Alexander Haig visits the Middle East to convince conservative Arab leaders of the need for a strategic consensus to counter the Soviet threat.

July: Through UN and Saudi intermediaries, the United States indirectly negotiates a PLO-Israeli cease-fire along the Lebanon-Israeli border.

August: Saudi Crown Prince Fahd of Saudi Arabia proposes an eight-point peace plan.

1982
January: Covert Israeli mission to Phalangists in Lebanon.

August: U.S. facilitates the evacuation of PLO forces from West Beirut.

The UN General Assembly conference on Palestine begins in Geneva; U.S. and Israel do not attend; calls for an international conference on the Middle East.

September: President Reagan announces a peace plan: the Arab-Israeli conflict should be resolved through negotiations, exchanging territory for peace; Palestinians should have full autonomy, associated with Jordan.

Arab summit meeting in Fès, Morocco, announces peace plan, including a Palestinian state and Israeli withdrawal from all territories occupied in 1967.

Brezhnev offers a peace plan, including the establishment of a Palestinian state, total Israeli withdrawal, and security for all states in the region.

1983
May: U.S. mediation in negotiations for Lebanese-Israeli agreement for Israeli withdrawal from Lebanon, security arrangements, and normalization of relations.

December: Yasir Arafat meets with President Hosni Mubarak in Cairo, to strengthen relations with Egypt to bolster bargaining power relative to Syria, Jordan, and Israel.

1984

November: PLO's Palestine National Council meets in Amman, Jordan, empowering Arafat and its executive committee to develop a strategy with Jordan for a negotiated Middle East peace settlement and to continue exchanges with Egypt; calls for international peace conference.

1985

January: Israel announces a phased withdrawal of forces from Lebanon.

February: Arafat and Hussein reach an accord in Amman on negotiating a Middle East peace settlement.

July: List of PLO nominees for Jordanian-Palestinian delegation to meet with the United States is revealed; the Reagan administration asserts that Israel will be consulted about the attendees but will not be allowed veto power.

1986

November: PLO delegation meets with nongovernmental Israeli delegation in Romania.

1987

April: Foreign Minister Shimon Peres meets with Al-Fajr editor Hanna Siniora and other pro-PLO Palestinians to discuss an international Middle East peace conference.

May: Secretary of State Shultz endorses international Middle East conference.

June: UN Under Secretary Marack Goulding visits the Middle East to discuss prospects for an international peace conference.

1988

February: Shultz undertakes a mission to Israel, Jordan, Egypt, and Syria to promote international peace conference.

June: PLO spokesman Bassam Abu Sharif releases statement favoring a Palestinian state alongside Israel.

November: Palestine National Council, meeting in Algiers, proclaims a Palestinian state, accepts UN Security Council resolutions 242 and 338, and rejects terrorism in all forms.

December: The United States announces the opening of dialogue with the PLO.

1989

April: Prime Minister Yitzhak Shamir states that Israel is willing to hold elections in occupied territories to produce a delegation to negotiate an interim self-governing administration.

September: President Mubarak offers a ten-point plan for holding Palestinian elections.

December: The United States issues the "Baker Plan" for Israeli-Palestinian talks regarding elections in occupied territories.

Since several de-escalation efforts may be going on at the same time, the same set of exchanges may involve actions at more than one phase of a conflict. Thus, at a summit meeting, one set of issues may be concluded while proposals to settle another set of issues are explored.[22]

Minor initiatives are not included in tables 3 and 4. *Minor* refers to either the issue in contention or the way a major matter is being addressed. Particularly in U.S.-USSR relations, many matters of contention are handled almost routinely. Whether a matter is major or minor depends finally on interpretation by the adversaries. For example, the establishment in 1949 of a committee—including Egyptians and Israelis—to open the blocked bank accounts of private citizens is often cited as an early de-escalation move in the Arab-Israeli conflict. Yet initiatives and negotiations over Soviet and U.S. fishing claims, leading to many agreements, are rarely mentioned.

Patterns of Initiatives

Four patterns are clearly distinguishable from the tables. First, a great many initiatives have been undertaken; just about everything, it seems, has been tried once. Uncompromising statements have been issued, as if to settle a conflict by fiat; conciliatory gestures have been offered unilaterally; tentative, indirect feelers have been issued and formal conferences called; and would-be intermediaries have issued peace plans or proposals on particular issues. Second, initiatives have been made more often in the American-Soviet conflict than in the Arab-Israeli conflict. Third, the frequency of the peacemaking efforts has varied over the course of the conflicts, many efforts occurring in some years and relatively few in others. They are particularly frequent shortly after an intensification in a conflict—for example, immediately after one of the Arab-Israeli wars—and seem more frequent after someone new assumes leadership of a country that is a primary adversary. Furthermore, there seem to have been more de-escalation efforts as the conflicts continued. Fourth, some parties to these conflicts have been especially active, while others have been generally inactive in undertaking peacemaking initiatives. In the U.S.-USSR conflict, the Soviets have engaged relatively frequently in peace initiatives, some of them including a series of concessions—as in the mid-1950s and late 1980s. In the Arab-Israeli conflict, until the late 1980s, the Palestinians have initiated relatively few de-escalation efforts, even after the PLO was formed. Among neighboring Arab states, the Syrian government has been comparatively uninvolved in de-escalation efforts directed at the Israelis.

Intermediaries have played important roles in de-escalation efforts. This is obvious in the Arab-Israeli conflict, since the United Nations has been a key element from the outset. The U.S. government has also undertaken many de-escalation initiatives in the Arab-Israeli conflict, being a principal in UN efforts during the early years of the conflict.

Even in the U.S.-USSR conflict, intermediaries have been key agents. In the United States, relations with the Soviet Union are popularly seen to be bilateral. In the immediate post–World War II years, however, the Big Four (the USSR, the United States, Great Britain, and France) constituted the primary set of actors in negotiation efforts. Although generally this has been an East–West division, sometimes differences among the Western powers have been such that one or another played a quasi-intermediary role.

Particular issues, especially those relating to nuclear disarmament, have been the subject of de-escalation efforts by countries allied neither with the United States nor with the USSR. The United Nations here too has provided a convenient setting for such initiatives.

In the next chapter, I apply the various explanations for de-escalation initiatives and assess how well they account for those efforts.

4

Accounting for
the Initiatives

Preconditions in three spheres are relevant in accounting for the variations in de-escalation initiatives: domestic circumstances, the international context, and relations between the protagonists. I examine the relevance of these factors in explaining the patterns previously described, noting strategic implications.

Domestic Circumstances

Populists and pluralists stress that government actions are a response primarily to a combination of domestic circumstances. Constituency pressures constitute one major circumstance.[1] For a government head, direct pressure comes from valued advisers and fellow officials, political party leaders, nongovernmental supporters, opposition political leaders, rivals, a variety of elite groups, and from the public at large. Indirect pressure comes from the competing demands for economic resources and social attention. To what degree does the public foster de-escalation efforts? The events listed in tables 3 and 4 reflect the presence or absence of domestic public pressure to both sets of initiatives.

Direct public pressure includes public opinion, as manifested in polls, social movements, social movement organizations, demonstrations, and votes for opposition parties.[2] Assessing the level of public support for de-escalation is certainly difficult; the public is not homogeneous in opinions or in influence; moreover, opinions vary over time on specific proposals. Direct indicators of public opinion are available for the United States and to a lesser degree for Israel; for Egypt and the USSR, they are indirect.

The United States

A few examples typify the relation between public pressure and government action.[3] For the United States, these include efforts on a nuclear weapon test ban (1955–63), the rise of détente (1969–72), the reduction of strategic nuclear weapons (1981–82), and the *absence* of U.S. government de-escalation initiatives in regard to Berlin and a nuclear free Central Europe in the late 1950s and early 1960s. For the USSR, they include its initiatives in the late 1950s and early 1970s, as well as its lack of responsiveness in the late 1960s on antiballistic weapon systems and strategic nuclear weapons. The role of domestic forces in the transformation of Soviet foreign policy in the late 1980s was crucially important.

For the Arab-Israeli conflict, illustrative cases are the Egyptian initiatives in the early 1970s and late 1970s, the PLO and Jordanian initiative of 1985, and the Israeli initiatives in the late 1970s and early 1980s. There were relatively fewer initiatives by the Egyptian and Jordanian governments in the early 1960s, by the PLO leadership in the 1960s and 1970s, and by the Israeli government in the early 1960s and late 1980s.

The trends in U.S. public opinion of the Soviet Union are clear.[4] In the 1950s, hostility toward the Soviet Union and an intolerance of communism were almost universal. This widespread, intense antagonism gradually declined in the 1960s but began to rise somewhat in the mid-1970s. Opinions on specific issues varied within that general context. Public concern over radioactive fallout from nuclear weapon tests emerged in the mid-1950s. Pressure for a test ban grew quickly and was expressed in the

resolutions of legislative bodies, petitions, mass demonstrations, and statements by prominent individuals. By 1957, as Glenn Seaborg noted, "perhaps most significant of all to the [U.S.] administration, the Gallup Poll
showed that 63 percent of the American public favored a test ban, as
contrasted to only 20 percent three years earlier."[5]

Negotiations for a comprehensive nuclear test ban went on for several
years, and the Soviet and U.S. governments halted testing for extended
periods. Public opinion in support of continued cessation or for an agreement to stop testing varied considerably according to how the matter was
presented.[6] While British public opinion strongly opposed testing in the
early 1960s, survey data indicated that American public opinion would
support President Kennedy whether or not he decided to resume testing.[7]
There was, nonetheless, overwhelming support for the treaty once signed.

Détente is another example. The U.S. government's shift toward détente
in the early 1970s followed a massive peace movement, which grew and
was consistent with a transformation in U.S. public opinion beginning in the
late 1960s and early 1970s. The lyric "give peace a chance," was sung at
many demonstrations, and the peace symbol was widely displayed; but
peace referred to ending the U.S. government's involvement in the war in
Vietnam. The connection with détente was made by the Nixon administration.[8]

When Richard M. Nixon took office as president in January 1969, he
faced many contradictory demands, which détente promised to help satisfy.
Opposition to the war had grown so that in late 1969, 58 percent of the
population thought the United States had made a mistake in sending troops
to Vietnam; only 32 percent thought it was not a mistake.[9] Once engaged, it
was not clear what should be done. Many people favored increasing military
intervention in order to win, others favored a military withdrawal. Nixon
sought withdrawal with honor. He saw that the Soviet Union and China
could help in encouraging the North Vietnamese to provide that honorable
way out. Approaching both nations, given their enmity, would make each
more eager to reach an accommodation with the United States.

Meanwhile, the level of violence against North Vietnam increased, and
U.S. troops were slowly withdrawn. Nixon knew that being a peacemaker
with the major communist countries would help him to deflect opposition
while continuing the war in Vietnam. Such calculations were necessary
because opponents to the Vietnam War had joined other forces and movements that would profoundly affect American society. A lack of confidence
in major institutions, including the military, had grown; increasingly Congress acted independently of the president and tried to control his decisions.

General trends in the 1960s toward increased liberalism and tolerance had reduced the public's animosity toward communism and the Soviet Union.[10] Together these developments fostered a movement toward détente by Nixon's administration.

A last example of a U.S. initiative is the Reagan administration's proposal to reduce nuclear weapons as part of Strategic Arms Reduction Talks (START) negotiations. Ronald Reagan had been elected president calling for vastly increasing U.S. military capability and condemning the SALT II treaty as "fatally flawed." The administration had showed little interest in reaching an arms control agreement on terms that seemed acceptable to the Soviets. When possible U.S. arms control positions were considered, they were defended by some department officials as negotiable but attacked by others on that very ground. A plausible position was all that was sought.[11]

The need to find this plausible position seemed to be a response to public pressure. In the late 1970s, public support for increased military spending had risen sharply as had antagonism toward the Soviet Union. Shortly after Reagan became president, however, immense increases in military spending and the militant rhetoric toward the Soviets spurred a reaction: public approval declined sharply. The nuclear freeze campaign grew quickly and gained the widespread active support of the public and Congress. The appearance of a willingness to negotiate an arms control agreement became politically necessary for the Reagan administration.

Public pressure in a country affects the likelihood that an adversary will undertake a de-escalation initiative. Popular support for accommodation can provide reassurance to an adversary that peacemaking overtures will be recognized and respected. For example, Soviet moves toward accommodation since 1985 may have been fostered by American popular and Congressional opposition to the Reagan administration's militantly anti-Communist policies.

Of the many periods during which no major peacemaking efforts were made, the U.S. lack of response to the 1957 Rapacki Plan to establish Central Europe as a nuclear free zone warrants consideration. In the United States, the early 1950s were marked by extreme fears of communism at home and abroad and anxiety over not appearing sufficiently alarmed by the threats of communism. McCarthyism came to epitomize what was later seen as hysteria.[12] By the mid-1950s, the intense anti-Communist sentiments of the cold war were beginning to decline, but the level of antagonism was still high and widespread. Peace movement activities were marginal amid the cold war consensus.

"Domestic pressure" in every country covers more than popular views;

those of elite groups and rival political leaders are important elements. In the United States, the cold war consensus extended beyond popular opinion to nearly all elite groups and political leaders and did not fundamentally break until the late 1960s under the impact of the Vietnam War.[13] Widespread popular opposition to the war provided the base for a break in the cold war consensus among elite groups. When present, the consensus made each administration wary of being attacked as soft on communism; Democratic party leaders often seemed particularly fearful of such a charge. Once the consensus broke down, there was more opportunity for possible accommodation with the Soviets, especially for government leaders who had previously established a reputation as hard-line anti-Communists. Nixon took advantage of this; Reagan failed to until the end of his second term.

The Soviet Union

Assessing public pressure in the USSR obviously has been much more difficult than in the United States. Until very recently, relevant survey data were not available, and there were hardly any autonomous social movements or demonstrations. General public views have probably been relatively stable and characterized by an easily understood dualism. First, there is and has been a profound concern to preserve peace and avoid the devastation of war. Second, being militarily strong was widely believed necessary for the preservation of peace.

Nevertheless, the Soviet perception of being threatened by Western powers has varied, as have its priorities other than military security and strength. A direct indicator of such variations is not available. The ebb and flow of mass media reports about threats of American imperialism, German militarism, or the need to strengthen Soviet military capability largely reflect elite views of what the public should think rather than actual popular opinion, which is, of course, influenced by the government-controlled media.

Periods of stagnation or decline in the growth rates of consumer goods per capita may correspond to pressures to reduce military spending.

In his memoirs, Nikita Khrushchev explained the decision to reduce substantially the size of the Soviet armed forces: "We didn't want to give our adversary an opportunity to exhaust us economically. . . . We could demonstrate our own peaceful intentions and at the same time free some of our resources for the development of our industry, the production of consumer goods, and the improvement of living standards."[14] The CIA has prepared estimates of annual Soviet GNP growth by various end uses. Although the value of per capita consumer goods—in 1970 rubles—rose from 279.2 in 1950 to 674.9 in 1980, there has been considerable fluctuation in the rate of growth during those thirty years. In 1951 and 1964, there were actual declines in the value of consumer goods per capita, and in 1961 there was virtually no growth. Among consumer goods, food is the largest component, and its value per capita shows more years of decline: 1951, 1964, 1972, 1976, and 1980, with no significant change in 1961. Overall, the average annual growth rates for food per capita were modest in the 1950s, weak in the early 1960s, stronger in the late 1960s, and then weak again in the 1970s, particularly in the late 1970s.[15]

Changes in military spending are associated with changes in housing construction and the production of durable consumer goods. Annual growth rates in housing construction, between 1950 and 1980, varied from 2.1 to 5.9 percent and were generally low in the late 1970s; in consumer durables they varied widely, from very low in 1963 (-0.4), 1961 (1.7), and 1978 and 1979 (4.2 and 4.1, respectively) to very high in the mid-1950s (30.6 in 1953 and 27.8 in 1954).

There is no perfect match between these indicators and Soviet de-escalation efforts, but possible links may be inferred. Declines in meeting food and durable consumer needs began before and continued during the thaw of the early 1960s. Declines in food availability also occurred at the outset of détente in the early 1970s. The deterioration in consumer conditions in the late 1970s, however, was not associated with major Soviet de-escalation efforts. Although consumer needs were also poorly met in the early 1980s, there was no de-escalation movement during that period, which was a period of Soviet immobility, as one infirm leader followed another as Communist party secretary general. After Mikhail Gorbachev became the dominant leader in the mid-1980s, the Soviets began a major foreign policy shift toward accommodation with the United States. They made significant arms control proposals and reduced their involvement in regional conflicts, such as in Afghanistan. They undertook domestic as well as foreign policy initiatives that were presented as major de-escalation efforts, which were explained by Soviet and U.S. analysts as reflecting the need for domestic economic and social improvements.

The Soviet's new thinking and readiness to make what U.S. officials regarded as major concessions cannot be understood as reactions to immediately preceding U.S. de-escalation efforts. They were primarily new responses to domestic problems; the means to solve them was by increasing access to Western technology, expanding trade, and relieving some of the burden of military expenditures. Domestic pressures, however, do not fully account for those decisions. Gorbachev, in his 2 November 1987 speech to the Central Committee of the Communist party of the Soviet Union (CPSU), spoke of Soviet initiatives as flowing from new thinking and not from domestic concerns: "The new concept of foreign policy . . . proceeds from the idea that for all the profound contradictions of the contemporary world, for all the radical differences among the countries that comprise it, it is interrelated, interdependent and integral. . . . The new thinking with its regard for universal human values and emphasis on common sense and openness, is forging ahead on the international scene, destroying the stereotypes of anti-Sovietism and dispelling distrust of our actions and initiatives."[16] The new thinking, he argued, recognized new world developments. As I will discuss in later chapters, the East–West de-escalation accords of the 1970s helped to provide the basis for the rapid transformations of the late 1980s.

Elite groups in the Soviet Union have been much less differentiated than in the United States. Nevertheless, they have never constituted a single homogeneous unit, and their solidarity has varied over time. During the years dominated by Khrushchev, the party government, managerial, and intellectual elite groups became more differentiated than they had been under Joseph Stalin after the purges.[17] Within the Communist party leadership, factional groupings emerged and persisted; major institutional interests also emerged, for example, among branches of the armed forces and ministries such as those for light and heavy industry. In addition, institutes for the study of international relations and foreign regions were established and the number of other groups interacting with people in the West increased. Although under Brezhnev there was some consolidation of the top leadership into a collective unit, the elite differentiation continued. With Gorbachev, the differentiation grew in a fashion unprecedented since the 1917 revolution.

These groups varied in their foreign policy orientations. Some stressed the need for military strength while others stressed consumer interests; some emphasized the threat from the imperialistic West and others the possibility of working out an accommodation with the West or segments of it. In general, dominant government and party leaders have not been able to move too far away from the existing consensus of the course of action to be pursued. Until the mid-1980s, this situation produced considerable stability and even rigidity in the foreign policy of the USSR. Since the late 1980s, however, the range of expressed foreign policy views has widened greatly, fundamental policy changes have been implemented, and great, unforeseen changes have followed—all resulting in the dissolution of the Soviet foreign policy consensus.

The Arabs

In the Middle East, direct indices of public opinion and public pressure for accommodation with adversaries are generally not available except for Israel and Egypt, where survey data are not adequate for analyzing trends. Again, indirect signs must be used. Acknowledging domestic considerations in taking foreign policy actions that may be viewed as conciliatory, Sadat wrote: "My 'Peace Initiative' of February 4, 1971 was submitted less than four months after I had taken office. . . . I believed that as military action was ruled out at the time, a diplomatic offensive had to be launched: the broad masses wanted to see action being taken all the time."[18] Here, being active and appearing decisive was seen as a way of consolidating support.

Although the general economic difficulties in Egypt are often pointed to as a source of pressure to make peace with Israel, there is not a necessary connection, since economic problems were severe during Nasser's presidency as well as Sadat's. What was different was that Sadat believed that reliance on Soviet assistance and models had not been successful, and he wished to turn to the United States for help. He believed that assistance from the U.S. government would require accommodation or at least the appearance of seeking an accommodation with Israel.

The role of the January 1977 bread riots in Sadat's decision to go to Jerusalem in November 1977 is revealing. The riots to protest the reduction in government subsidies and consequent increases in the prices of bread and other basic commodities were extensive, and troops had to be called to quell them. Sadat was in Aswan when the riots erupted and had to disguise himself to get out; back in Cairo, he had the price increases repealed.[19]

The riots reflected economic distress that required action. The action might have been a further move toward peace with Israel, thus reducing the need for military expenditure and gaining access to substantial U.S. assistance. But some Egyptian intellectuals and government advisers have interpreted the impact of the riots differently.[20] They argue either that the riots had no impact or that Sadat was insulted by them and the slogans chanted against him and decided to disregard the Egyptian people. Instead, he turned to the West for an audience, taking advantage of his popularity there. The move toward peace with Israel, then, was made possible by Sadat's break with his own people.

Sadat may have been offended by the riots, but not so much that he became indifferent to the Egyptian masses. He undoubtedly wanted to remain president and secure sufficient domestic support to do so. The riots, therefore, possibly indicated something else to Sadat. After the great contribution that Egypt had made to the Arab cause, particularly in the October 1973 war with Israel, the petroleum-rich Arab countries had not provided enough assistance to solve Egypt's economic and social problems. Egypt had to find its own way, without relying on other Arab countries.[21] In any case, the riots put pressure on Sadat to do something. Given the choices he had already made, reliance on the U.S. would have appeared increasingly vital.

In Egypt, elite groups include intellectuals, Islamic leaders, government officials, high-ranking members of the military forces and business. Their relative importance and impact on the direction of Egypt's foreign policy has varied, as has the nature of the constituency to which each feels obligated or presumes leadership. Thus, it is significant that Nasser—unlike Sadat—considered his constituency to include the "Arab nation" as a whole, not only Egypt. To maintain that role, championing the Arab cause by encompassing the Palestinian cause was critical. Moreover, the domestic policy of opening the Egyptian economy to Western business, the policy of *infallah*, increased the role of the business elite and supported a foreign policy linked to the United States rather than to the Soviet Union.[22]

The domestic pressures on Jordan's King Hussein and his supporters and on the PLO's Yasir Arafat were quite different. For King Hussein, the presence of large masses of Palestinians constituted great pressure against any accommodation with Israel that the Israeli government was likely to accept without many changed conditions.[23]

In the period between 1948 and 1967, the Jordanian government controlled and then annexed East Jerusalem and the West Bank. Residents could become Jordanian citizens. They included not only those living there before the 1948 war but also those who had fled from their homes in what had become Israel; these refugees wanted a settlement with Israel that would enable them to return to their homes. After the June 1967 war, the West Bank and East Jerusalem came under Israeli control. Even within the remaining Jordanian territory on the east bank of the Jordan River, the Palestinians constituted the majority of the population. They included many who lived in refugee camps with the hope of returning to places they had left after the 1948 and 1967 wars.

Who would speak for the Palestinians has long been a matter of contention. The Jordanian government and other Arab leaders have presented themselves at various times as representatives of the Palestinians. Not until October 1974 did the Arab League, meeting in Rabat, Morocco, endorse the PLO's claim to be the sole legitimate representative of the Palestinian people.

The PLO developed in the mid-1960s, and its leadership was dependent in many ways on people in refugee camps who opposed an accommodation with Israel on terms acceptable to most Israelis.[24] The leaders of the PLO sought to represent all Palestinians, but Palestinians comprise people who differ significantly by country of residence, class, and religious orientation. Fundamental differences of interest in relation to Israel arise from their different places of residence. Some Palestinians live within the State of Israel or in the Israeli-occupied West Bank, East Jerusalem, or Gaza Strip; some are in Jordan, dispersed in Lebanon, the Persian Gulf states, and throughout the world. The armed groups have usually come from refugee camps, particularly those in Lebanon.

For most Palestinian Arabs living under Israeli military occupation in the Gaza Strip and the West Bank, greater autonomy or full independence alongside Israel has become a primary goal. For many living in camps who were denied citizenship in host countries, returning to where they or their parents or grandparents were born is a primary objective. Most Palestinians living in countries where they have become citizens, as in Jordan or in the West, do not seek to return to Palestine, but they lend their support to other Palestinians.

The PLO is a confederation of organizations, the leaders of which are potential rivals. Arafat established himself as the leader of the largest group, Al Fatah, but faced rivalry from within and without. These rivals generally took more extreme positions than his core group. As the "moderate," he seemed reluctant to take any de-escalation initiative for fear of being outflanked by groups more extreme in their demands against Israel.[25]

Shifts in the relative importance of different constituency groups help to account for changes in the policy of the leaders of the PLO. After the Israeli invasion of Lebanon in June 1982 and the subsequent siege of Beirut, PLO fighters were withdrawn from Lebanon. In 1983, Chairman Arafat was also attacked by the Syrian government and PLO factions supported by the Syrian government. Arafat and his associates thus found that the Palestinians on the West Bank and Gaza Strip, together with support from the moderate Arab governments, had become more important than ever. This clarifies somewhat the 1985 agreement between Arafat and Hussein to cooperate in forming a joint delegation to negotiate with Israel.

In 1987, a further shift in the constituency of the PLO developed. Palestinian Arabs of the West Bank, frustrated by the preoccupation of the Arab governments with the continuing Iran-Iraq war and the failure of past PLO-Jordanian efforts, felt that they were on their own more than ever before. An uprising began in December 1987 that surprised nearly everyone.

As it continued, the claims of the West Bank Arabs took on increasing primacy within the PLO. The leadership came to believe that it had to use the uprising to achieve goals particularly sought by the Palestinians in the Israeli-occupied territories. Expressing a willingness to settle for a Palestinian state in a part of Palestine alongside Israel solved many dilemmas. It promised quick political gains in the form of a dialogue with the U.S. government; it responded to the most pressing concerns of the Palestinians in the occupied territories; it demonstrated leadership; and it could forge links with major groups and governments throughout the world. In November 1988, the PLO leadership announced its acceptance of a two-state solution, declared Palestinian independence, and renounced violence—all of which led to the opening of a dialogue with the U.S. government. Many Palestinian leaders had long-favored a two-state solution but sought assurance that this would be accepted before they would risk making the offer.

Israel

On the whole, a broad consensus has existed in Israel for a long time.[26] Peace with neighboring Arab states was desired, but the Arabs were believed to be uninterested in peace with Israel—there was "no one to talk with." Even the changes in Egypt following Sadat's succession to the presidency in 1970 were not initially viewed as signs that a negotiating partner had appeared. Israeli political parties had different programs and orientations, suggesting that they had different terms for an acceptable peace agreement. As long as no Arab government nor the PLO would recognize Israel, however, even that did not matter.

After the Likud party came to power in Israel in the spring of 1977 and Sadat signaled a readiness for peace by flying to Jerusalem in November 1977, the Israeli consensus began to break. Then, after the failure of a conference in Ismailia, Egypt, in December 1977, a peace movement emerged in Israel that pressured the government not to lose the opportunity represented by Sadat's visit.[27]

In Israel, elite groups are heterogeneous, being linked to a variety of sectors of Israeli life: religious, ethnic, ideological, and economic; political parties tend to reflect coalitions of the various sectors. For example, the Likud drew support from expansionist nationalists and from the oriental rather than Western ethnic community. It was shut out from political power until it was brought into a unity government in 1969–70. The Likud gradually grew in strength, and the split in the Labor party in 1977 enabled it to win an electoral victory and assume leadership of the government.

The prevailing Israeli consensus that there was no one to talk with on the Arab side meant that the differentiation among elite groups had no significant impact. As consensus broke down, the differences among elite groups became more relevant. Even the divisions within the ruling labor coalition in the early 1970s blocked decisive action in response to tentative overtures by Sadat. Labor's desire to maintain unity and hence remain in power tended to immobilize the government.[28] But with the Likud newly in power and the grand gesture of Sadat, the government was free to act in a conciliatory manner. The Likud was the dominant government party, and the party's militant nationalism made it less vulnerable than the Labor party would have been to charges of giving up too much to the Arabs.

The Israeli government's de-escalation initiatives in 1985 were also grounded in domestic shifts. Following the 1982 Israeli invasion of Lebanon, Israeli consensus deteriorated even more severely. The invasion of Lebanon, the siege of Beirut, and the Christian militia's massacre of Palestinians in refugee camps in territory controlled by the Israeli army, produced widespread dissatisfaction with Likud government policies. At the next election, the Likud party lost enough seats in the Knesset that it no longer could form a government without the Labor party. The leaders of the Likud and Labor parties agreed to govern together until the next election in four years. For the first two years, the head of the Labor party, Shimon Peres, was prime minister and Yitzhak Shamir was foreign minister; after two years they would exchange offices. Prime Minister Peres quickly sought to warm the cold peace with Egypt and to pursue negotiations with the Jordanian government about the future of the occupied territories.

Peres's time as prime minister ran out without ever starting direct or even substantive indirect negotiations with the Jordanian government. With Shamir as prime minister, the Israeli government demonstrated reduced interest in making de-escalation overtures toward the Jordanians or the Palestinians. At the end of his two-year term, new elections were held. The results again produced an unclear outcome, revealing that the country was polarized with no clear mandate for either the Labor or the Likud party. To avoid a Likud coalition government formed with the religious parties, the Likud and Labor parties formed another coalition; this time the slight edge held by Likud allowed it to have the dominant role in the government. Shamir was prime minister with no mandate for decisive foreign policy action. The Palestinian uprising in the occupied territories further increased the polarization of political views within Israel.

Global Context

Inasmuch as the international system provides an important context for de-escalation efforts, variations in the patterns of initiatives are explicable in large degree by changes in the global context. In the case of the American-Soviet conflict, the tight bipolar world of the immediate post–World War II era gradually gave way to a much looser bipolar system and then to an almost multipolar system—that is, the division of the world into two clearly bounded camps, each with a dominant single power, gradually dissolved. In the 1960s, third world countries asserted their independence from the cold war by founding the Non-Aligned Movement. France began to play a somewhat independent military role and in 1969 left the unified command of NATO. The tight alliance between China and the Soviet Union was shattered, and at the end of the 1960s, military skirmishes were fought along the border.

In the Middle East in the mid-1950s, the United States became the dominant nonregional power, replacing Great Britain and France. By then, the Soviets had begun to penetrate the Middle East by supporting Egypt, and thus the cold war was superimposed upon regional conflicts.[29] Nevertheless, the United States was able to maintain diplomatic relations and important economic and military ties with Arab governments as well as with Israel, as indeed did the Soviet Union.

For the American-Soviet conflict, these changes in the international system gradually introduced the possibility of more intermediaries. Nonaligned governments as well as governments playing a quasi independent role within an alliance could and did serve as intermediaries. Moreover, they were potential recruits as allies and therefore were likely targets for appeals; demonstrating reasonableness and willingness to be accommodating is an important form of appeal.

The loosening bipolarity of the world system was associated with a decline of the U.S. government's dominance of intergovernmental institutions such as those affiliated with the United Nations.[30] The United Nations, then, could more readily play an independent intermediary role in the U.S.-USSR conflict; and an expansion in the number of third world countries and the formation of voting blocs facilitated trade-offs between them. A different consequence affected the Arab-Israeli conflict: UN General Assembly resolutions were passed that relegated Israel to marginal status, which handicapped the United Nations in playing an intermediary role in the conflict.

Generally, however, the United Nations has been a key figure in de-escalation initiatives. Whatever coalition of governments can shape a resolution in the Security Council or the General Assembly is likely to use that power to undertake the initiatives it wants. From the beginning of the Arab-Israeli conflict, the United Nations has figured predominantly. It was the UN vote that partitioned British-mandated Palestine into a Jewish and a Palestinian state. When the partition was rejected by neighboring Arab states and they attacked Israel, many efforts were made through the United Nations to mediate and resolve the conflict.

The American-Soviet cold war became a major context for the Arab-Israeli conflict beginning in the mid 1950s. The interjection of the cold war into the Middle East meant that great reservoirs of military and economic resources were made available to the regional adversaries. That enabled partisans in the conflict to anticipate future assistance, which encouraged escalation. Each could think it had reason to hold out and better its position before seeking a settlement.

Inter-Arab rivalry has also affected the Arab-Israeli conflict.[31] This rivalry has been fed by personal ambition, national aspirations, and ideological differences. Influence and control over Palestinians and the land of Palestine has been one object of the rivalry; in addition, governments have jockeyed for influence and dominance in the Arab world. Consequently, resolution of the Israeli-Palestinian conflict favoring one Arab government over another would be unacceptable.

Changes in Egyptian-Soviet relations are illustrative. Beginning in the mid-1950s, Nasser led Egypt into a collaborative relationship with the USSR; the Soviets provided military and economic assistance, such as aid in building the Aswan High Dam. After Nasser died in 1970, Sadat gradually shifted away from collaboration with the Soviets and leaned toward the United States, changing the context for the U.S. government's role in the Egyptian-Israeli conflict.

Each dispute that Israel has had with an Arab antagonist has been connected to many other conflicts. Superimposed conflicts can inhibit de-escalation beginnings. Thus, the escalation of the Egyptian-Israeli conflict in 1967 into open warfare and the increased U.S. fighting with North Vietnam interfered with possible U.S.-USSR de-escalation movements in the Middle East. The reduction in U.S.-USSR antagonism in the late 1980s greatly affected the Arab-Israeli conflict, as it did other regional conflicts. The Soviets encouraged the PLO leadership to announce positions that might facilitate a dialogue with the U.S. government, which made it easier in turn for the U.S. government to do the same without seeming to yield to Soviet pressure or to be aiding a Soviet ally.

Adversary Relations

According to both the conflict resolution and statist approaches, adversary relations are particularly important in determining whether initiatives take place. For statists, the relative power of each adversary is the significant aspect. Thus, government leaders calculate what they think they can get from their adversary at a given time and make offers based on that assessment. The conflict resolution approach usefully adds that the interdependence between adversaries is also key and is the source of potentially productive negotiations. In addition, the views expressed by leaders and other groups in each adversary party may reveal points of conflict and possible settlements.

U.S.-USSR Relations

Relations between the U.S. and Soviet governments have shown considerable continuity, but they have also changed in several major ways since the beginning of the cold war. Each country is highly significant to the other. Both peoples partly define themselves in terms of the other: in the United States, "Americanism" has been defined by many as anti-Communist and "un-American" as pro-Communist—that split perception has affected the extent of popular support for military and foreign policies. In the Soviet Union, although the United States has been popularly viewed as the major capitalist country and sometimes as a threat, it is also seen as an advanced and industrially progressive country compared to a backward Soviet Union.

In the early years of the cold war, the leaders of the U.S. and Soviet governments regarded the world as essentially bipolar; neutrality was not possible. In later periods, the leaders in each country have at times regarded their adversarial relationship as embedded in a much more complex set of multilateral relations—ones less clearly ideological. Since the late 1980s, a transformation to a new relationship has been under way.

The ideological appeal of each power has undergone significant shifts. The appeal of communism grew in the 1960s as newly independent countries overthrew their ties with Western colonialism.[32] Later, the economic troubles of countries trying to apply the Soviet model reduced communism's attractiveness. The emergence of independent communist parties offered new ideological philosophies, but they sometimes competed with Soviet influence. Since 1990, communist ideology has lost much of its attractiveness even within the Soviet Union itself.

The relative military strength of the USSR and the United States has changed greatly. Initially, the United States was the dominant world military power, able to destroy the Soviet homeland without fear of comparable retaliation. Yet by the end of the 1960s, the USSR had achieved the capacity to strike or retaliate with devastating effect; by the mid-1970s, it had established itself as a superpower. Since the late 1980s, however, the USSR has been reducing its military capability in Europe and elsewhere. As a result of these and other changes, the relationship between the U.S. and Soviet governments has become increasingly complex. Apart from a continued capacity to wreak nuclear ruin, each has become more related to the other. Both powers now confront new problems.

Alterations in the world economy and the economies of individual countries have made economic and technological exchanges increasingly attractive. The growth of multinational corporations and an increase in foreign investment has increased the search not only for markets but also for investment. Beginning in the late 1960s, countries of the socialist camp have become suitable for such purposes. A Soviet desire for rapid economic growth and the promise of speedier development using Western technology has contributed to its faith in the benefits of exchange. Together these changes—according to the conflict resolution approach—are conducive to de-escalation initiatives.

Beginning in 1945, the World War II alliance against Nazi Germany provided the basis and procedures for ongoing meetings for the exchange of proposals. After several years of failure, however, those meetings ceased. Gradually, new forums for exchange developed, primarily in UN bodies but also at bilateral meetings where discussions became almost routine and seemed to require the presentation of de-escalation proposals, however meaningless.

American-Soviet relations have been marked by crises and indirect military confrontations. In 1948, the Soviet land blockade of West Berlin— to prevent its integration in the West German economy—was a severe crisis. Then, in the spring of 1950, North Korean forces invaded South Korea; the United States fought against the North Koreans with the avowed purpose of stopping communism. The struggle between communism and the West seemed to widen when U.S. military units moved near the North Korean–Chinese border, triggering Chinese intervention. In 1958 and 1961, crises erupted over Soviet threats regarding the status of West Berlin. In October 1962, the U.S. response to the Soviet deployment of missiles in Cuba threatened actual warfare. Beginning in the mid-1960s and escalating for several years, U.S. military forces were engaged in a struggle against communist North Vietnamese forces, which were being aided by China and the Soviet Union. At the end of 1979, the Soviet Union invaded Afghanistan to support the friendly government endangered by Afghan rebels. The fighting escalated, with assistance from the United States and other governments for the Afghan rebels.

Arab-Israeli Relations

Relations between Israel and its several Arab neighboring peoples have also undergone major changes. Although the roots of Zionism and Arab nationalism are deep once their conflict began, each shaped the other. Zionism in its early manifestations was socialist and European in its cultural background. Jewish militancy increased in reaction to the experience of the Holocaust, the fight against the British control of Palestine, and then the struggle with the Arabs. Jews who fled Arab countries after the establishment of the State of Israel became increasingly important elements of the Israeli population.

For Arabs in Palestine, a sharpened nationalism seemed to preclude acceptance of a Jewish state in that territory; its actual establishment accelerated and deepened the identity of non-Jews as Palestinians.[33] Many other political and ideological currents have affected Arab identity and Arabs' characterization of Israel. For example, socialist and Marxist ideologies fostered the view of Israel as an outpost of Western imperialism and influenced those countries where new elite groups, often military, had overthrown traditional, authoritarian regimes—as in Egypt, Syria, Libya, and Iraq. In the 1980s, the Islamic revival gave a religious meaning to resisting Zionism.

Many of these changes have been marked by wars. In 1948, Arab armies marched against the newly founded State of Israel to counter its establishment. In October 1956, Israeli forces, in collaboration with British and French military units, attacked Egypt and occupied Sinai and the Gaza Strip. Under pressure from the United States, the United Nations, and the USSR, Israeli forces were soon withdrawn. UN peacekeeping forces (UNEF) were stationed in the Gaza Strip, along the Sinai demarcation lines, and in the Sharm al-Sheikh area overlooking the Strait of Tiran.

Between 1948 and 1967, Israel could offer little in exchange for recognition and acceptance by the Arabs. Only with Jordan did a mutually beneficial exchange seem possible. The land on the West bank of the Jordan River could be divided between Israel and Jordan by both governments; Jordan would gain access to the Mediterranean through special port rights at Haifa granted by Israel. In June 1967, however, in the Six-Day War, Israeli military forces defeated Egyptian, Jordanian, and Syrian forces and occupied Sinai and the Gaza Strip, East Jerusalem and the West Bank, and the Golan Heights in Syria. The United Nations was active in terminating the war and in initiating efforts to settle the conflict.

After the war Israel had more to offer. Land for peace exchanges could be made with Egypt over Sinai, with Syria over the Golan Heights, and with Jordan over the newly occupied West Bank. The situation with the Palestinians was quite different. Jordan was forced to yield control over the portions of formerly mandated Palestine that it had annexed in 1948. It was conceivable that the Palestinians could now exchange recognition of Israel for a small Palestinian state alongside Israel and Jordan. Hardly anyone on either side, however, championed such an exchange.

The War of Attrition began in March 1969 with Egyptian artillery shelling across the Suez canal. It escalated first with Israeli air attacks, including raids into Egypt, and then with Soviet combat assistance against the Israelis. The fighting went on until a U.S.-mediated cease-fire agreement was reached in August 1970.

In addition to these relatively clearly defined wars, there have been many episodes of airplane hijackings and attacks on Israeli and non-Israeli Jews by armed Palestinians. In reprisal, Israeli military forces have bombed or otherwise attacked Palestinians and Palestinian targets. There has also been fighting among Palestinian groups and between Arab government and Palestinian militia forces.

The October 1973 war launched by Egypt and Syria brought about a new set of conditions. Not only did the Egyptians achieve some military success, the Arab petroleum exporting countries (OPEC) exercised effective economic power. The fighting left the Israeli and Egyptian armies intertwined on both sides of the Suez canal and Arab military honor somewhat restored. The need to disengage military forces was clear, as was a readiness to lend political significance to any agreement to do so. The fighting ended in a deliberate deadlock engineered by Secretary of State Henry Kissinger in conjunction with UN and Soviet efforts.

Relations between Israel and the various Arab governments and people are complex and have changed in different ways. After the October 1973 war, Israel and Egypt had much to offer each other. Moreover, each had demonstrated it could impose costly military engagements; neither had reason to expect that in the foreseeable future it could triumph by renewed escalation. The relations between Israel and the PLO, Syria, or Jordan, however, were not as significantly changed in the 1970s.

The 1979 peace treaty between Israel and Egypt increased the primacy of the Israeli-Palestinian conflict for both sides. The Israeli invasion of Lebanon in 1982 to destroy the PLO infrastructure there and disperse PLO fighters was one response to the shift in the focal conflict.[34] Following this invasion—as after the 1967, 1969, and 1973 fighting—there were many de-escalation initiatives. Most of them were undertaken by *would-be* intermediaries. The United Nations is an obvious instrument for such efforts. Many other parties, either wishing to play a role in the world scene or having a special interest in the region, have also undertaken initiatives.

Patterns of Initiatives

Various theoretical perspectives seek to explain the patterns of de-escalation efforts, but they are not all equally applicable. They all recognize but give different stress to the three sets of factors—domestic conditions, the international context, and relations between adversaries.

Many Initiatives

The first pattern is one of very many de-escalation initiatives, some even during the years of greatest antagonism. The conflict resolution approach, emphasizing the variety of possible peacemaking actions and initiators, particularly applies here. The populist perspective suggests that the multiplicity of initiatives reflects widespread public support for peacemaking: Peace is popular; government officials generally want to be seen to be striving for peace. Pluralists suggest, however, that government heads balance popular preferences with other interests in selecting the kind of initiative, if any, to be taken. The statist approach adds that governments may offer peace initiatives only for the sake of appearance. The possibility of duplicity increases the sources for de-escalation initiatives.

Clearly, there are many grounds for de-escalation efforts; many are infertile seeds and many fall on barren ground, which is why so many of them fail to take root and result in actual negotiations.

Variation among Conflicts

That the conflicts differ in the frequency of de-escalation efforts is the second pattern to be explained. More efforts have been made in the U.S.-USSR conflict than in the Arab-Israeli conflict. The pluralist and conflict resolution approaches suggest that the international context is more conducive to the initiation of de-escalation efforts in the Arab-Israeli conflict than in the American-Soviet conflict. Because of the United Nations' involvement in establishing Israel and in the U.S.-USSR rivalry in the region, more intermediaries are available and have reason to intervene in the Middle East conflict than in the American-Soviet conflict.

Adversary relations in the Arab-Israeli conflict, however, are much less conducive to de-escalation efforts than in the U.S.-USSR conflict, where the primary adversary governments at least officially recognize each other— making the discussion of issues easier. In the Arab-Israeli conflict, however, the primary adversaries generally have not recognized one another's legitimacy, which precludes direct discussion of even marginal matters. Furthermore, direct threats to vital interests have been more evident in the Arab-Israeli conflict than in the American-Soviet conflict, while the possibility of nuclear war appeared to promise mutual suicide.

Domestic sources of pressure have also been more conducive to de-escalation efforts in the U.S.-USSR than in the Arab-Israeli conflict. The burden of military preparations, particularly in the Soviet Union, constituted pressure—as did the popular protests for peace in the United States—which sometimes made government peace initiatives almost mandatory. There has been no comparable pressure in the Arab countries. Even in Israel, until Egypt appeared as a negotiating partner after Sadat visited Jerusalem, there had been no significant peace movement.

Variation over Time

The third pattern of initiatives is their relative frequency over the course of the conflict, responding to constituency considerations; they do not primarily seek reciprocation from an adversary. Even when undertaken by intermediaries, they are more often expressions of intermediaries' concerns than of adversaries. As the conflict resolution approach suggests, such bases for initiatives are likely to reduce their efficacy because often they are shaped to be plausible to an initiator's constituency but not to the adversary.

De-escalation initiatives are particularly likely to occur immediately after a conflict has intensified (for example, after one of the Arab-Israeli wars), suggesting that they are reactions to conflict escalation. Unfortunately, they are relatively rare over extended periods of conflict intensification and after the flurry of activity that immediately follows the eruption of a crisis or war. The conflict resolution perspective gives particular attention to alternatives to a negotiated settlement. After a violent exchange, at least some elements will regard movement toward agreement as more attractive than continuing violence.

De-escalation initiatives are also likely when one of the protagonists has new leadership, it then being freer of past commitments. New leaders, moreover, by such initiatives, demonstrate that they are indeed in charge. The American presidential system, with a fixed four-year term, adds the pressure for quick movement at the outset of an administration.[35] New government heads are also more likely to undertake initiatives (hostile as well as accommodative) because they and their supporters remain confident of their effectiveness.

In addition, an adversary may regard the appearance of a new leader for the other side as an occasion for a de-escalation initiative, believing the adversary is now willing and able to break with the past. These explanations suggest that many de-escalation initiatives are true problem-solving efforts and not merely responses to constituency considerations.

Variation among Adversaries

The fourth pattern to be explained is the varied frequency with which different adversaries undertake peace initiatives. The tendency of the Soviets to undertake de-escalation efforts and the PLO not to until the late 1980s is noteworthy. Here the statist approach is less helpful than the pluralist perspective.

Paradoxically, domestic factors are particularly important in explaining the greater frequency of Soviet peace initiatives than American initiatives. Public opinion and pressure has been much more influential in the United States than in the Soviet Union, which has two major implications. One, the Soviet government has been more able to affect American foreign policy by influencing the American people than the reverse. Both the Soviet and the American governments have behaved as if they believe this to be true, and the accessibility of the U.S. public has been attractive for Soviet peacemaking offers. Two, the power of the American public can be a disincentive for the U.S. government to undertake peace initiatives. Many American leaders believe that peacemaking efforts toward the Soviets would lead the public to think that expanding or even maintaining military strength is not necessary. In the past, the weakness of public pressure in the Soviet Union made this a less substantial fear for Soviet leaders.

As the populist approach suggests, the dominant ideologies of both societies encourage peace initiatives by government officials. Appeals to the people or the toiling masses are appropriate according to both democratic and communist ideologies. In both countries, too, peace is a highly esteemed intrinsic value and a central element of their political ideologies; military preparations have always been justified only as a means of defense or to ensure peace. The Communist party of the Soviet Union also has historical reasons for stressing the value of peace. It came to power in the October 1917 revolution on the ground that it would bring peace, taking Russia out of World War I. Then came the war against Nazi Germany; the "Great Patriotic War," was devastating. As Soviet citizens repeatedly remind themselves and others, 20 million of their compatriots died in that war.

The international context ordinarily should foster peace initiatives for Middle East adversaries as it does between the United States and the USSR. Yet the PLO made relatively few de-escalation gestures until the end of 1988. PLO leaders, their major constituencies, and the relations between them were primarily responsible. As the PLO developed, the leaders' emphasis upon armed struggle contributed to and was shaped by their dependence on fighters from refugee camps whose bitterness sustained their militancy. The goals initially sought, they correctly believed, would be nonnegotiable for the Israelis; as the goals changed toward a two-state solution, the possibility of a movement toward settlement was at least conceivable.

Rivalry among the leaders in the coalition making up the PLO made those leaders who would seek an accommodation with Israel vulnerable. They risked the loss of constituency support and even the loss of their lives. For example, Issam Sartawi, a PLO leader who had met with many Israeli leaders, was assassinated in Lisbon, Portugal, on 10 April 1983. A rival Palestinian group, led by Abud Nidal, and based in Syria, claimed it had executed this "criminal traitor."[36]

The Palestinian uprising in the Israeli-occupied territories gave prominence to the PLO leadership associated with Arafat and at the same time increased the importance of the Palestinians in the occupied territories, relative to those in camps or elsewhere in the diaspora.

Implications for De-escalation Strategies

Although these findings have strategic implications, no formula for peacemaking efforts emerges. Rather, we need to consider the many alternative configurations of domestic conditions, the international context, and relations between adversaries to explain de-escalation initiatives. Since many different configurations can be the basis for peacemaking efforts, many different strategies might be pursued to bring about an appropriate set of ameliorating conditions.

De-escalation initiatives primarily responsive to domestic pressure are usually formulated to gratify those concerns, sometimes resulting in pseudo-de-escalation initiatives; though plausible, they do not adequately take into account the interests of the adversary. Such formulations obstruct or even preclude an accommodative response from the adversary.

The circumstances discussed here are not merely the result of historical processes unaffected by the actions of particular human beings. Leading officials can choose actions that help to create the conditions supportive of peace initiatives. Other people can influence those officials or replace them.

The global context is generally conducive to peacemaking initiatives but being relatively stable contributes little to explaining variations in one country's tendency to undertake accommodative initiatives toward its adversary. Changes in the international context, however, can significantly affect the balance of power among adversaries and also can increase or decrease the salience of the particular conflict.

Intermediaries play an important role in making initiatives, as indicated by the conflict resolution and pluralist approaches. They are freer than principal parties to do so, since they risk less. Whether UN agencies or governments, intermediaries not of the primary adversaries are not vulnerable to domestic pressures for seeming weakness in the face of an enemy in proposing a de-escalation move.

Furthermore, intermediaries such as UN agencies have routine pro-

cedures for making de-escalation initiatives. Even intermediary governments, having diplomatic representation with each of the adversary parties,
can readily transmit messages. The effectiveness of these possibilities is
another matter, discussed in the next chapter.

Initiatives for de-escalation vary in many ways, as discussed in the next
chapter. The preconditions fostering or inhibiting initiatives differ, varying
according to the nature of the initiatives. For example, to conduct an
extended series of peace initiatives with some unilateral concessions requires a shift in domestic conditions, involving strong popular support for
the policy or a commitment by a risk-taking leadership.

Strategic alternatives are constrained by the preconditions that have been
outlined here. Circumstances conducive to de-escalation initiatives are not
rare; indeed, there are many opportunities. Knowing precisely what objectives are desired and whether conditions are conducive for different actors
can determine the timing of a de-escalation initiative, as well as what
changes are needed to bring about the preconditions for later negotiations.

5
Starting Negotiations

Even though all the pieces seem to
fall into place and de-escalation initiatives are finally undertaken, negotiations do not always follow. Sometimes it is the substance of the proposal
that dooms the initiative to failure; sometimes it is the way the initiative is
presented. It may be the international context, domestic conditions, or the
structure of adversary relations that determine whether negotiations can
start, regardless of the nature of the initiative.

Much of the writing and research about conflict resolution has focused on
the negotiation and mediation processes. The problem of reaching an agreement, once the adversaries are at the negotiating table, is becoming much

better understood. We have less understanding, though, and less policy guidance on the problems of getting adversaries to the table.[1] In this chapter I examine how the content, form, and context of initiatives affect the likelihood that they will lead to negotiations.

We must first recognize when a process is to be called a negotiation. The word *negotiation* can refer to a great variety of conduct.[2] Here, negotiations are explicit interactions between representatives of adversaries in which proposals for an agreement are exchanged and mutually modified. This excludes implicit bargaining in which each adversary modifies its conduct toward each other until a stable condition is reached. In negotiations, an adversary's representatives must exchange verbal or written messages; exchanges may be conducted directly by representatives of the adversaries or indirectly through intermediaries. Furthermore, negotiations must include at least the appearance of a mutual discussion of proposals and go beyond an exchange of proposals and their rejection.

Even though I have defined negotiation, it is difficult to mark the beginning and end of a negotiation sequence. Some matters can be the subject of meetings carried on for decades, with periods of intense negotiation activity interspersed with periods of little activity. I will concentrate on short periods of relatively intense de-escalation activity and exchanges on the introduction of new proposals, which may be embedded in the longer stream of formal negotiations and many other interactions.

Explanatory Ideas

To suggest which circumstances, tactics, and strategies are most important to the start of negotiations, I draw from the conflict resolution approach as well as from the statist, populist, and pluralist approaches.

The conflict resolution approach recognizes that mediation and negotiation skills are effective only when most appropriate for the conditions of the conflict. Strategic choices involve considering the efficacy of coercive and noncoercive inducements as well as targets and focal issues.

Statism stresses a balance of coercive strength and a calculation of national interest by the leaders of each party to a possible agreement. This conventional view is challenged by the populist approach, which emphasizes that mutual trust is created among leaders and the public by conciliatory gestures, new ways of thinking about the issues, and the mutual benefits to be gained by open-minded exploration. The pluralist approach also stresses the multiplicity of actors and the overlapping and crosscutting character of conflicts—often with little specification of which factor is likely to be important or which method effective under particular conditions. The analysis presented here will contribute to such specification.

For de-escalation initiatives to lead to negotiations, they must be recipro-cated; strategies must be pursued that encourage an opponent's positive response. Strategies combine variations in the blend of inducements, selection of parties for negotiation, and the choice of issues.

Inducements

Three basic types of inducements can be combined in waging a struggle or ending it: coercion, positive sanctions, and persuasion. Coercion, under-standably, has received the most attention in the study of conflicts. Noncoer-cive inducements—rewards and persuasion—however, may play a signifi-cant role, particularly in de-escalation. The form and magnitude of positive sanctions vary greatly, of course, from making future benefits contingent on unilateral concessions to symbolic and material sanctions; some may be granted magnanimously and others begrudgingly. Finally, inducements may be part of the peace proposal's substance or may accompany proposals without explicit linkages.

The relative value of coercive and noncoercive inducements for initiating de-escalation has long been a matter of controversy. Some theorists and practitioners note the particular contribution positive sanctions or noncoer-cive inducements can make to de-escalation efforts.[3] Government officials often require *deeds,"* not words from adversaries. The deeds called for usually refer to conciliatory actions such as ceasing hostile acts, but even an acknowledgement of past errors may serve as well. Sadat explained his journey to Jerusalem in 1977 as a "deed" that would break the "psychologi-cal barrier" blocking negotiations.

Taking a populist perspective, to interrupt a conflict characterized by long-standing animosity and mistrust, one party must make significant conciliatory gestures. Thus, the Graduated Reciprocation in Tension-reduction (GRIT) strategy emphasizes the need to initiate de-escalation with a concession and then to persist with additional cooperative moves, even if they are not reciprocated; the actions should be publicly announced in advance, and the other party invited to reciprocate.[4]

Many statists argue that conciliatory gestures made by one side are likely to be seen as signs of weakness by the other, which will respond with increased demands.[5] These analysts argue that only if the gesture is com-bined with sufficient strength will the adversary be deterred and the conflict not escalate; with coercion, the adversary will be brought to the negotiating table and a sound agreement will be reached. Government officials are likely to assume this stance and publicly assert that they must remain firm and increase their own strength in order to avoid appeasement and force the adversary to the table for serious negotiations.

The pluralist approach provides the too-often neglected ground to criticize both of these sets of ideas. The peace-through-strength approach is often provocative, and the adversary will respond by escalating the conflict. Critical of the populist approach as well, pluralists would argue for a mixture of positive and negative sanctions, of carrots and sticks. One form this may take is a "tit-for-tat strategy."[6] That is, after an opening de-escalatory move, one party matches the other side's conciliation with conciliation and a coercive demand with an equally coercive demand.

In addition to positive and negative sanctions, persuasive inducements may also be employed. Persuasive inducements refer to symbolic communications in which one party tries to alter another's views of what its interests and values should be. For example, a party may argue that justice will be served by accepting its claims and that the antagonist would advance its own values by agreeing. This reasoning was the basis of the anticolonial claims of leaders of national liberation movements reaching out to peoples and governments in the colonial motherlands.

Persuasive efforts are frequently made in conflicts, even though the people responding, and particularly their leaders, deny that they have been persuaded of anything by their enemies.[7] These same people, nevertheless, try to persuade their antagonists. It is true that evaluations of one's interests do change over time and to some extent as a result of the adversaries' arguments. A major acknowledgment of the efficacy of such persuasion comes from Soviet leaders in the change in their position between 1968 and 1972 on the utility of antiballistic missile systems. American arguments on their de-stabilizing effects helped to convince the Soviets that a treaty banning their further development and deployment would be mutually advantageous.

The change in American views of the Soviet Union at the end of the 1980s was largely in response to the Soviet withdrawal from Afghanistan, the encouragement of self-determination in Eastern Europe, and unilateral changes in military posture. These deeds were given meaning, however, by the words of Gorbachev, which in turn were given substance by the deeds. The transforming changes in the Soviet Union were the culmination of many social processes. The drama of the manifested changes transformed the American people's perception of the Soviet Union.

Choosing Parties to De-escalation

In addition to inducement choices, strategies differ in choosing which parties shall participate in de-escalation efforts, the number and character of the major parties represented in the negotiations, and whether intermediaries will participate.

Within a country, various domestic groups may not be consulted about an initiative. For example, in 1963 Kennedy prepared his American University speech without extensive consultation in order to avoid objections that might have blocked the speech.[8] More drastically, Sadat announced his readiness to go to Jerusalem in 1977 without prior consultation with foreign allies and without domestic advisers, presenting them with an accomplished fact.[9] Usually, of course, major initiatives and responses to them are subject to extensive internal consultations.

Since conflicts are always multiple and interlocked, de-escalation negotiations involve various combinations of adversaries. Each adversary is part of a coalition of parties; initiatives may be made by some members of a coalition to certain members of the opposing coalition. Indeed, just which parties should be invited to negotiate is often a matter of policy dispute.

For example, in the initial post–World War II years, many efforts at negotiation were conducted by the Big Four, which meant that meetings were held with the Soviet representatives facing the U.S., British, and French delegations alone. In the late 1950s, the Soviets insisted on parity in such meetings: either the Soviet and the U.S. representatives would meet on a bilateral basis or the USSR and the United States would meet, with each accompanied by its European allies. These two sets of negotiating partners replaced the Big Four settings.

Negotiations can also be between a major party on one side and an ally of its primary adversary on the other. Thus, Soviet leaders, even though they saw the United States as their chief enemy, sometimes made initiatives directed at one or more governments of Western Europe. For example, Soviet moves toward a peace treaty with the Federal Republic of Germany, signed in 1971, were thought by Soviet officials to promise more than the acceptance of existing borders. As a former high Soviet official has reported,

> Gromyko and others often remarked that although the Federal Republic belonged to the West, its geopolitical interests would gradually push it toward neutrality and eventually perhaps closer to the Soviet Union than to the United States. This view was based on the assumption that our propaganda and blackmail would influence pacifist sentiment in the FRG to such an extent that fear of nuclear war would prevail over any other possibilities. . . . We intended to support the theme with a refrain that Moscow was Germany's natural and historic economic partner. Finally, on a firmer note, the case would be made that it was Moscow—not Washington—that held the key to German aspirations for reunification or, at least for the time being, to widening contacts with East Germany.[10]

When intransigent parties, whose interests are centrally involved in a possible settlement, are excluded from a settlement effort, the initial stages of negotiations may be facilitated. Their exclusion, however, may ultimately hamper reaching an agreement or undermine the fairness of any resulting agreement. In the Arab-Israeli case, for example, many negotiation initiatives have been suggested and negotiations undertaken that did not directly include Palestinian representatives. Their interests, consequently, were not fully taken into account. Even in the early Big Four discussions on Austria, Berlin, and Germany, Austrian and German representatives were often not directly engaged.

The importance of unofficial diplomacy is being increasingly recognized.[11] It includes private individuals acting at the behest of a government, as in the case of the Iran-contra covert arms-for-hostages diplomacy during the Reagan administration; it also includes private individuals who act as mediators and represent, for example, churches or voluntary associations. Some speak for informal groups and act relatively independently, as was true of some Israelis who met with PLO representatives, or Westerners like Armand Hammer, who met with Soviet officials as a private individual. On occasion, private organizations have engaged in negotiating de-escalation agreements, as between U.S. nongovernmental organizations and Soviet government agencies in cultural and scientific exchanges.

Choosing Issues

It may seem that the conflict itself will determine the choice of issues for de-escalation efforts. But conflicts always comprise many issues; selecting those for emphasis in de-escalation efforts is a matter of strategy.[12] These issues vary in at least two qualities: centrality and linkage. A major strategic choice is whether to set an agenda of central issues or peripheral ones. The argument for dealing with peripheral or minor matters is that such negotiations are more likely to be successful and can increase mutual trust, leading to improved relations and therefore to more significant de-escalations in the future. Thus, in the U.S.-USSR conflict, negotiations were successfully conducted, long before détente, to ban the use of Antarctica for military purposes.

Some argue that dealing with minor issues is a waste of time, having little impact even if an agreement is reached. Sometimes, indeed, an agreement has little substance and promises more than seems possible; it might even be used by an adversary for unilateral advantage, as when that adversary seems to have been granted legitimacy and even parity simply from negotiation meetings. Some Western analysts have made the charge regarding early arms-control agreements that they served only the Soviet political goal of gaining respectability.[13] In the Middle East, for a long time even minor matters could not be discussed with the enemy since to do so would constitute de facto recognition; the Arabs did not want to acknowledge "the Zionist entity," and the Israelis refused to acknowledge the PLO.

Similarly, in the mid-1950s, the U.S. government sought to mediate an agreement between Israel, Jordan, Lebanon, and Syria over the use of water in the Jordan River valley. Although a formal agreement was almost reached, the Arab League regarded it as a form of recognition of Israel and blocked the agreement.[14] Nevertheless, portions of the understanding were implemented in a tacit agreement.

These examples indicate that whether an issue is vital or trivial is often difficult to determine and sometimes irrelevant. The *symbolic* meaning assigned to an issue by one or several major adversaries must be respected in practice and analysis. Shared assessments are the focus here; when parties do not agree, an issue will be treated as vital if a major party claims it to be.

The second strategic choice is whether to treat a matter of contention by itself or link it with other matters. A single issue can be more readily handled, but linking many issues together makes possible a "package deal" based on trade-offs. Sometimes linkage is made explicitly by the party making a proposal or by the responding party. Sometimes negotiating parties may not agree that there is or should be a link between particular issues; such connections then become obstacles to starting de-escalation negotiations.

Linkage may be explicitly part of a single set of negotiations or may occur between different sets of negotiations and be only implied. Whether or not to link issues has been frequently debated in regard to the U.S.-USSR conflict. From the U.S. perspective, Soviet conduct in emigration and freedom of speech matters should be linked to arms control and trade agreements. For example, during the early 1970s, as the several negotiations pertaining to the beginning of détente were under way, Kissinger used linkage extensively. He did this through "back channels" while formal negotiations about each matter were being conducted separately by official delegations.[15] Linked negotiations are likely to be seen as an effort for comprehensive settlement, either of a dispute or a major portion of a general conflict. They are more effective once the conflict has begun to be transformed and a broad accommodative movement is under way. The argument for de-linking issues and de-escalating only a portion of a conflict—particularly early on—is that when successful they breed confidence in continued efforts. Without such confidence and trust, no comprehensive agreement is possible.

Each of these arguments has been used by different antagonists and intermediaries in the Middle East conflict. Debates have long raged over the wisdom of seeking a comprehensive settlement or following a step-by-step approach. Kissinger pursued the latter strategy in the aftermath of the October 1973 war: first, he mediated a disengagement agreement between Egypt and Israel, then between Syria and Israel, then another disengagement agreement between Israel and Egypt, and (unsuccessfully) sought a partial settlement between Israel and Jordan. Carter, critical of this approach at the outset of his administration, sought a comprehensive settlement,[16] striving to convene an international peace conference among the major adversaries cochaired by the U.S. and the Soviet governments. The result, however, was but another step in peacemaking, albeit a giant one: an Israeli-Egyptian peace treaty.

Tactics

Many choices regarding the inducements used are more tactical than strategic; that is, they entail short-term considerations such as who is to present the inducements, to whom are they addressed, the clarity of the message, how publicly are they to be offered, and the degree to which they should appear irrevocable. Arguments for different ways of presenting an inducement so that it will be effective can be readily formulated. On the one hand, a public announcement may not be taken seriously or dismissed as propaganda; on the other hand, it might be considered as a serious commitment precisely because it is publicly proclaimed. Of course, if the public is the speaker's constituency, it might be taken as more binding than if the public is the adversary's constituency.

A de-escalation message is often deliberately ambiguous and subject to interpretation in order to reduce risk. If the desired response is elicited, the sender is applauded; if the message is not well received, the sender will not appear to his constituency to have been weak. What makes a message easy to send, however, is less likely to be effective. Uri Avnery, a member of the Israeli Knesset, reports making such an argument to Said Hammani, a PLO official, in a confidential meeting in 1975. He argued that to effect a change in Israeli official policy, it was necessary to change Israeli public opinion, which, he argued, required dramatic events—"cautious diplomatic texts, coded statements and speeches were not enough."[17]

The complexity of these matters is readily illustrated in the Arab-Israeli conflict. For several years Yasir Arafat and other Palestinian leaders indicated in interviews with Western journalists that the PLO had, in effect, recognized Israel and accepted UN Security Council resolution 242. Israeli officials were quick to point out that such messages were not convincing because they were not made unequivocally in statements to the Arab press.[18]

The Palestinian uprising that began in the occupied territories in December 1987 provided a major incentive for the PLO to take action. Some political direction and achievement, Palestinians believed, should result from the new conditions created by the *intifada*. The Palestine National Council (PNC) of the PLO met in Algiers and on 14 November 1988, by a majority vote, declared Palestinian independence, called for support of the intifada, rejected terrorism, including state terrorism, and affirmed the necessity of holding an international conference on the Middle East on the basis of UN Security Council resolutions 242 and 338.[19]

An objective of the PNC declaration was the opening of a dialogue with the U.S. government, which had long declared that the PLO must recognize Israel, reject terrorism, and embrace negotiations as the key to a Middle East settlement. U.S. State Department officials, however, characterized the PNC declaration as too ambiguous in its recognition of Israel to begin any dialogue. On 7 December, a delegation of American Jews met with a Palestinian delegation led by Arafat and issued a joint statement that more clearly and less conditionally stated U.S. requirements. Secretary of State Shultz, recognizing progress, still noted ambiguities. On 13 December 1990, Arafat made a speech at the United Nations, restating the PLO position but still not satisfactorily meeting U.S. conditions. Finally, the next day, another PLO statement was released that Shultz declared did meet U.S. requirements and authorized the U.S. ambassador to Tunisia to enter a substantive dialogue with PLO representatives. The Israeli government, however, rejected the PLO statements as deceptive and expressed shock and disappointment over the American move.

Background Circumstances

The background circumstances discussed in the previous chapter shape the consequences of de-escalation strategies and tactics. The significance of domestic conditions varies at different stages of a conflict and de-escalation effort. The effects of various initiatives and the significance of constituency considerations obviously also differ with the political structure of the countries involved. Domestic changes have a dynamic of their own and are not readily affected by the actions of foreign governments. Public preferences and particularly those of leading groups in the long run will shape a government's foreign policy and its reaction to the initiatives of its adversaries. Most significantly, the relations between adversaries will determine whether particular initiatives will lead to negotiations by providing the context and defining the nature of a conflict. Furthermore, the impact of a de-escalation effort will vary according to the different stages of a fight: when it is escalating, when it is stalemated, during a crisis, and with a decline in antagonism.

Believing that a satisfactory agreement is attainable and that a settlement will be better than the alternative is necessary to serious negotiations.[20] This means an effective de-escalation effort must contribute to the perception by the adversary that the likely benefits will be greater than the costs of an agreement, while losses relative to gains will be excessive if no agreement is reached.

Finally, in the international context, allies, potential allies of an adversary, mediators, adversaries in other fights, and external groups all may act to enhance the role of constituency groups in fostering government peace-making efforts. Certain international actors can oblige governments to negotiate. Thus, the United Nations, through the Security Council or General Assembly, can instruct the secretary general to explore possible conflict settlements. Through representatives of that office the views of adversaries can be exchanged, constituting prenegotiations or rudimentary negotiations. Refusal to participate in such exchanges is difficult for any government. The Egyptian and Israeli governments were always responsive to the efforts of Gunnar Jarring, for example, even if slowly and with great qualifications, when he represented the UN secretary general in accordance with the 1967 Security Council resolution 242.

Patterns of Starting Negotiations

Why have initiatives in the U.S.-USSR and Arab-Israeli conflicts resulted in negotiations in some cases and not in others? It may not always be clear that negotiations have followed an initiative, and an initiative may need to be reiterated over several years before movement begins. Sometimes, an initiative that promotes a proposal on a particular set of issues may be followed, after a long time, with negotiations on a similar but not identical set of issues. Even in the course of negotiations, major new proposals may be introduced, but they will not be regarded as a new initiative and are discussed in the context of ongoing negotiations.

With these ambiguities in mind, the interpretations provided by the adversaries themselves will be accepted initially for the purpose analysis. Cases are not treated in a single way; the same event in a different context will elicit a different perspective. Major negotiations in U.S.-USSR and Arab-Israeli relations are listed in tables 5 and 6 according to the same four time periods as the initiatives in tables 3 and 4. The negotiations cited in this chapter can be compared to the initiatives listed in chapter 3. Some initiatives have been followed by negotiations but often only after many years and in a different form than originally proposed. This chapter compares those followed with those not followed by negotiations within one year.

Of the initiatives in the U.S.-USSR conflict given in table 3, several were not directly followed by negotiations; for example: the 1950 USSR proposal for a meeting of the Big Four foreign ministers to negotiate a peace treaty for Germany was not followed by significant negotiations for two decades. Many more of the initiatives in the Arab-Israeli conflict did not result in negotiations; such instances include the 1965 Israeli proposal for direct negotiations between Israel and the Arab governments that signed the armistice agreements of 1949 and the 1982 UN General Assembly call for a conference on Palestine.

My examination is not a statistical one; far too much ambiguity and dispute among conflict protagonists exist in defining an initiative and a negotiation to make precise comparisons. To extract a single instance from the continuity of most negotiating efforts would not be a reliable method. Nevertheless, many cases are clear-cut and do yield strong patterns, providing the basis for the interpretations made here. First, I describe how major aspects of initiatives (inducements, parties, and issues) may be related to the initiation of negotiations in order to account for the effects of interrelated aspects.

Inducements

This discussion of inducements focuses on the use of various positive and negative sanctions, though it is not always clear what constitutes positive and negative sanctions. When an adversary makes a harsh demand or threatens coercion and then later withdraws it, is the withdrawal a positive sanction? Such withdrawals are generally regarded here as concessions and positive sanctions, since that is how they are usually presented. For a specific dispute over a short period, the withdrawal of a threat is appropriately regarded as a concession.

In assessing the effects of different sanctions, an act or speech cannot readily be designated as a major unilateral gesture of conciliation, a minor conciliatory concession, an offer of a benefit contingent upon reciprocation, a forced concession, or as a demand politely phrased. Although there is some conventional understanding about how to identify a conciliatory gesture, there is not universal agreement. Apart from disagreements motivated by partisan interests, differences in understanding can be based on

Table 5. Major U.S.-USSR Negotiations, 1948–1989

Dates	Participants	Issues
1948–1957		
June 1948–September 1949	Big Four foreign ministers, U.S.-USSR	Berlin blockade; status of Berlin
January 1952	UN Disarmament Commission (UNDC) replaces UN Atomic Energy Commission and the Commission for Conventional Armaments	Disarmament
January–February 1954	Big Four ministers	Security in Europe and peace treaty for Germany—unified and demilitarized
April–July 1954	France, U.K., PRC, and USSR meet in Geneva	Indochina armistice
May 1954–September 1957	UN disarmament subcommittee	Anglo-French, Soviets, Americans, for disarmament with elimination of all nuclear weapons, reduced conventional forces, aerial inspection
August–October 1955	Geneva Conference of Heads of Government (U.S., U.K., and USSR)	Open skies, disarmament, unification of Germany, denuclearized zone in Germany, military budget reduction, nuclear test ban, twenty-six-nation European security treaty, and dissolution of NATO and Warsaw Pact
March–September 1956	Multilateral, with primary U.S.-USSR interaction; forum expanded to include all UN members	Germany, disarmament, and peaceful co-existence
February–May 1955	Austria-USSR, within context of Big Four	Austrian Peace Treaty

Date	Participants	Topics
March–August 1957	UN Disarmament Commission Subcommittee, (U.S., USSR, France, Canada, and U.K.); bilateral talks (U.S.–USSR) West Germany	Cutoff in production of fissionable material; limits on nuclear testing; inspection and verification system; staged reduction in conventional arms and military budgets; prohibition on use of nuclear weapons and aerial inspection; bomb reduction and limitation, tied to German rearmament and reunification
October 1957	U.S.–USSR	Educational, cultural, and scientific exchanges
1958–1967		
May 1958–December 1959	U.S., USSR, and ten other countries	Antarctica as demilitarized zone
July–December 1958	Two conferences of East–West experts; and Geneva conference on the discontinuation of nuclear weapon tests (U.K., U.S., USSR)	Prevention of surprise attacks and verification, discussed separately at two conferences; limited test ban
October 1958–January 1962	U.S., U.K., USSR	Nuclear test ban
May–August 1959	Big Four ministers	Status of Berlin
August 1959–April 1960	Ten-Nation Disarmament committee led by U.K., France, U.S., and USSR	Limitations and reductions of armaments and armed forces
September 1959	U.S.–USSR summit, Camp David	Status of Berlin, nuclear test ban, disarmament, trade, and credits
May–September 1961	U.S.–USSR summit, Vienna (June 1961), followed by negotiations	Disarmament, Berlin status, nuclear test ban, Laos; formation of Eighteen-Nation Disarmament Committee (ENDC)
March 1962	ENDC formed, including members of Ten-Nation Disarmament Committee and eight neutral countries	Initially focused on GCD and partial measures, later on test ban and collateral issues

Table 5 (*Continued*)

Dates	Participants	Issues
July 1962–June 1967	ENDC	Confidence-building measures to reduce the risk of war by accident; verifiable freeze
November 1962–February 1967	UN General Assembly	Prohibition of nuclear proliferation in Latin America
1968–1977 June 1963	U.S.-USSR summit	Establishment of U.S.-USSR hot line
June–July 1963	U.S., USSR, U.K., trilateral negotiators	Partial nuclear test ban
September–December 1963	U.S.-USSR	Consular rights and practices; grain sales; civil aviation
October 1963–January 1967	UN General Assembly, U.S.-USSR	Outer-space weapons ban
September–July 1968	ENDC, UNDC, General Assembly	Non-Proliferation of Nuclear Weapons Treaty linked to FRG's use of nuclear weapons and hesitation of France
June 1967	U.S.-USSR summit, Glassboro, N.J.	Middle East and Vietnam wars; ABM and SALT I
November 1967–February 1971	U.S.-USSR, UN ad hoc committee, ENDC (1969)	Preservation of ocean floor for peaceful purposes
September 1969	ENDC enlarged to twenty-six nations, name changed to Conference of Committee on Disarmament (CCD)	Comprehensive test ban and other avenues to international disarmament
August 1969–April 1972	UN General Assembly, UNDC, U.S.-USSR, CCD	Chemical and bacteriological weapons ban

Date	Parties	Subject
October 1969	U.S.-USSR	Secret talks on peace in the Middle East
November 1969–May 1972	U.S.-USSR summit, Moscow	SALT I: antiballistic missile systems and strategic offensive arms
March 1970–September 1971	Big Four ambassadors	Status of Berlin
September 1971	U.S.-USSR	Hot line and measures against nuclear accidents upgraded
May 1972	U.S.-USSR summit, Moscow	Continuation of SALT talks: basic principles of relations; economic relations; Europe, Middle East, Indochina; medical science; environmental protection; cooperation in space; prevention of incidents at sea; chemical weapons
May 1972–June 1979	U.S.-USSR	Continuation of SALT II talks
November 1972–July 1975	Negotiations, U.S.-USSR and thirty-three other nations begin (July 1973)	Conference on Security and Cooperation in Europe formed (CSCE); talks between NATO and Warsaw Pact forces
December 1972	U.S.-USSR	Standing Consultative Commission (SCC) formed as by-product of SALT agreement; two sessions a year
June 1973	U.S.-USSR summit, Washington	Peaceful use of atomic energy; SALT II principles; bilateral cooperation; CSCE; basic principles reaffirmed; peaceful ties; prevention of nuclear war; commercial and economic relations; bilateral cooperation
October 1973–1989	Warsaw Pact and NATO	Talks on MBFR in Europe
March 1974–June 1974	U.S.-USSR summit, Moscow	SALT II; CSCE progress, Middle East and Vietnam; UN effectiveness; economic matters; chemical warfare; bilateral cooperation; threshold nuclear test ban; Protocol for 1972 ABM Treaty; comprehensive test ban
November 1974–June 1979	U.S.-USSR	SALT II; Cyprus; UN resolution 338 and Middle East

Table 5 (*Continued*)

Dates	Participants	Issues
November 1974	U.S.-USSR summit, Vladivostok	SALT II
August 1975	CSCE Helsinki summit	Final act of CSCE in three major categories: military security in Europe; cooperation in economics, science, technology, and the environment; human rights and cultural and educational exchanges
March 1976	U.S.-USSR	Peaceful nuclear explosions (PNE)
July 1976–August 1976	U.S.-USSR and CSCE	SALT II and the Middle East
September 1976	UN Committee on PNE	Peaceful explosion of nuclear weapons
March 1977–June 1979	U.S.-USSR	Conventional Arms Transfer Limitations; antisatellite (ASAT) arms control
October 1977–March 1978	CSCE follow-on, Belgrade	No first use of nuclear bombs
February–August 1977	CCD	Cessation of nuclear weapons test; prohibition of chemical weapons; and prohibition of new types of weapons of destruction
July 1977–November 1980	U.S., USSR, U.K. tripartite negotiations; UN ad hoc committee of scientific experts meets concurrently	Comprehensive test ban: verification by national technical means, on-site verification and agreement in principle (July 1979); arrangements for verification negotiations continues until November 1980
1978–1989		
May 1978–August 1979	UNDC and UN special session on disarmament; UNDC continues annual meetings, primarily to discuss issues	Prohibition of ASAT systems

Date	Forum/Location	Topics
June 1979	U.S.-USSR summit, Vienna	SALT II agreement; SALT III guidelines; comprehensive test ban; non-proliferation; MBFR; ASAT, and CSCE progress; conventional arms transfers; chemical and radiological weapons ban; Indian Ocean; Middle East; peaceful use of oceans and outer space
May 1981–November 1983	U.S.-USSR	Elimination of INF
May 1982	Ad Hoc Committee on Disarmament	Verification and compliance
June 1982–December 1983	U.S.-USSR	Strategic Arms Reduction Talks; focus changed from limiting number of launchers to reducing number of missiles and warheads
April 1983–July 1984	U.S.-USSR	Hot line upgraded to facsimile machine
August 1983	U.S.-USSR	Negotiation of new cultural and scientific exchange agreements begins
January 1984–September 1986	Conference on Disarmament in Europe (CDE), part of CSCE, all thirty-five members	Confidence and security-building measures
February–August 1984	Conference on Disarmament, U.S.-USSR	Chemical weapons; nuclear test ban; prevention of nuclear war; nuclear disarmament
March 1985–December 1987	U.S.-USSR	INF treaty negotiations as part of umbrella negotiations covering INF, START, and defense and space weapons
November 1985	U.S.-USSR summit, Geneva	Hot line upgraded, crisis stations established; SDI tied to 50 percent reduction in nuclear weapons, separate from INF negotiations; nuclear non-proliferation; chemical weapons; regional conflicts; cultural exchanges; consulates; human rights
November 1985–September 1987	U.S.-USSR	Crisis stations
October 1986	U.S.-USSR summit, Reykjavik, Iceland	INF, 50 percent reduction of strategic nuclear arms; SDI; crisis stations

Table 5 (*Continued*)

Dates	Participants	Issues
November 1986	CSCE follow-on, Vienna	Humanitarian issues, European security, Mediterranean follow-up, and economic issues
December 1987	U.S.-USSR summit, Washington	Elimination of intermediate nuclear range weapons; limitation of strategic weapons; SDI; Afghanistan; ABM treaty interpretation; limitation of ballistic missiles
January 1988	U.S.-USSR	Continuation of nuclear and space talks (START and Space Weapons), with submission of joint draft START treaty and an associated protocol, and joint draft protocol to the ABM Treaty
May 1988	U.S.-USSR summit, Moscow	Notification of ballistic missile launches, joint verification experiment; cultural exchanges; student exchanges; regional conflict; human rights; joint ventures in radio navigation; search and rescue at sea; experimentation and use of outer space for peaceful purposes; peaceful use of atomic energy; transportation research and technology; and fishing
January 1989	151 nations	Prohibition of chemical weapons
March 1989	U.S.-USSR and members of Warsaw Treaty Organization and NATO	Conventional Armed Forces in Europe (CFE) negotiations begin

Table 6. Major Arab-Israeli Negotiations, 1948–1986

Dates	Participants	Issues
1948–1957		
January–February 1949	Israel and Egypt and UN mediator, Bunche, at Rhodes	Cease-fire; troop, disengagement
January–March 1949	Israel and Lebanon and UN mediator, Bunche	Armistice lines
March–April 1949	UN Conciliation Commission for Palestine (U.S., France, and Turkey) meet to mediate indirect talks between Israel and Arab states	Israeli borders and Palestinian refugees
Winter 1949/50	Israel and Jordan	Settlement of borders
September 1951	CCP meets in Paris with Israeli and Arab government representatives	Settlement of borders test ban
March–June 1953	Egypt and Israel through official and nonofficial U.S. intermediaries	Possible direct meetings and specific matters discussed, e.g., return of ship or crew inadvertently reaching the other's shores
October 1953	Israel, Jordan, Syria, Lebanon mediated by U.S. representative Eric Johnston	Jordan River valley project
1958–1967		
May 1961–October 1962	U.S. special representative Joseph E. Johnson is intermediary between Israel and Arab states	Palestinian refugees

Table 6 (*Continued*)

Dates	Participants	Issues
September 1963	King Hussein meets secretly in London with Prime Minister Levi Eshkol's general-director Yaacov Herzog	Solution to the conflict between Jordan and Israel; mutual security
1968–1977		
January 1968–March 1969	UN special representative Gunnar Jarring intermediary between Israel, Jordan, and Egypt	Implementation of UN Security Council resolution 242
December 1969–March 1970	U.S. Secretary of State Rogers, intermediary with Israel, Jordan and Egypt	"Rogers Plan" based on resolution 242
June–August 1970	U.S. Secretary of State Rogers and Egypt and Israel	Cease-fire along Suez canal, ending War of Attrition
February 1971—March 1972	Public and private Egyptian and Israeli statements and mediation by Jarring and Rogers	Partial Israeli withdrawal from Sinai and opening of Suez canal; Rogers' peace proposal
December	At Geneva, foreign ministers of U.S., USSR, Israel, Jordan, and Egypt	UN Security Council resolution 338 and disengagement of military forces between Israel and Egypt, and Israel and Syria

November 1973–December 1974	Kissinger mediates between Egypt and Israel	Disengagement of Israeli-Egyptian forces, partial withdrawal by Israel from Suez canal
February 1974–May 1974	Kissinger mediates Syrian-Israeli disengagement	Disengagement of Golan Heights
Summer 1974	Kissinger mediates Jordanian-Israeli disengagement	Disengagement
December 1977	Egypt and Israel	Comprehensive peace
1978–1986		
July 1978	Egypt, Israel, and ;u.s. (Leeds)	Areas of agreement
September 1978	Egypt, Israel, and u.s. summit (Camp David)	Comprehensive peace
March 1979–June 1982	Egypt and Israel with mediation by U.S	Autonomy and future of West Bank and Gaza
May–July 1981	Habib shuttle between Israel, Syria, Lebanon, Saudi Arabia, and indirectly with PLO	Cease-fire between Israeli and Lebanon territory
June–August 1982	Israel, Lebanon, and u.s.	Israeli-Lebanon security; PLO withdrawal
December 1982–May 1983	Israel, Lebanon, and u.s.	Israeli-Lebanon security agreement, Israeli withdrawal
September 1985–March 1986	Egypt and Israel	Disputed Taba area on Red Sea

Table 7. Cases of Initiatives with Inducements and the Start of Negotiations

Inducements with Initiative	Negotiations Begin	
	Yes	No
Major unilateral gesture with initiative	Sadat's visit to Jerusalem, November 1977	
Small positive gesture		Israeli peace plan October 1968
No significant inducement with initiative		Rapacki plan October 1957
Coercion accompanying initiative		Soviet Berlin proposal June 1961

differences in culture, ideas on the equivalency of concessions, and how quickly a gesture should be reciprocated. When the Israelis debated an appropriate response to Sadat's Jerusalem visit, cultural expectations were elements in the debate.[21] The Egyptians considered that certain matters would be sullied by "profane" negotiations, and therefore concessions involving Egyptian soil were unthinkable. The Israelis felt that Arab nomadism would diminish the significance of the territory and regarded Sadat's insistence on a complete Israel—withdrawal from all occupied Arab territories—as a high opening-bid bargaining position.[22] Lack of agreement on the nature and magnitude of a conciliatory measure can obviously reduce the usefulness of a reciprocal strategy.

There is evidence that, at least among Americans, certain aspects of initiatives are generally viewed as indicative of the seriousness of a proposal. Some evidence comes from a survey of U.S. international relations professionals and college students, which used brief scenarios that included various de-escalation proposals and gestures. The survey indicates that some ways of conveying de-escalation initiatives are assessed similarly, whether they are made by the Soviet or U.S. government.[23] For example, proposals made through confidential channels are generally more likely to be considered as serious than those made publicly on television.

The initiatives listed in tables 3 and 4 indicate the variety of inducements and their relative frequency. Four kinds of de-escalation initiatives, varying in their use of noncoercive elements, can be distinguished (see table 7). The first entails the use of a major unilateral gesture accompanied by an explicit interpretation of the act as conciliatory. The most notable example of such a gesture was Sadat's trip Israel, which yielded something the Israelis deeply wanted: public recognition by an Arab country, a gesture that Sadat could not, after all, rescind.[24]

If not quite as grand, there are several other gestures that exemplify a positive inducement. A frequently noted example is Kennedy's June 1963 speech at American University, which included concessions and the contingent promise of other benefits.[25] Reading the speech now, we see that it includes much cold war rhetoric; at the time, it marked a break with the cold war and included much that the Soviets wanted to hear.

> Let us reexamine our attitude toward the Soviet Union. . . . Among the many traits the peoples of our two countries have in common, none is stronger than the abhorrence of war. . . . We have never been at war with each other. And no nation in the history of battle ever suffered more than the Soviet Union in the course of the Second World War. . . . Let us reexamine our attitude toward the Cold War. . . . We are not here distributing blame or pointing the finger of judgment. We must deal with the world as it is.[26]

Kennedy went on to announce that U.S., British, and Soviet high-level representatives would shortly meet in Moscow to discuss an early agreement on a comprehensive test ban treaty. "To make clear our good faith and solemn convictions on the matter, I now declare that the United States does not propose to conduct nuclear tests in the atmosphere so long as other states do not."

There are other examples of U.S. conciliatory gestures accompanying de-escalation initiatives. In November 1969, Nixon renounced the use of bacteriological weapons in order to advance negotiations to ban such weapons. The Soviet peace offensive of the mid-1950s is a major case; it included a large-scale Soviet reduction of soldiers in uniform, withdrawal from bases in Finland, establishment of diplomatic relations with West Germany, and proposals for de-escalation agreements. A four-power summit meeting was consequently held in Geneva in 1956, but no equivalent reciprocated concessions and no extended negotiations followed. Generally, however, when major conciliatory gestures have been made, de-escalation negotiations have followed.

The transformation of U.S.-USSR relations at the end of the 1980s certainly would not have happened without the dramatic and radical actions taken by the Soviet Union. They made possible the reopening of INF negotiations, which had been broken off in 1983, and the renewal of negotiations in a wide variety of areas, including environmental matters, regional conflicts, trade, and investment.

The second set of cases entails instances in which positive sanctions were unilaterally made. Although small or unaccompanied by a clear presentation of their de-escalation character, positive gestures were made as evidence of good faith and seriousness in seeking a de-escalation accord. Thus, in 1964, President Lyndon Johnson announced that the United States would reduce the production of fissionable nuclear materials as an inducement to negotiations with the Soviets for a mutual cutback.[27] Thus, too, when Israeli Foreign Minister Abba Eban presented an Israeli peace plan to the UN General Assembly in October 1968, he included an announcement that his government would "intensify and accelerate action to widen the uniting of families scheme and to process 'hardship cases' among refugees who had crossed to the east bank during the 1967 fighting."[28] Another example is Sadat's peace initiative early in 1971 when he proposed a partial Israeli withdrawal from Sinai, offering in exchange to reopen the Suez canal. In each of these cases, the positive inducements were relatively minor.

Unilateral positive actions have sometimes been taken without claiming them to be de-escalation efforts, though they might have been. Carter's 1977 decision not to proceed with the production of B-1 bombers is an illustrative case. He explained his decision in terms of cost effectiveness, not as a conciliatory gesture—nor did he use it as a negotiating chip. A Soviet arms control negotiator told his U.S. counterpart that he was surprised at the announcement, commenting that Carter could have gotten something for not producing the bombers.[29] These instances of small concessions and ambiguous claims, however, have generally not led to reciprocated concessions and de-escalation negotiations.

Parties playing a mediation role sometimes provide positive inducements to one or more of the primary adversaries. They can add resources, expanding the size of the pie so that each adversary may get much of what they want without having the other pay the price. This is particularly true of the U.S. government's mediation of the Arab-Israeli conflict where it has provided financial compensation for certain concessions and assurances of compliance for others.

The third set of peace initiatives is relatively large. It includes the many cases in which de-escalation proposals have been presented but without any significant conciliatory deeds by the proponent. An example is the proposal made in October 1957 by Polish Foreign Minister Adam Rapacki for a nuclear-free Central Europe, including Czechoslovakia, the two Germanys, and Poland, known as the Rapacki Plan. The plan itself was offered as mutually beneficial. This set of initiatives also includes secret meetings and conversations, unaccompanied by either significant gestures or public explanations. For example, Israeli representatives have met several times with Jordanian and other Arab government representatives without public acknowledgment.[30] The instance involving the most extensive private negotiations was in 1949 between the Israeli government and King Abdullah of Jordan regarding a draft peace treaty.

In the Arab-Israeli conflict, because the protagonists do not in principle recognize one another, intermediaries have generally initiated de-escalation efforts. UN representatives, the UN General Assembly, U.S. officials, journalists, and others have made proposals or transmitted proposals from one or another adversary party. These have often not included any coercive or conciliatory actions and have generally not resulted directly in de-escalation negotiations. Initiatives undertaken by the United Nations, particularly in the early years of the conflict, resulted in negotiations, even if only indirect ones. When the U.S. government has taken the initiative, promises of later benefits or compensations for the risks of an agreement have often been made. As in the case of the United Nations, some negotiations often followed those initiatives.

Very often in the Soviet-American conflict, however, negotiations have been undertaken without having been preceded by a significant conciliatory unilateral gesture. This is particularly the case in the years since the late 1960s, except during the renewed cold war of the early 1980s. On many matters, negotiations had become so routine that positive gestures at the outset were unnecessary. Initiatives undertaken by parties other than primary adversaries—for example, UN committees—have often led to negotiations. It may be that these initiatives hold the promise of reward. Indeed, the simple approbation of parties such as a UN body has value.

Finally, in many cases an adversary may claim to seek de-escalation negotiations, accompanying that claim with warnings of possible punishment or of increasing its capability to do so. This kind of peace effort can be made even when a conflict is not being waged through open warfare or is not at a crisis stage. Thus, even during periods of relatively stable confrontation, one or both parties may hope to bring the other to the bargaining table by gaining a position of strength or by threatening to harm an adversary's interests. For example, in 1961, Khrushchev threatened that if the Berlin situation were not "normalized," the Soviets would turn over access to West Berlin to the German Democratic Republic.[31] At that time, the West did not even diplomatically recognize the GDR.

More recently, the Reagan administration argued that it had brought the Soviets back to arms control negotiations in 1985 because of its firm line and deployment of cruise missiles and Pershing II's in Europe while pursuing the Strategic Defense Initiative (SDI). Similarly, Soviet officials have argued that the U.S. government's willingness to reach arms control agreements in the 1970s reflects its recognition of the Soviet Union as an equal superpower owing to a shift in the correlation of forces.

Certainly, such developments sometimes contribute to the subsequent onset of de-escalation negotiations. In many other instances, of course, intransigence and threats have been returned, and a conflict has escalated or remained locked in antagonism. This is the case for most of the de-escalation efforts in the conflict between the Israeli government and the PLO. It was also so with Soviet efforts to "normalize" the status of Berlin; the pressures to bring about negotiations created the Berlin crises of 1957–62.

Parties

For the negotiations and theoretical issues discussed here, five combinations of protagonists are usefully distinguished. They are based on the partisanship and number of official and major participants and include their various roles, whether governmental or nongovernmental.

The first type is bilateral; it encompasses negotiations between two primary official adversaries, for example, between the U.S. and Soviet governments. Type two is an expanded bilateral negotiation consisting of dealings between two sets of adversaries, though one side may be alone and the total number of negotiating parties only three or four. A conference of the Big Four nations is an example. Type three is a two-sided and multilateral negotiation. It consists of coalition partners from each side without formal intermediaries; a conference of only NATO and Warsaw Pact members is an example. Types four and five include parties who take the role of intermediaries. In type four, two adversary parties meet with an intermediary party; the U.S. government mediation in the 1978 Israeli-Egyptian negotiations is illustrative. In pattern five, many parties are engaged in the negotiations, including one or more formal or informal intermediary parties. In the 1958 negotiations leading to the Antarctica treaty, for example, twelve governments were represented, some of which provided intermediary services for particular issues in dispute.

Many de-escalation initiatives do not call for negotiations; they essentially announce a gesture or a peace plan. It may be intended that they foster negotiations already under way or make a statement that will strengthen the position of a party before or during negotiations. Many initiatives, however, do include calls for beginning talks. Whether initiatives that require specific negotiations are more or less likely to lead to negotiations can now be considered.

In the U.S.-USSR conflict, bilateral negotiations between U.S. and Soviet representatives have been the type most frequently requested, often in de-escalation initiatives, particularly since the late 1950s, and often have occurred. Expanded bilateral negotiations have been relatively frequent, particularly in the early post–World War II years. Two-sided, multilateral negotiations have been relatively rare; when sought, they have not been held. Several times Khrushchev had suggested negotiating a nonaggression pact between NATO and Warsaw Pact members.

Conversely, initiatives to undertake negotiations involving intermediaries generally have resulted in meetings. The United Nations has been an effective vehicle for bringing U.S. and Soviet representatives together in multilateral negotiation settings, including parties not allied with either major adversary. Such initiatives and negotiations were relatively frequent in the 1960s, as in the Eighteen-Nation Disarmament Committee (ENDC).

Since 1948, proposals for negotiations and actual negotiations have become more frequently bilateral. In the immediate post–World War II years, meetings of the Big Four constituted the usual negotiating format. During the cold war, the United Nations and its committees provided the major negotiating setting. Only in the 1960s did bilateral meetings become increasingly frequent, and in the 1970s they became the usual negotiating format. The patterns for the Arab-Israeli conflict are very different. While some de-escalation initiatives specified holding negotiations, most did not, stating only a desired position. Most such initiatives did not result in any negotiations.

A different format for the meetings has typically been proposed by each side. Generally, the Israelis have called for direct, bilateral negotiations between governments, seeking to reach an agreement with one Arab government at a time and avoiding recognition of the PLO. The Arab states, not wanting to appear ready to make a separate peace with the Israeli enemy, have generally suggested multilateral conferences, including intermediaries and in recent years the PLO. The negotiations that have been conducted have rarely been multilateral and have never been multilateral without intermediaries. Most frequently, they have been bilateral with intermediaries.

The role of nonstate actors, particularly the PLO, deserves attention, although Israel has not recognized that the PLO has a legitimate claim to participate in negotiations on peace settlements in the Middle East. During the years in which East Jerusalem and the West Bank were part of the Kingdom of Jordan, the Palestinians had no widely recognized representation of their own. Only in October 1974, at the Rabat Conference, did the Arab governments affirm "the right of the Palestinian people to set up an

independent national authority under the leadership of the Palestine Liberation Organization, in its capacity as the sole legitimate representative of the
Palestinian people, on any liberated Palestinian land."[32]

Some indirect, prenegotiation exchanges have occurred between Israeli
and PLO officials. In 1985, the U.S. and Jordanian governments discussed
the representation of Palestinians in a Jordanian-Palestinian delegation to an
international peace conference. Palestinian representatives were proposed
by the PLO and reviewed by the Israeli government, having been transmitted
through Jordanian and U.S. government channels. Other indirect negotiations took place in 1981 on a PLO cease-fire agreement for the Lebanese-
Israeli border.[33] After the U.S. government had opened a dialogue with the
PLO in December 1988, it began, in effect, indirect prenegotiations between
the PLO and the Israeli government. These discussions were not only about
the modalities of possible negotiations but included the substance of negotiations and possible settlements.

Despite repeated failures to enter full-scale negotiations, many meetings
have been held between Israeli officials and a few Arab governments. Most
have been direct, bilateral meetings, particularly between Israeli and Egyptian representatives and, covertly, between Israeli and Jordanian representatives.[34] Officially, Israel has not engaged in multilateral negotiations with
Arab governments without intermediaries.

Intermediaries have been effective figures in efforts to negotiate settlements in the Arab-Israeli conflict. The conflict is of sufficient seriousness and
duration that many governments, international organizations, and private individuals and groups have believed they should offer suggestions and be
ready to intervene to de-escalate the conflict. When adversaries do not recognize each other's legitimacy and will not openly meet face to face, intermediaries are necessary for negotiations. This has been the case in the Arab-Israeli
conflict. Negotiations often have been conducted through intermediaries
who have shuttled between the adversaries. Representatives of the United
States and the United Nations have been particularly active in this way.

Intermediaries have also participated in open, direct bilateral negotiations, as in Israeli-Egyptian negotiations since the mid-1970s. In a few
cases, mediators have also participated in multilateral negotiations that have
included direct private talks and formal meetings. The UN's Conciliation
Commission for Palestine (CCP) was such an intermediary. Consisting of
representatives of France, Turkey, and the United States, it hosted meetings
in Lausanne in 1949 and in Paris in 1951.

International governmental organizations like the United Nations have
played important roles, not only as intermediaries but as vehicles of repre-

sentation for nonstate actors. Such accessibility is striking since international governmental organizations are generally reluctant to recognize nonstate actors. This reluctance was manifest at the United Nations before the change in its composition with the admission of the newly independent states of Africa and Asia. The changed composition led to new voting groups and coalitions. Thus, support from Arab and Muslim countries of African-initiated pressure against South Africa could be traded for African support against the Israeli government. One form this has taken is recognition of the PLO as the sole representative of Palestinians. The United Nations in the early post–World War II years did not attempt to give a continuing role to Palestinians after the effort to set up a Palestinian state failed in 1948.

Frequently, nongovernmental actors have also been active intermediaries. They have been based outside the countries of the primary adversaries, as U.S. citizens are who engage in intermediary actions in the Arab-Israeli conflict. They also include citizens of primary adversary countries, as when American and Soviet academics and research scientists meet with others in the context of Pugwash or Dartmouth conference meetings.[35] The Dartmouth conferences are a forum for regular meetings between Soviet and U.S. academicians, writers, former officials, and scientists. They began in October 1960 at Dartmouth College. Like the Pugwash conferences, many participants have attended meetings over many years and have establish enduring personal relationships.

Historically, nongovernmental actors claiming to be parties to a conflict have generally not joined negotiations, nor has their claim for participation been recognized by either side. This has been true for the Palestinians and the PLO; in the U.S.-USSR conflict, it was an important issue at the outset of the cold war. Organizations of refugees from Estonia, Latvia, Lithuania, Poland, and other nations in Eastern Europe have sought to influence U.S. policy but have had no official role in negotiations. Even when nonstate actors are major fighting groups, they often do not officially or directly participate in negotiations for the settlement of conflicts in which they are engaged, as in ending the wars in Vietnam or Afghanistan.

Issues

Matters about which negotiations may be conducted are as numerous as the issues about which people fight. Specific negotiations may pertain to trade, cultural exchanges, refugees, borders, or arms control. Each of these matters has many subparts that can be combined in various ways. In light of the theoretical considerations discussed here, two dimensions of negotiation subjects claim our attention: centrality and isolation.

Centrality refers to matters that one or more of the parties regards as vital to its existence. In the cases under consideration, this certainly includes recognition of a state's claim to legitimacy and its survival. For governments, matters of state and military security are generally regarded as vital. Matters affecting social, economic, and cultural conditions have usually been held as peripheral, unless they are so massive as to involve the survival of the society.

In both major conflicts considered here, initiatives that propose negotiations are more likely to refer to fundamental interests or to political and security matters than to matters less central, such as trade and cultural exchange. This is particularly true in the Arab-Israeli conflict. Both parties have felt their existence as cohesive entities so threatened that nonvital matters have relatively rarely been the subject of de-escalation initiatives since they take on exaggerated significance.

The other significant dimension is the degree to which an issue is isolated from other matters. Initiatives may contain an offer on a single issue or may present several matters as a package. Issues have been raised in isolation as often as they have been proposed as part of a comprehensive settlement or linked with other issues. Issues have been raised in isolation more often in the U.S.-USSR conflict than in the Arab-Israeli conflict, where calls for a comprehensive settlement have been relatively common.

The relationship between the issues proposed for negotiation and the actual initiation of talks is similar for the two conflicts examined here. In both, issues that are not vital and that do not deal with major political or military security matters when proposed for negotiations are more likely to result in negotiations than those that do.

In many other ways the relationship is dissimilar. Certainly, proposals have been much more likely to result in negotiations in the U.S.-USSR conflict than in the Arab-Israeli conflict. Furthermore, patterns have changed in different ways since 1948. In the U.S.-USSR conflict, the initiatives leading to negotiations were more often about peripheral matters in the years of the cold war; as the cold war thawed, matters of greater centrality took their place. In the Arab-Israeli conflict, since the primary adversaries did not accord one another recognition, nearly every initiative entailed vital issues. Only in Israeli-Egyptian relations after the peace treaty could relatively peripheral matters be the subject of negotiations.

Accounting for the Patterns

To explain the relations between the kind of initiatives made and the actual undertaking of negotiations, strategic choices are stressed. The possible effects of selecting different inducements, parties, and issues discussed earlier will now be assessed.

Inducements

The lack of a strong relationship between either unilateral concessions or coercive threats and the beginning of de-escalation negotiations does not necessarily indicate irrelevancy. The effects of various inducements differ depending on how they are combined with issues and parties in particular historical contexts. The four patterns in the use of initiatives in de-escalation efforts warrant explanation.

Major Conciliatory Gestures First, both the infrequent use of major conciliatory gestures and their relative success in starting de-escalation negotiations need to be explained. Government leaders often hesitate to make bold conciliatory motions toward an adversary—with good reason. They are susceptible to charges of appeasement, of having yielded to an enemy, and of cowardliness. This susceptibility indicates the importance of supportive domestic conditions—especially popular readiness, if not pressure, to lower the level of a conflict.

In general, leaders of nondemocratic countries are in a better position than democratic leaders to risk major conciliatory gestures that mark new policy directions. The intense ideological confrontation between Nazi Germany and Stalinist USSR would have been difficult to halt as abruptly as it was by the German-Soviet nonaggression pact of 1939 had the countries involved been democratic. Relatively sudden major conciliatory gestures, such as those by Sadat in 1977 and Khrushchev in the mid-1950s, could be conducted without great concern for possible popular opposition.

Government leaders can more safely make a conciliatory gesture without losing constituency support if they have already demonstrated toughness in dealing with an adversary. Witness the case of Sadat after the Egyptian and Syrian attack against Israel in October 1973, of Kennedy after the Cuban missile crisis, and of Nixon after a career of being vehemently anti-Communist.[36]

A conciliatory gesture may have increased significance after a drastic coercive action, in line with the theoretical argument for the use of both coercive and noncoercive inducements. Note, however, that the inducements should not be simultaneous; combining major conciliatory actions with confrontational ones often obscures the meaning of both and reduces their effectiveness. Such a situation contributed to the failure of the U.S. government to respond significantly to the Soviet peace offensive of the late

1950s—Khrushchev had coupled it with demands that were readily seen as threatening.

The extreme cold-war consensus in the United States in the 1950s required major, consistent, and reiterated conciliatory gestures from the Soviets to have yielded an accommodative response consistent with the GRIT strategy. In 1953, the Soviet government did make many cooperative moves and adopted a relatively conciliatory tone in UN disarmament negotiations. The Chinese and the North Koreans made some concessions, and in July an armistice was signed. The U.S. response, however, was slight.[37]

Under Khrushchev's leadership, a series of even more significant conciliatory moves were made, notably leading to the Austrian State Treaty on terms that the Soviets earlier had rejected. Again, the U.S. response was limited, leading only to a Big Four summit conference in Geneva in May. The muted response was partly attributable to U.S. Secretary of State Dulles, who was suspicious of the Soviet Union and inflexible about recognizing any new information that might damage the image he held of Soviet communism.[38]

Nevertheless, Khrushchev's peace offensive and coexistence policy probably contributed to the gradual decline in anti-Soviet sentiment among Americans that began in the mid-1950s.[39] Gorbachev followed a relatively consistent conciliatory policy in the late 1980s, saying yes to U.S. government proposals until the Reagan administration could not say no.

These observations further indicate that the constituency as well as the government of an adversary country should be the targets of peace initiatives. Sadat had the Israeli public government in mind with his dramatic and highly visible visit to Jerusalem. He also sought to influence the U.S. public and government, and he succeeded very well. In a U.S. national survey conducted in October 1977, only 37 percent of the respondents believed that Egypt really wanted peace; in November, after Sadat's trip, 58 percent thought so.[40]

The role of preliminary private communications between government heads before major de-escalation initiatives is more important than the theories previously discussed acknowledge. It may be that such exploratory, confidential communications help to convince an adversary that the initiatives constitute more than propaganda.

Because nongovernmental players are sometimes significant in these circumstances, government officials may request private persons to explore possible conciliation moves. This is particularly important between protagonists who lack official channels of communication. For example, in the past when the U.S. government has wished to communicate with the PLO, it has often done so through public announcements or through officials from

Saudi Arabia or Jordan, but it has also requested private U.S. citizens to make tentative investigations.[41] Private individuals or nongovernmental groups themselves sometimes initiate communications. A significant example of this began at a meeting of the Dartmouth conference held during the Cuban missile crisis. In the course of that conference, a representative from the Vatican explored the usefulness of an intervention by the Pope. After U.S. and Soviet participants at the conference consulted with their respective government officials, the Pope issued a statement calling for moral responsibility in the crisis.[42]

After the conference, Norman Cousins, editor of the *Saturday Review* and co-chair of the American delegation at the conference, was approached by Vatican and Soviet representatives to visit Khrushchev in Moscow in December 1962 on behalf of the Vatican. Cousins informed Kennedy about the planned meeting and was invited to the White House. The president said he wanted Soviet officials to understand that he was eager to get beyond cold war animosities. Cousins met with Khrushchev and in April 1963 reported on his Moscow visit to Kennedy; he told the president that "what was perhaps needed was a breathtaking new approach toward the Russian people, calling for the end of the cold war and a fresh start in American-Russian relationships."[43] Cousins's intermediary activities contributed to the decision to renew the effort to reach a nuclear weapon test ban agreement and to initiate the effort with Kennedy's June 1963 speech at American University.

Modest Gestures The use of modest conciliatory gestures or gestures that are not clearly claimed to be conciliatory also needs to be explained. These gestures are usually unreciprocated and do not lead to de-escalation negotiations. Yet grand gestures are often avoided—not only because they may seem to be a surrender to the enemy, but because if unreciprocated, the leader who took the initiative will look foolish as well as weak. This risk was minimal for Kennedy in 1963 because there had already been extensive negotiations on a nuclear test ban agreement and because messages had been conveyed informally about the possibility of a de-escalation move. Even Sadat's seemingly abrupt visit to Jerusalem was preceded by preliminary direct and indirect soundings.[44] In short, small gestures or concessions, though not claimed to be so, may be probes to seek out conciliatory reciprocation safely. Still, a tentative probe may undermine this goal, and the modesty of the concession may be too small to win the de-escalatory response being sought. The results of a survey made of U.S. international relations professionals and college students also indicate that small positive gestures contribute little to making de-escalation proposals appear serious.[45]

No Gestures In the third set of cases, de-escalation proposals are pre-sented—but without unilateral conciliatory actions. There are many such cases, and although they often do not lead to de-escalation negotiations, they sometimes do. The most fundamental explanation for entering de-escalation negotiations without inducements is that conditions are right—in the conflict and globally—to make de-escalation attractive. This was cer-tainly the case at the beginning of détente.[46]

Circumstances may be so compelling that de-escalation negotiations are desired by both adversaries, even though for quite different reasons. Often in these circumstances, each adversary envisages some future benefit from the other or at least from a reduced level of conflict. Thus, the Soviet and American governments in the first year or two of détente anticipated com-plementary benefits, including expanded markets for the U.S. and aid in gaining North Vietnamese agreement for an honorable U.S. exit from South Vietnam, and for the USSR, access to advanced technology, acceptance of the post–World War II status of Eastern Europe, and prevention of a U.S.-China anti-Soviet alliance.

When conditions do not obviously converge toward de-escalation, one actor may have to take relatively dramatic action to initiate de-escalation moves. Without that, an offer will not generate the desired response. For example, although the Rapacki Plan could be seen to offer security benefits to the West as well as the East, it was not given serious attention by the U.S. government and its allies. Suspicions of Soviet intentions, the mind-set that required the placement of nuclear weapons in the FRG, and the lack of a policy on Central Europe to loosen Soviet control did not encourage think-ing about the possible benefits of the Rapacki Plan.[47] A series of extraordi-nary Soviet conciliatory gestures would have had to accompany the pro-posal. It did not.

Threats Finally, there are many cases in which one or both sides in a conflict seek de-escalatory negotiations by coercing the other. In the U.S.-USSR conflict, this situation was particularly prevalent during the 1950s and again in the early 1980s. In Israeli relations with the Arabs, particularly with the PLO and the Syrian government, coercion has consistently been the prevailing inducement. Short of war or extensive, organized violence, coercion alone has not generally prompted de-escalation moves. Constitu-ency considerations may be the reason.

Leaders believe they must be careful not to appear to back down under enemy pressure. Such care needs to be greater where domestic groups have great influence in affecting government policy. This concern is truer for U.S. government leaders than Soviet officials and explains in part why the

Soviets have yielded on several occasions and entered de-escalation negotiations after the U.S. government had remained firm or even increased
coercive pressure. Note the Austrian State Treaty in 1955, the Berlin crises
of the late 1950s and early 1960s, and the elimination of intermediate-range
nuclear weapons in the 1980s.[48]

Under certain circumstances, then, coercion does contribute to initiating
negotiations. To do so, however, it must be combined with offers of possible
benefits. The combination must not be so mixed that the threats and promises reduce each other's credibility; alternating over time is one way to avoid
the problem of confusion and misunderstanding. The more diverse and
significant the constituency groups, the more difficult it is for the leadership
to manage the appropriate combination of conciliation and confrontation.
Its moves are subject to criticism and challenge if reciprocation is inadequate; diversity in the target society, however, can encourage greater commitment to making conciliatory moves. In the late 1980s, a new Soviet
leadership's accommodative moves could be safely made since it could
believe that U.S. domestic forces would restrain the government from
taking advantage of unilateral Soviet concessions.

Adversary Parties

Initiatives toward an agreement usually include proposals about who should
participate in the meetings; whether negotiations will follow often depends
on who is included. Proposals for meetings involving intermediaries more
regularly lead to negotiations than proposals that do not—something especially true of the Arab-Israeli conflict. Several processes account for this
regularity. First, intermediaries usually ensure that there will be at least the
appearance of negotiations. Second, leaders who may be concerned about
accusations of being too soft with the enemy can explain their willingness to
enter negotiations by their relationship with the intermediary. Thus, the
Israeli government may express interest in talks proposed by the U.S.
government for the sake of its relationship with the United States. Similarly,
the PLO may say it is ready to search for a formula for negotiations with
Israel when it believes it must seek support from an Arab government that
wishes to show it is seeking negotiations. Negotiations are also more likely
with intermediaries because they may add resources to make a successful
negotiation conceivable and reduce the risks and costs of reaching an
agreement. This is most evident of the U.S. government's role in Middle
East peacemaking efforts.

The number of official parties represented in negotiations in the Arab-
Israeli conflict has usually varied from the U.S.-USSR conflict. Multilateral
negotiations, even with intermediaries, have rarely been held in the Middle

East conflict, largely owing to the multiplicity of interconnected conflicts. In the first years after the establishment of the State of Israel, the United Nations, through the CCP, was able to bring about some multilateral negotiations.[49] These negotiations occurred before the conflict had become embedded in the East–West conflict, before inter-Arab rivalries had become profoundly important, and before Palestinians had begun to make their own claims effectively. Since then, the conflict has become more intractable and multilateral negotiations more difficult to realize.

Bilateral meetings with an intermediary have become the basic format for negotiations between the Israeli government and any Arab adversary. In Israeli-Jordanian relations, bilateral negotiations without an intermediary were conducted in secret at the outset of the conflict. Since then, secret bilateral negotiations have been held. There are implicit understandings and occasional secret meetings between King Hussein and Israeli officials, but these do not constitute negotiations as defined here. In Israeli-Egyptian relations, negotiations were usually bilateral with intermediaries. Only after Sadat's visit to Jerusalem did bilateral meetings without intermediaries become the typical mode of negotiations. This was possible once mutual recognition and some common understandings had been achieved, providing an essential context.

In U.S.-USSR relations, the patterns have been significantly different. American-Soviet bilateral negotiations were always possible even in the early post–World War II era and were conducted; as expected, their frequency increased as the cold war waned. During the 1950s and much of the 1960s, negotiations that involved other governments (aligned with neither the USSR nor the United States) were held more often than were U.S.-USSR bilateral negotiations. It appears that when the conflict was relatively intense and its management less institutionalized, having participants who could play intermediary roles was important.

Issues

Generally, initiatives pertaining to relatively isolated or peripheral issues are more likely to result in negotiations than are comprehensive or central issues, because they seem safer to government officials—since they reduce the risk of being charged with selling out to an enemy. It also reduces the risk of losing something important if negotiations fail and even if they succeed and an agreement is later violated. As an adversary relationship becomes more accommodating, initiatives relating to more comprehensive and central matters can and do become subject to negotiations. For example, the comprehensive Egyptian-Israeli peace treaty negotiations of 1978–79 were preceded by two limited disengagement agreements on the Sinai.

There is one area of negotiations that does not fit this generalization. Violent engagements such as wars would certainly seem to involve vital issues, yet cease-fire and armistice agreements must be negotiated while a conflict is still intense. A cease-fire may be a step in one side's surrender to the other, constituting the beginning of a comprehensive settlement of vital issues. This has not been the case, however, for negotiations in the major conflicts examined here. In the Middle East, there are two other ways of regarding cease-fires: First, it may be treated as an isolated matter, involving limited military issues; it may even be viewed as only an interruption in ongoing violent antagonism, the adversaries awaiting an opportunity to fight again. Second, the cease-fire is limited but is often regarded as a possible first step toward resolving major issues in the future.

Implications

The initiatives and negotiations examined here suggest several things. First, no one combination of inducements, parties, and issues will necessarily lead to de-escalation negotiations. Innumerable combinations are conceivable, depending on the background circumstances of the conflict. Conducive conditions in conjunction with an appropriate strategic formula bring adversaries to the negotiating table.[50]

Leaders with substantial constituency support are more able to enter de-escalation negotiations—not only because they can afford to take risks, but because for serious negotiations the adversary's leaders must believe their counterparts can indeed make binding agreements. For example, an argument of some Israeli Jews against dealing with Arafat is that he cannot effectively control his constituency if an agreement between the PLO and the Israeli government were reached. Leaders often emphasize a capacity to take decisive action and to commit their constituency and ask the same of their counterparts. This belief was critical in Sadat's decision to go to Jerusalem; after Begin became prime minister of Israel in early 1977, Sadat contemplated seeking a major de-escalation move with this new Israeli government headed by a hard-line nationalist. In his autobiography, Sadat reports on his visit to Romania's President Nicolae Ceauşescu shortly after Begin had visited Ceauşescu: "His emphasis on Begin's desire for peace, on Begin being a 'strong man,' confirmed my conclusion that a change was urgently needed—a change in the position of both sides."[51] Shortly thereafter, Sadat announced his readiness to go to Israel.

Strong leadership obviously is not the only relevant aspect of domestic conditions. Popular support for de-escalation is critical and is not only a pressure on leaders to negotiate seriously but an enticement to the adversary's leaders. Believing that the other side's leaders lack such pressure or can ignore it, discourages entering de-escalation negotiations. Some U.S. critics of negotiations on arms control with the Soviet Union argue that the lack of political freedom in the Soviet Union would enable Soviet leadership to exploit or violate any agreement. The strength of that view in the Reagan administration, especially in his first term, limited the extent and nature of the U.S. arms control position and its negotiations.

A demonstration of popular support and commitment to de-escalation not only enhances a leader's readiness to enter negotiations but also an adversary's security and hence readiness to do so. Domestic sentiments as articulated by social movement organizations also frame the issues in dispute. Public pressure in the United States and the United Kingdom for a nuclear weapon test ban illustrates this power. In the mid-1950s, organizations like the Federation of American Scientists, United World Federalists, American Friends Service Committee, the Women's International League for Peace and Freedom, the Fellowship of Reconciliation, and the World Council of Churches were all actively opposed to nuclear weapon testing. In 1957, the leaders of some of these organizations met to plan a strategy for the peace movement, deciding to focus on nuclear testing and to form new coordinating organizations.[52] This decision led to the formation of the Committee for Non-Violent Action and the broader, educationally oriented, National Committee for a Sane Nuclear Policy (SANE). Through advertisements in the *New York Times* and other newspapers and through rallies, SANE rapidly grew in membership and support. It focused on the issue of radioactive fallout from nuclear weapon testing.

On 16 April 1962, SANE published a full-page advertisement in the *New York Times,* with a large picture of the famed pediatrician Benjamin Spock gazing down on a small child, with the caption: "Dr. Spock is worried." *Time* and *Newsweek* carried articles on the advertisement and twenty-five thousand reprints were distributed throughout the country. On 5 July 1962, an advertisement showed a bottle of milk with a poison label of a skull and crossbones and the caption, "Is this what it's coming to?" The campaign continued until the Partial Nuclear Weapons Test Ban Treaty was signed and ratified.

Relations between adversaries constitute another condition fundamentally affecting the likelihood of entering negotiations, and they are always changing. Both of the major conflicts examined here have followed a course of development that has included periods relatively conducive to de-escalation negotiations. In U.S.-USSR relations, notably, there has been a gradual though fluctuating movement toward mutual accommodation since the depths of the cold war.

In a period of moving toward increased accommodation, initiatives are more likely to result in negotiations than in periods of frozen or escalating animosities. Therefore, the initiatives themselves can be modest and still be effective. An important policy implication follows. To enter significant de-escalation negotiations during periods of growing confrontation requires a long-run strategy together with a consistent and persistent implementation. Sadat, for all his readiness for surprising acts, pursued a general and extended strategy of accommodation with Israel through reliance on the United States.

The balance of power among the adversaries is often a decisive factor. Relevant parity makes the start of negotiations more likely than do large power inequalities. Parity, however, is not an absolute matter; it is always relative to a given set of issues within a given time frame. Obviously, for example, U.S. military power was much greater than the power of the North Vietnamese, and that of the Soviet army was greater than that of the guerrilla forces contesting the Soviet-supported government of Afghanistan. Nevertheless, for the limited goals sought by the opponents of the great powers, their strength was adequate.

A fitting formula for de-escalation negotiations must be based on the combination of parties and issues that yield an adequate equivalence of power. For example, the PLO has not gained adequate allies to threaten Israel into negotiating the establishment of a Palestinian state. Palestinians seeking only autonomy on the West Bank and Gaza Strip, however, may have generated enough power to induce Israel to enter serious negotiations for such a goal but lacked the ability to commit a significant constituency. Only in December 1988 did the PLO leadership, representing a wide variety of Palestinians, articulate terms of a possible settlement that seemed plausible—given existing conditions—and that included an ongoing uprising in the Israel-occupied territories. The terms were sufficient to open a dialogue with the U.S. government, which might then serve as a mediator. Nevertheless, the Israeli government, resisting Palestinian statehood, still refused to start negotiations with the PLO.

Creating an appropriate formula is a social construction. Important leaders and segments of relevant publics must agree that a particular combination of issues, parties, and inducements could lead to an acceptable settlement, often entailing a redefinition of a conflict, as Khrushchev's emphasis on "peaceful coexistence" and Gorbachev's stress on "new thinking" illustrate.

Political officials and leaders are obviously critical forces in constructing new formulas. Social movement organizations, intellectuals, leaders in established institutions, and many others in an adversary country or in an intermediary country can also contribute new definitions of the conflict and therefore suggest possible formulas for de-escalation. Moreover, informal and back-channel explorations of possible settlements make public initiatives more credible and increase the likelihood they will be reciprocated. These are important elements in the prenegotiation phase of conflict resolution.

Whether conditions are right for de-escalation negotiations depends, therefore, on the terms of the settlement. An adversary is likely to avoid negotiations that do not appear to produce an acceptable settlement. Such avoidance is likely to occur unless to do so would prove too costly; under such circumstances, a party may agree to negotiations if they can easily be pursued without reaching an agreement.

Finally, once having undertaken negotiations, adversaries may unwittingly be on a slippery path to an agreement. That possibility inhibits some parties from beginning negotiations altogether, as Israeli's refusal in 1989 to begin talks with the Palestinians illustrates. The extent to which talks end in agreements is the subject of the next chapter.

6
The Negotiation
of Agreements

hy do some international nego-
tiations result in de-escalation agreements and others do not? Why do many
negotiations, after months or even years of meetings, fail to produce any
agreement? Sometimes negotiations do not conclude with a signed accord
because the negotiators do not want one—intending only to give the appearance of seeking de-escalation—as when a government enters negotiations simply to deflect domestic opposition to its militant policy or to
forestall domestic pressure to make a unilateral conciliatory move. For
example, many observers argue that the U.S. government entered into
negotiations in 1973 on the reduction of conventional military forces in

Europe in order to undermine support for U.S. Sen. Mike Mansfield's amendment, which would have required a reduction of U.S. armed forces in Europe.[1] A treaty was finally concluded in November 1990 but only after the Soviet Union unilaterally undertook large-scale military withdrawals from Europe.

Sometimes negotiating partners seem to fail to reach an agreement, yet are satisfied in failing to do so, the lack of accord being an implicit agreement. In another example of counterintent, some critics of the U.S. and Soviet governments argue that the failure to conclude any disarmament treaty in the 1950s, 1960s, and 1970s was what both parties really wanted.[2]

Nonetheless, for our purposes here, all meetings regarded by the parties as negotiations will be so regarded here and treated as efforts to reach a mutually accepted explicit agreement. Once engaged in negotiations, presumably each party would at least be willing to reach an agreement—on its own terms. Furthermore, negotiations once under way often have their own momentum and even when not undertaken seriously, can yield results.

Explanatory Ideas

Numerous descriptions of negotiation processes and prescriptions about how to negotiate have been made. Analysts follow theoretical perspectives that stress background circumstances, tactics, and strategy in varying degrees. Many point out that reaching an agreement depends on the background of the conflict and minimize the role of negotiation skills. This view is stressed particularly by statists, who emphasize the coercive balance of power. Those using a populist approach stress the negotiation tactics and skills used in reaching an agreement.

Strategy is the focus in this book, drawing especially from the pluralist and conflict resolution approaches. Much depends upon the strategy used in selecting the issues, parties, and inducements for negotiations. The combination of those most effective in reaching an agreement depends on the particular state of the ongoing conflict.

Background Conditions

Whether or not meetings conclude with an agreement often depends on the timing of negotiations and on whether conditions are ripe for a settlement.[3] Conditions are defined as ready when the actions of at least one party to the conflict or an intermediary would result in an acceptable settlement among a significant set of adversaries. Such conditions may result from a convergence of domestic forces in one or more of the adversary countries, relations between adversaries, and the international context.

A de-escalation agreement may be reached when one or more governments experience powerful domestic pressure to settle. For example, the U.S. government's steps in the early 1970s toward accommodation with the Soviet Union can be explained in part as Nixon's response to the anti–Vietnam War movement in the United States.[4] It can also result from changes in the balance of forces between adversaries; both sides recognize that neither can unilaterally force the outcome preferred and hence seek mutual accommodation. For example, the Soviets contend that détente agreements in the early 1970s reflected a shift in the correlation of forces, which established a strategic parity that the United States had to recognize. But the collapse of détente demonstrates that such a balance was not itself sufficient to generate new agreements.

Finally, a de-escalation agreement may result from the convergence of several factors in the international environment. The initial agreements of détente, for example, including the ABM and SALT I treaties, were responses to the confluence of several international developments, notably the intensification of the Sino-Soviet conflict and the emergence of the West German *Ostpolitik* policy of accommodation with Eastern Europe and the USSR. Conversely, the absence of supporting conditions explains the failure to reach an agreement between the Israeli and Jordanian governments in 1985.[5]

The argument that background factors strongly influence whether or not a de-escalation agreement is reached can be strengthened in noting that sometimes aspects of domestic circumstances, relations between adversaries, and the international context together almost compel agreements. As the examples indicate, such a case might be made for the beginning of détente. Domestic circumstances take on importance in the course of negotiations as representatives become increasingly aware of gaining constituency support and, in some countries, of achieving formal ratification of any accord reached in negotiation.

Tactics

According to those analysts who emphasize tactics, background factors do not determine the reaching of an agreement; rather, the skills and techniques of negotiators are decisive.[6] Even under favorable background conditions, they say that poorly conducted negotiations can produce delays and that conditions can become unfavorable before an agreement is reached. But with sufficient skill, a de-escalation agreement can be reached even when background factors are not compelling or even conducive. Skills include *listening*: to discover the underlying interests of the negotiating partner;

analyzing the conflict: to discover possible common gains; and *creating new options* when negotiations become stalemated.

An emphasis on skills tends to promote a problem-solving approach to negotiation. Other techniques that contribute to reaching agreements sometimes include problem solving; some are difficult to pursue at the same time that other valued methods are used. For example, it is often urged that before negotiations each side rank the priority of its own preferences. In international negotiations, this is usually done even though it entails a locking in of positions. In turn, this procedure may obstruct attention to the preferences of negotiating partners and make it difficult to be responsive.[7]

Many techniques can be useful, whether or not a problem-solving approach is taken, and include establishing good personal relations with negotiating partners—often through informal exchanges—arguing against positions not persons. Specific techniques include taking responsibility for one's own feelings instead of blaming the other side and attending to what the other side is saying. In addition, particular tactics include setting the opening negotiating position to support a mutually acceptable agreement and concessions at an appropriate rate. In the course of negotiations, other specific techniques govern disagreements, as, for example, putting aside difficult items for later trading. Finally, agreement can be promoted by creating timely deadlines for completing negotiations.

Of course, negotiations have sometimes not concluded with an agreement even in periods that seemed most promising, while other negotiations have resulted in accords when the conditions were not conducive. For example, during détente in 1973, negotiations to reduce conventional military forces in Europe were unsuccessful. Yet during the cold war, agreements were concluded, for example, the Austrian State Treaty.

Tactics are important even if only to speed negotiations in order to take advantage of conducive background conditions. The alignment of supporting conditions, however, is not fixed; if an agreement is not reached when conditions are appropriate, it may be delayed for a very long time, if not forever.

Strategy

Although the strategic approach has been relatively neglected in explaining de-escalation, an appropriate strategy can produce an agreement on a particular matter even when a more general accord is not possible. In 1959, for example, in spite of the cold war, the U.S., Soviet, and several other governments signed the Antarctica Treaty, banning nuclear weapons on that continent. The cases examined here will provide tests of the sometimes contradictory expectations from strategic choices involving issues, parties, and inducements.

In selecting issues for de-escalation negotiations, some analysts and practitioners stress the utility of dealing with peripheral, nonvital matters in the early stages, while others concentrate on central and vital concerns— even if only in principle—in order to assure serious negotiations. The choice must also be made between dealing with one contentious issue in isolation or several at the same time.[8] Although negotiating one issue separately simplifies the task and enhances the likelihood of reaching an agreement, negotiating several linked issues allows gains on one to offset losses on another. Such trade-offs can actually facilitate reaching an agreement. Often failure to reach an accord is a failure to discover a formula for an appropriate set of issues for negotiation.[9]

Linkages vary in two ways. First, matters may have a negative or positive connection. In negotiating one issue, another matter may be raised in the form of a positive benefit or a demand. In the former case a concession on a secondary matter is offered if the negotiating partner will yield some on the primary issue in dispute. In the latter case, a concession on the primary issue is denied until the other side concedes something. The other characteristic of linkage pertains to its form: several issues may be made part of the same negotiations or may be divided among different negotiations. For example, negotiating about strategic nuclear weapons involves many interrelated matters; these must necessarily be linked. Other issues, such as trade matters or conventional weapons, however, may or may not be linked with those relating to strategic nuclear weapons.

In addition to the selection of agenda items, a de-escalation strategy requires a careful choice of the parties to the negotiations. Although this choice is related to the array of issues, if the negotiations are about several issues, more interested parties are likely to be involved, making the selection potentially crucial. For example, a major debate about de-escalation of the Middle East conflict is deciding whether Israel should negotiate with the PLO, with a particular Arab government, or at an international conference including all who claim to have an interest in the conflict. In the latter case, although a comprehensive peace might be sought and perhaps attained, it is more likely that no agreement would be reached. Other choices involve the negotiating teams: how many persons should constitute the delegations, how diverse should they and their constituencies be, and what political rank within their own societies should they have?

The third area of strategic choice pertains to the mixture of inducements that will accompany negotiations. These may include coercion (such as threats), positive sanctions, and persuasion. Some analysts and practitioners stress that agreement is most likely when positive sanctions accompany negotiations. These include concessions offered, promises of future benefits, or unilateral conciliatory gestures.[10] Negative sanctions, including making demands and threatening dire consequences if no agreement is reached, are considered essential by some observers. Still others argue that a "tit-for-tat" strategy is best, matching the other side's positive and negative sanctions.[11] Finally, much commentary focuses on the rate of concessions of each negotiating partner, stressing how much each side gains in the final settlement.[12]

Of course, background conditions, negotiation skills, and strategic choices all contribute to success in reaching agreements. Their relative significance, however, is not obvious. Although no hierarchy of factors can be established, the relative importance of conditions, skills, and strategies can be clarified.

Patterns of Negotiation

Major American-Soviet and Arab-Israeli de-escalation agreements are listed in tables 8 and 9; these can be compared to the negotiations presented in tables 5 and 6 to reveal which negotiations are considered to have concluded in agreements. The list omits many U.S.-USSR accords. Some of these are important, even though they did not receive much attention— either at the time of signing or since—and consequently are not seen to have played a major role in advancing peacemaking.[13] An exception to this argument is that a little-noted agreement may serve to prevent conflicts from escalating; the U.S.-USSR agreements on fishing rights are examples.

The distinction between negotiations that result in agreements and those that do not is not always clear. Does agreement mean negotiators signing, governments ratifying, and countries complying? Here, when official representatives sign an accord, an agreement is taken to have been reached. Although reaching an explicit, signed agreement may be clear, failure to do so often is not. Some negotiations go on for many years because of interruptions and shifts in topics before finally concluding in an agreement. Such a long series of meetings may be viewed as a single case of negotiation or as several failed and one successful instance of negotiations. President Johnson and Soviet Premier Aleksey Kosygin, for example, began discussions on ABM systems in 1967, but negotiations made little progress. Yet later, when they were renewed between Nixon and General Secretary Leonid Brezhnev, the new negotiations were able to build on earlier efforts. It is useful in comparing major negotiations to remember that later ones are

Table 8. Major U.S.-USSR Agreements, 1948–1990

Date Signed	Parties	Agreement
May 1955	U.S., USSR, U.K. and France	Austrian State Treaty
January 1958	U.S., USSR	Cultural, technical, and educational exchange
December 1959	U.S., USSR, and ten other governments	Antarctica demilitarization
June 1963	U.S. and USSR	Hot line established
August 1963	U.S., USSR, and U.K.	Partial Test Ban Treaty (PTBT)
December 1964	U.S. and USSR	Fishing operations
January 1967	U.S., USSR, and sixty other countries	Outer-space treaty bans nuclear weapons in outer space
July 1968	U.S., USSR, and many other governments	Non-proliferation of nuclear weapons (NPT)
February 1971	U.S., USSR, U.K., and several other governments	Seabed arms control
May 1972	U.S. and USSR U.S. and USSR U.S. and USSR	ABM Interim Agreement (SALT I) Basic Principles of Mutual Relations
April 1972	U.S. and USSR and over eighty other governments	Biological Weapons (BW) Convention
May 1972	U.S. and USSR	Prevention of incidents on the high seas
July 1972	U.S. and USSR	Grain sales
October 1972	U.S. and USSR	Trade Agreement
June 1973	U.S. and USSR U.S. and USSR	Expand commercial facilities in U.S. and USSR Prevention of Nuclear War Agreement
July 1974	U.S. and USSR	Threshold Test Ban Treaty (TTBT) limiting size of nuclear tests
August 1975	U.S., USSR, and thirty-three other governments	CSCE, Helsinki Accords
May 1976	U.S. and USSR	Peaceful Nuclear Explosions Treaty
June 1979	U.S. and USSR	Treaty limiting strategic missiles (SALT II)
August 1983	U.S. and USSR	Peaceful uses of atomic energy
November 1985	U.S. and USSR	Agreement on grain sales

Table 8 (*Continued*)

Date Signed	Parties	Agreement
	U.S. and USSR	Program of cooperation and exchanges
September 1986	U.S., USSR, and thirty-three other governments	Pact to ease Europe war threat
December 1987	U.S. and USSR	INF
September 1989	U.S., USSR	Monitoring chemical weapons
November 1990	U.S., USSR, and twenty other governments	Conventional Armed Forces in Europe (CFE)

affected by earlier ones. Sometimes negotiations have failed in a comprehensive form and yet have contributed to an agreement on a subset of issues. The distinction in such cases is arbitrary, even if necessary for analytic purposes. In many other cases, however, the distinction between negotiations that have and have not lead to agreements is unequivocal. Negotiations have gone on for years and broken off or withered without an agreement; others have been conducted for only several months or less and ended with a treaty.

Four patterns are clear from the agreements listed in tables 8 and 9 and the negotiations in tables 5 and 6. First, de-escalation negotiations in the Arab-Israeli conflict have rarely resulted in agreements, while there have been many de-escalation agreements in the U.S.-USSR conflict. Second, in both the Arab-Israeli and American-Soviet conflicts, negotiations undertaken in the early years of the conflicts proved less likely to lead to agreements than those undertaken in later years. Third, intermediaries played important roles in reaching agreements. In the U.S.-USSR conflict, intermediaries were significantly involved in fewer agreements than in the Arab-Israeli conflict. Interestingly, intermediary involvement was less frequent in the later stages of the U.S.-USSR conflict. Fourth, in both cases, the issues of agreements were generally not comprehensive and dealt with peripheral issues until later stages of the conflict.

U.S.-USSR Agreements

Table 8 begins with the Austrian State Treaty, which ended the Soviet, American, British, and French occupation of Austria. The negotiations that resulted in that agreement were conducted in 1954 and 1955; they followed intensive discussions between the Austrian and Soviet governments, par-

Table 9. Major Arab-Israeli Agreements, 1948–1986

Date Signed	Parties	Agreement
February 1949	Egypt and Israel	General armistice agreement
March 1949	Lebanon and Israel	General armistice agreement
April 1949	Jordan and Israel	General armistice agreement
July 1949	Syria and Israel	General armistice agreement
June 1953	Egypt and Israel	Agreement to return any ship or crew inadvertently reaching the other's shores
August 1970	Egypt and Israel	War of Attrition cease-fire
January 1974	Egypt and Israel	Accord on Sinai
May 1974	Syria and Israel	Disengagement of forces on Golan Heights
September 1975	Egypt and Israel	Accord on Sinai, includes undertaking not to use force against each other and Israeli withdrawal from Sinai passes
September 1978	Egypt and Israel	Framework for peace treaty between Egypt and Israel and for comprehensive settlement
March 1979	Egypt and Israel	Peace treaty
July 1981	Lebanon, Israel and PLO	Cease-fire between Lebanese and Israeli territories
May 1983	Lebanon and Israel	Security agreement
September 1986	Egypt and Israel	Arbitrated agreement regarding Taba

ticularly over the neutralization of Austria.[14] The Antarctica Treaty of 1959 originated in the 1957–58 International Geophysical Year (IGY). The twelve countries having territorial claims or that had established scientific bases in Antarctica during IGY negotiated a treaty to ban nuclear weapons there. Since 1955, several rounds of meetings have been held by the U.S. and Soviet governments on a comprehensive ban on the testing of nuclear weapons; no such agreement has yet been reached. In the summer of 1963, however, the Soviet Union, United States, and United Kingdom did negotiate the Treaty Banning Nuclear Weapons Tests in the Atmosphere, in Outer Space and under Water, although it did not prohibit underground tests.

The negotiations culminating in the Non-Proliferation Treaty, signed in 1968, involved the U.S., Soviet, West German governments, and other members of the UN Eighteen-Nation Disarmament Committee. Another treaty resulting from negotiations in a multilateral setting was the treaty signed in 1971 to ban weapons of mass destruction from the seabed.

The evolution of arms control thinking in the United States spurred discussions on stopping the development of antiballistic weapon systems and on limiting strategic nuclear weapons,[15] energetically emphasized by Secretary of Defense Robert McNamara and Johnson to Kosygin at the 1967 meeting in Glassboro, New Jersey. After Richard Nixon became president, negotiations for limits on ABM systems and strategic nuclear missiles were renewed, and in 1972 the ABM and SALT I treaties were signed. Arms control negotiations were linked to negotiations on trade, regional conflicts, and cultural and scientific exchanges.

In the early 1970s, two matters about which possible agreements had long been discussed became the subjects of separate, multilateral meetings. One sought to reduce conventional military forces in Europe—the Mutual and Balanced Force Reduction (MBFR) talks; the other sought to normalize relations throughout Europe—the Conference on Security and Cooperation in Europe (CSCE). The initiation of the two conferences was linked. MBFR negotiations did not result in an agreement, but CSCE negotiations were concluded with the Helsinki accords, signed in 1975. Negotiations to limit strategic nuclear weapons more comprehensively than was accomplished by the interim agreement of SALT I were pursued throughout the 1970s. The result was SALT II, signed by Jimmy Carter and Brezhnev in 1979.

Yet by the end of the 1970s détente was over. The Carter administration had begun major increases in military expenditures.[16] The Reagan administration escalated this movement and increased U.S. government opposition to regimes and movements in the third world that it charged were supported by the Soviet Union. Nevertheless, in spite of the renewal of the cold war, the momentum of arms control talks was not totally broken. After several months, new negotiations to reduce strategic weapons were begun (START talks), and negotiations to reduce intermediate-range nuclear weapons in Europe were also begun (INF talks). These negotiations were broken off in 1983 by the Soviet government following the deployment of U.S. cruise and Pershing II missiles in Europe.[17] In early 1983 Reagan announced his hopes for a Strategic Defense Initiative. Although widely ridiculed as unrealistic, SDI became a centerpiece of Reagan's policy, which alarmed the Soviets.

The INF and START talks were renewed in January 1985. These and other matters were discussed by Reagan and Gorbachev—as the new head of the Soviet Union—at summit meetings in Geneva in 1985 and then in Reykjavik. Later, the Soviets agreed to separate INF from SDI and START and to accept the Reagan administration's zero-option proposal to destroy both classes of weapons entirely: the intermediate and shorter range nuclear weapons. The INF treaty was signed by Reagan and Gorbachev in 1987.[18]

Arab-Israeli Agreements

The parties to negotiations in the Arab-Israeli conflict, have been more varied than in the u.s.-ussr conflict. Shortly after the 1948 war, which established the State of Israel, King Abdullah of Jordan and the Israeli government conducted secret negotiations for an agreement that would entail recognition of the State of Israel and of Jordanian control over the West Bank and East Jerusalem. Because King Abdullah failed to gain support in Jordan for the proposed agreement, it was never concluded.[19]

In 1952, King Farouk of Egypt was overthrown by nationalist military officers. The new government, led by Nasser, entered into indirect talks with the Israeli government. Mediation efforts included those by Ralph Bunche of the United Nations, President Tito of Yugoslavia, Dom Mintoff of Malta, British M.P.s Richard Crossman and Maurice Orbach, and unofficial diplomats such as Elmore Jackson.[20] The U.S. government was a major mediating party; one mission was that made by Robert B. Anderson, who for a few months in 1955–56 sought to mediate the Egyptian-Israeli conflict. These discussions did not result in any agreement.

In 1954–55, Eric Johnston, representing the U.S. government, helped to negotiate a plan for the development of water resources associated with the Jordan River. Although an agreement was nearly reached by the governments of Israel, Jordan, Lebanon, and Syria, it was never fully concluded.[21] The territories occupied by the Israelis following the June 1967 war provided a new basis for agreements based on exchanging land for peace. Negotiations, however, did not quickly follow. The Israeli government waited for a telephone call from the Arabs that would suggest discussions based on the new, postwar, realities—a call that did not come.

In March 1969 Egypt, under the leadership of Nasser, began the War of Attrition by shelling Israeli positions across the Suez canal. The escalated war was ended in August 1970 through a cease-fire agreement mediated by Secretary of State Rogers. Anwar el-Sadat became president of Egypt after Nasser's death in September 1970. In the early 1970s there were several indirect negotiation efforts between the Israeli and Egyptian governments; most notably, Rogers attempted to mediate an interim agreement. Gunnar Jarring, a Swedish ambassador appointed special representative of the UN secretary general, independently conducted two major mediation missions to bring about a peace settlement. None of these efforts resulted in an agreement.

The October 1973 war in which the Egyptian and Syrian military forces attacked Israel ended with Egyptian and Israeli military units on both sides of the Suez canal. Secretary of State Kissinger mediated a disengagement of forces agreement in 1974 (Sinai I) and then mediated a further withdrawal of Israeli forces in the Sinai in exchange for a greater Egyptian commitment not to wage war against Israel (Sinai II).[22]

Sadat's visit to Jerusalem in November 1977 opened a new series of negotiations. Initial bilateral negotiations between the Israeli and Egyptian governments in early 1978, however, came to a dead end. Carter's mediation led to the Camp David accords in 1978; he engaged in mediation efforts again for the Israeli and Egyptian peace treaty that was concluded in 1979.

The Camp David accords included a framework for negotiating an agreement on the status of the West Bank and Gaza Strip. Those negotiations made little progress and were ended in 1982. In 1985 a new set of negotiations was initiated between Prime Minister Peres and President Hosni Mubarak and separately between King Hussein, Arafat, and Mubarak. These talks were mediated by Egyptian and U.S. officials and constituted preliminary indirect negotiations between Israeli officials and Jordanian and Palestinian leaders. These indirect negotiations collapsed in 1986.[23]

Accounting for the Findings

The four general patterns identified need explanation. First, I have noted the greater likelihood of negotiations resulting in agreement in the U.S.-USSR conflict than in the Arab-Israeli. Second, later negotiation efforts are more likely to result in agreements than earlier ones. Third, intermediaries play more important roles in the Arab-Israeli than in the U.S.-USSR cases but become somewhat less important in the later stages of the Egyptian-Israeli component of the Arab-Israeli conflict. Fourth, the issues about which agreements were reached were initially less vital than those dealt with in later stages. Within these general patterns there was significant variation in nearly every period and within each major conflict, with some negotiations failing to result in an agreement and some agreements being reached.

The first issue is the relative significance of background factors, negotiating skills, and strategic choices in reaching agreements. By considering only those negotiations that were explicitly initiated, I have omitted cases where the background conditions were so forbidding that negotiations were not undertaken. Nevertheless, background conditions seem to account in large measure for the discernible patterns. The negotiations between the U.S. and Soviet governments more often resulted in agreements than those between the Israelis and Arabs, first because the international setting of the two conflicts has been significantly different. In the Arab-Israeli conflict, in contrast to the American-Soviet conflict, often outside actors were able to initiate indirect negotiations. The intervention of intermediaries meant that talks occurred when the adversaries themselves were not ready, making successful negotiations unlikely.

The structure of the conflicts have also been fundamentally different. For neither the U.S. nor the Soviet government has the destruction of the other been an immediate goal; the matters in contention did not threaten each other's vital interests. Furthermore, by the late 1960s each had the capacity literally to destroy most of the other's population; and the vulnerability of each to the other meant that they had a common interest in finding ways to avoid a double suicide.

Negotiations undertaken at later stages of the conflict more frequently ended in agreements than those initiated at earlier stages. This is most evident in the Arab-Israeli conflict; only since the 1973 Yom Kippur War have any significant accords beyond cease-fires and armistices been reached. One reason for this is that later negotiations are dependent on earlier ones. Some negotiations, even failed ones, prepare the ground for later talks that do succeed. Once some agreements are reached, additional accords are more likely unless the supporting conditions change greatly.

It is possible that negotiation skills improve over time. It is more likely, however, that in the course of many failed talks, negotiating partners better understand one another, which itself improves the likelihood of successful negotiations. It is also possible that the circumstances of the conflict change in its later years. Of special interest is the possible role of varying negotiation skills and strategic choices. To assess the role of such differences, negotiations on similar matters will be compared, necessarily holding some background conditions constant and giving greater weight to strategic choices and skills.

U.S.-USSR Negotiations

Talks on the status of Austria were conducted unsuccessfully for several years after the end of World War II, but in late 1954 and early 1955 negotiations moved quickly to a conclusion. What changed? Certainly, some background conditions were different. Within the Soviet Union, Joseph Stalin had been succeeded by Khrushchev, who had proclaimed a policy of peaceful coexistence, which at least meant greater flexibility in the means of struggle.[24] The international context had also changed; especially significant was the implementation of the policy by the Western powers to rearm West Germany.

There were also changes, however, in the de-escalation strategy and, perhaps, in negotiation skills. Austrian government officials played a major role in those changes. They stressed the option of Austrian neutrality, ensured through an agreement that would be in the USSR's interest. This proposal constituted a shift in strategy and tactics by emphasizing new inducements and considering the important interests of all parties concerned.[25]

The success of the partial nuclear weapon test ban negotiations and the failure of comprehensive test ban negotiations may be attributed to a shift in strategic choices, particularly the choice of the issue about which to negotiate. There was also a shift in the use of inducements. Kennedy in his American University speech skillfully gave the Soviets some of the benefits they sought.[26] Particular negotiation skills were absent at crucial times in negotiations on the comprehensive test ban and present in partial test ban negotiations. Thus, in the former, misunderstandings about the number of on-site inspections the U.S. government would require arose and were not surmounted.[27] In the concluding partial test ban talks in Moscow, however, Averell Harriman, representing the U.S. government, effectively used many negotiation techniques; for example, at the first meeting, when Khrushchev brought up the idea of a nonaggression pact between the NATO and Warsaw Pact states, Harriman pointed out that that would require extended consultations with allies, but he assured Khrushchev that the United States would consult with its allies in good faith on such a pact.[28]

Background factors, however, were also important. As public demonstrations revealed, concerns in the United States and the United Kingdom over radioactive fallout from nuclear weapon testing were strong. The Cuban missile crisis was another incentive for both the Soviet and American governments to reduce a level of tension that might otherwise have engendered one more severe crisis. The failure of the ABM and SALT negotiations in 1967–68—compared to successful ones in 1970–72—is largely attributable to the disruptive effects of external events and to the lack of available time. The earlier negotiations were abortive owing to the 1968 Soviet invasion of Czechoslovakia and the ending of Johnson's term in office. A major negotiation effort in this series was the Glassboro meeting between Johnson and Kosygin. Kosygin, however, was most concerned with discussing the consequences of the June 1967 war in the Middle East, and his domestic position was not such that he could initiate a new strategic nuclear weapon policy. American arguments on the destabilizing effect of ABM systems, nevertheless, contributed to their credibility for Soviet leaders and helped in later negotiations.

The talks on ABM and SALT in the early 1970s were conducted in a context in which concessions by one party could be linked to concessions by a negotiating partner on matters outside negotiations. This linkage was conducted through the "back channel" meetings conducted by Kissinger and the Soviet ambassador to the United States, Anatoly F. Dobrynin.[29] Deciding which issues to include in the final agreement and which to exclude reflects the strategies for deciding which issues were negotiable. Trade-offs were made, for example, in the inclusion of forward-based weapons, MIRVs, and mobile missile launchers. In addition, the trade-offs made reflect external realities, especially the Soviet nuclear weapon building program.

It is useful to give special attention to agreements reached when conditions were not conducive and to negotiations that failed to produce agreements, although general conditions appeared conducive. Even in the years of the cold war, some agreements were reached by the U.S. and Soviet governments. The Antarctica Treaty, signed in 1959, illustrates one way this was accomplished. The issues involved did not entail vital concerns or major differences of interest; the issues dividing other sets of governments were more salient, such as competing land claims. The multilateral nature of the negotiations facilitated minimizing U.S.-USSR differences.

The Non-Proliferation Treaty involved issues of more salience to the U.S. and Soviet governments, although more symbolic than substantive.[30] Yet, here too, other parties played an important role. The UN Eighteen-Nation Disarmament Committee, which convened in 1962, played a continuing role in sustaining negotiations and providing options. In addition, European Community members and particularly West Germany advanced their own interests as the Soviet and U.S. governments pursued theirs in seeking common positions with European governments. The multiplicity of conflicts provided the basis for developing formulas that could be subscribed to by the United States and the USSR.

The negotiations leading to the Seabed Arms Control Treaty and CSCE, which produced the Helsinki accords similarly benefited from the participation of representatives from countries other than the United States and the Soviet Union.[31] These were the early years of détente, moreover, and the international context was generally more conducive to agreement.

The SALT II treaty requires a different explanation. The negotiations were essentially bilateral; they were concluded in a period of declining détente; and they concerned issues regarded as substantively and symbolically important. The success in reaching a signed agreement needs to be understood in the context of the momentum that previous agreements had created. SALT I was an interim agreement. After Nixon's resignation, Gerald Ford reached an understanding with Brezhnev in 1975 in Vladivostok about the general form of a SALT II treaty. They did not, however, complete their negotiations and sign a treaty.

Jimmy Carter took office as president intending to reach agreements on arms control and even on arms reduction. There were difficulties in the conduct of the SALT II negotiations, notably over the choice of an opening position by the new U.S. government seeking significant cutbacks in nuclear weapons beyond the Vladivostok understanding.[32] Even during negotiations, misunderstandings arose from mutual suspicion and great attention to constituency concerns, such as the U.S. Air Force's insistence on the right to have shelters over the Minuteman silos at the Malstrom Air Force base.[33] Such difficulties slowed the completion of negotiations; that tardiness contributed to the subsequent failure to win ratification by the U.S. Senate.[34] On the whole, these negotiations on complex matters were conducted skillfully and intensively. In the final phase, a two-track approach was adopted: formal negotiations between teams in Geneva took place alongside private exchanges between Secretary of State Vance and Ambassador Dobrynin in Washington. Despite deteriorating relations between their governments, the treaty was signed in June 1979.

Before U.S.-USSR relations were transformed, two sets of East–West negotiations that did not conclude in agreements warrant discussion: MBFR meetings, begun in 1973, and the START meetings, begun in 1981.[35] Beginning in 1968, negotiations on the mutual and balanced reduction of conventional military forces in Europe were urged by NATO, while the Warsaw Pact sought a conference on European security. In the early 1970s, there was movement toward the reciprocal acceptance of proposals to begin both negotiations.[36]

MBFR meetings made little progress despite apparently conducive background conditions, strategic choices of issues having posed several obstacles. Conventional forces were difficult to discuss without considering nuclear forces—tactical, theater, and strategic. The ambiguous role of France in relation to NATO added complexities. Problems also arose from the conduct of the negotiations: for example, the lack of confidence in official data was partly due to information on force levels being submitted before definitions of forces were agreed to. Major unilateral actions could have provided incentives for accord, but only minor ones were undertaken late in the stalemated negotiations.[37] Only after fundamental, unilateral Soviet withdrawals from Eastern Europe were under way was an agreement reached.

Finally, the START and INF talks initiated during the first term of the Reagan administration could hardly have been expected to result in treaties. Background conditions were certainly not favorable: the United States was engaged in a large-scale military expansion. Specifically, in regard to the

INF negotiations, the Soviets were hoping that the deployment of Pershing II missiles and cruise missiles would be prevented by popular resistance in Europe. The Soviet government was generally immobilized as it moved from one set of infirm hands to another. Most fundamentally, the U.S. government sought the removal of Soviet missiles (SS20s) targeted on Europe while offering little compensation. Its proposed zero option—that it would not deploy any Pershing II's or cruise missiles in Europe if the USSR would remove its SS20s—did not seem to represent equal concessions to the Soviets.

Nevertheless, the chief U.S. and Soviet negotiators, Paul Nitze and Yuli Kvitsinsky, found a formula in their walk in the Geneva woods that each thought would serve his country's interests.[38] After deliberation, however, that proposal was not accepted by either government. The formula developed by the negotiators indicates that an accord might have been reached serving many of both government's interests. Its failure to be approved—or even used as a basis for further negotiations—revealed how rigid the positions staked out before negotiations were. Once U.S. cruise missiles and Pershing II's had actually been deployed, Gorbachev revived the zero-option proposal. He did so, he said, not as a concession but as part of what he presented as "new thinking." The Soviets offered to destroy short-range as well as intermediate-range missiles and suggested comprehensive on-site verification procedures.

The first START negotiations in 1981 were also marked by bargaining from fixed positions that were very self-serving. At least for the U.S. government, the objective seemed to be to make proposals that would appear plausible, but their nonnegotiability was widely recognized.[39] After the renewal of START negotiations in 1985, new proposals were put forward that were within new contexts.

Arab-Israeli Negotiations

The patterns of negotiations between the Israeli government, Arab governments, and representatives of the Palestinians are quite different than those of U.S.-USSR negotiations. Many de-escalation negotiations were begun after the establishment of the State of Israel, but except for cease-fires and armistices, until the 1970s they all failed to result in agreements. Most of these negotiations were undertaken through intermediaries, often representatives of the U.S. government.

Soon after the establishment of the State of Israel, King Abdullah of Jordan secretly negotiated with the Israeli government toward a pact. An agreement was initialed privately by officials of both sides in February

1950.[40] It included a five-year renewable nonaggression pact; Jordan would gain transit rights and a free-port zone in Haifa; and committees would explore issues on the protection of holy places and compensation for confiscated land. For over a year, King Abdullah unsuccessfully sought approval from his government for the agreement, but he was threatened by other Arab governments and received little support from the U.S. and British governments; the agreement was not signed. Then, in July 1951 the king was assassinated in East Jerusalem with his grandson, the future King Hussein, at his side. Abdullah's negotiations had involved core issues for each government, treating Jordanian-Israeli relations comprehensively. But Israeli relations with other Arab governments or with the Palestinians were not so treated. Talks, when they did take place, were bilateral, without major involvement by intermediary parties that could have served as guarantors or represented the interests of other parties.

Mediated negotiations in the 1950s also failed. In retrospect, that period seems to have been a relatively good time for reaching agreements. Some critics argue that intermediaries should have put more pressure on Israel to make enough concessions on boundaries and refugees to reach an agreement.[41] Others feel that if the intermediaries had allowed the adversaries to fight further, the fighting would have forced a settlement.[42] Still others maintain that if the mediators had pushed all parties harder, insisting on face-to-face meetings, an agreement would have been reached.[43] A more feasible strategic choice would have been for a mediator or one of the adversaries to work with those parties willing to reach an agreement, rather than hold out for a comprehensive settlement; for example, facilitating and supporting an Israeli-Jordanian agreement seemed feasible.[44] The terms of any settlement would differ depending on the strategy adopted.

The Israeli-Egyptian negotiations of the early 1950s concerned peripheral as well as core issues, but none of these was pursued. The intermediaries were transmitters of information, but none was able to exert pressure or add significant inducements. Certainly, the positions of the primary adversaries were far apart, and each had little confidence in the effectiveness of mediation. For example, consider the last notable mediation effort of this period, the secret U.S.-sponsored mission of Robert Anderson between December 1955 and March 1956: Nasser demanded that Israel's borders be based on the 1947 UN partition plan, not the 1949 armistice lines, and that territorial contiguity between Egypt and Jordan be established (see figure 2). The Israelis would accept only minor border changes from the 1949 armistice lines. Perhaps the conditions precluded any agreement, but there was limited probing; the primary adversaries lacked a sense of urgency to find a solution and lacked the conviction that an acceptable settlement was possible or even that U.S. government mediation would be useful.[45]

The effort to establish the Jordan Valley Authority, mediated by Eric Johnston, sought an accord on matters of mutual benefit and aside from core security concerns. After many months of negotiation, an agreement was nearly concluded to share in the development and use of water resources by the Israeli, Jordanian, Syrian, and Lebanese governments; the U.S. government would provide assistance to realize these ambitious plans. Yet, this accord too, failed to be accepted. Many of its provisions, however, were adhered to in the unilateral development of water resources subsequently carried out by the Israeli and Jordanian governments.[46] The formal acceptance of the agreement was opposed by the Arab League, whose approval was sought by the Arab governments involved in the negotiations. A reference in a speech by Secretary of State Dulles to the agreement as carrying political implications may have contributed to the Arab League's rejection of the plan.[47]

The 1967 war fundamentally changed the bargaining structure, providing Israelis land to exchange for peace. The UN Security Council passed resolution 242 and Gunnar Jarring, was designated "to establish and maintain contacts with the States concerned in order to promote agreement and assist efforts to achieve a peaceful and accepted settlement in accordance with the provisions and principles in this resolution."[48] Neither the Egyptian nor the Israeli government wanted mediation: the Egyptians wanted Jarring to oversee Israeli withdrawal, and the Israelis wanted direct negotiations with the Arab governments. In his first mission, Jarring essentially transmitted messages; although the parties moved somewhat closer together in their positions, they remained far apart, and the mediating efforts were not effective. The United Nations lacked resources and influence; with an unclear mandate, Jarring acted carefully to avoid offense to either the Israeli or the Egyptian government.

In his first mission, he began with limited objectives: helping to exchange prisoners and to release ships stranded in the Suez canal. In his second mission, Jarring acted with more initiative. He proposed a memorandum that described a settlement of the Israeli-Egyptian conflict. Although he succeeded in moving each government closer to an agreement, he was not able to persist in mediation and bring significant resources to bear in support of a settlement. His actions were superseded by U.S. mediation efforts for an interim agreement.

In 1969, the U.S. government began a series of active mediation efforts.[49] Initially, there were conversations with the Soviets, seeking a common move to bring about a comprehensive settlement. These efforts were conducted by Secretary of State Rogers and Soviet ambassador Dobrynin in Washington. When these proved unsuccessful, Rogers announced on 9 December 1969 the terms for a settlement in what came to be called the "Rogers plan." The plan, however, had already been rejected by the Israeli and Egyptian governments.[50]

Mediation policies shifted to a less comprehensive formula. In March 1969, Nasser began the War of Attrition to force the Israelis to withdraw from a part of the Sinai. The war gradually escalated and the losses for both sides were heavy, providing an opportunity for effective U.S. government mediation. Despite Egypt's reliance on military support from the Soviets, Rogers was able to be an effective mediator. In June 1970 he proposed the terms of a cease-fire, which were accepted in July by Egypt and Israel, with the addition of compensatory commitments by the United States to Israel.

To undermine that accord, militant Palestinian groups, notably the Popular Front for the Liberation of Palestine (PFLP) and the Popular Democratic Front for the Liberation of Palestine (PDFLP) increased attacks on Israel and Western targets from bases in Jordan.[51] On 6 and 9 September, the PFLP hijacked four airlines, forcing three down in Jordan. Although Arafat had cautioned restraint, he felt that he could not discredit this action. Jordanian suppression of the Palestinian armed units in Jordan began on 15 September; with a death toll estimated to be as high as 3,400 Palestinians, the PLO and Palestinian commandos were driven from Jordan. At a subsequent conference, it appeared that Nasser had managed to restore Arab unity; he then collapsed and died on 28 September 1970.[52] Sadat succeeded him to the presidency of Egypt.

In November 1970, Israeli Minister of Defense Moshe Dayan suggested the withdrawal of Israeli forces from the east bank of the Suez canal in exchange for opening the canal and continuing the cease-fire. In February 1971, Sadat, speaking to the Egyptian parliament, hazarded a similar suggestion. Despite the apparent convergence of views, when Rogers attempted to mediate such an interim agreement, he failed. Israel saw these negotiations not as an isolated agreement but as a step toward the implementation of the Rogers plan. Evidently, U.S. attempts to pressure the Israeli government into making the necessary concessions to reach an interim agreement were counterproductive.[53]

The beginning of the movement toward peace between the Israeli government and at least one Arab government followed the war of October 1973. The war was forced to an end by the U.S. government with the Egyptian and Israeli armies entangled.[54] The Egyptian Third Army was almost completely surrounded by Israeli forces on the west side of the Suez canal, while Egyptian forces retained some positions on the east side. This outcome was in part the result of U.S. government policies as orchestrated by Kissinger.[55] A disengagement of forces was necessary; Egypt and Israel each had its own requirements in seeking an agreement. They did so in face-to-face meetings and with relatively few mediation efforts. The second disengagement agreement (Sinai ii) was reached with much more difficulty. In fact, the first effort failed in March 1975 and was successful only later; an agreement was initialed on September 1975.

All of these efforts followed a gradualist strategy; Kissinger believed that such a step-by-step process was necessary, and indeed under the circumstances that strategy was effective. Nevertheless, within that approach, tactical skills are important. Thus, the failure to reach an agreement in March 1975 is in part attributable to tactical errors. For example, Prime Minister Yitzhak Rabin's interview in *Haaretz* on 3 December 1974 discussed "Israel's desire to drive a wedge between Egypt and Syria," which probably stiffened Sadat's position.[56] In a later interview, Rabin indicated possible final terms of the agreement, but these were taken by Egypt as an opening position, subject to further concessions. Israel's apparent unwillingness to make further concessions was then seen as rigidity.

The major breakthrough in Egyptian-Israeli relations followed Sadat's visit to Jerusalem in November 1977. That visit opened up a new stage in negotiations, although they did not move smoothly to a peace treaty. The Israeli and Egyptian delegations met in Ismailia, Egypt, at the end of December but were unable to make progress toward an agreement.[57] Political and military committees were established to continue talks. This device also failed to lead to an agreement, as did meetings with a U.S. mediation team at the foreign ministers' level.

Apparently, Egypt's position and Israel's position were incompatible, despite the major concession Sadat's visit was taken to be. A fundamental difference was their opposing views on the scope of the negotiations. Sadat resisted making a separate peace and sought to couple the Sinai issue with a settlement of the claims of the Palestinians and of Jordan and Syria. Prime Minister Begin's government did not believe that King Hussein's government or the PLO would concur in the kind of resolution the Israelis wanted on the West Bank. Israel wanted a separate peace with Egypt, hoping it might change the realities of the conflict so that eventually the Israeli terms of settlement for the West Bank would be accepted. In addition, there were many specific issues of disagreement about the terms of a peace treaty between Israel and Egypt, for example, the status of Israeli airfields and

Jewish settlements in the Sinai. Within Israel, the exultation over Sadat's visit to Jerusalem was followed by widespread disappointment when the chance for a peace treaty with Egypt stalled and seemed to slip away. A major social movement quickly emerged in Israel, "Peace Now." Its members held mass demonstrations supporting policies that would be more forthcoming than those of the current Israeli government, now that there was "someone to talk to."

In the end, persistent mediation by Carter at Camp David was needed to find a formula that would provide an acceptable separation between the Israeli-Egyptian peace treaty and the future of the West Bank and Gaza Strip.[58] The Camp David meeting culminated in two accords, the "Framework for the Conclusion of a Peace Treaty between Egypt and Israel" and the "Framework of Peace in the Middle East." Carter and the U.S. representatives structured the negotiations and provided the skills and resources critical to reaching the accords; the diversity of views and the skills of Egyptian and Israeli representatives also played important roles. Members of the U.S. mediation team would often rely on an Israeli delegation member to persuade Begin to be less rigid; however, they would deal directly with Sadat and avoid his advisers.[59] Even after the Camp David accords, difficulties remained, and Carter had to engage in additional mediation efforts to conclude the actual treaty. The peace treaty was signed at a public ceremony at the White House on 26 March 1979, while protesters demonstrated nearby.[60]

Negotiations for peace in the Middle East to resolve the status of the West Bank and Gaza and Israel's relations with Jordan, Syria, and Lebanon soon proved fruitless. The Camp David Framework for Peace in the Middle East provided the details for the many steps to be taken to negotiate and achieve peace. In resolving the Palestinian problem, it was expected that Egypt, Israel, Jordan, and the representatives of the Palestinian people would have to participate in negotiations to establish transitional arrangements. The Israeli military government and its civilian administration would be withdrawn when a self-governing authority had been freely elected by the area's inhabitants. The transitional period would not exceed five years.

Disagreements quickly emerged about the powers the to-be-elected authority could exercise and the conditions of elections. Meanwhile, the Israeli government continued to establish new Jewish settlements in the occupied territories, violating what the Egyptians regarded as a commitment by Israel not to. The Likud-led Israeli government was creating conditions that would be recognized as fact, the reality of Jewish communities throughout the West Bank, what they called Judea and Samaria.[61] By early 1980, the talks had withered and been suspended by a frustrated Sadat. U.S. mediation was no longer credible.

A fundamental difficulty in negotiating a settlement for the West Bank in the context of the Camp David accords was that the Jordanian government and representatives of the Palestinians did not participate in the negotiations. Of course, efforts were made at the outset to involve the Jordanian government and some Palestinians, notably those living in the West Bank. Although the United States, Egypt, and Israel each made an effort, none was successful.

In retrospect, it is possible to argue that the gesture of halting new Jewish settlements or other evidence of an Israeli willingness to foresee the end of its control of the West Bank and Gaza Strip would have brought about Jordanian and Palestinian participation. It might also be argued that if Palestinian representatives or Jordanian leaders had risked entering the discussions and thus recognized the State of Israel, they might have transformed the nature of the negotiations by changing the political reality in Israel and in the United States. Ideological commitments, fears of an adversary's likely response, and concerns about maintaining constituency support prevented the leaders of each party from taking necessary steps.

New exploratory talks began in 1985, following the Israeli elections that produced a government formed of the Labor and Likud parties. In the new government, the prime minister's position was held by the Labor party leader, Peres, for the first two years of the government's four-year term and then rotated to the Likud party's leader, Yitzhak Shamir. Peres initiated efforts to warm the cold peace that had developed between Egypt and Israel. Mubarak responded and also undertook mediation efforts in talks between Arafat and King Hussein, who reached an agreement that foresaw a Palestinian entity in the West Bank and Gaza within a Jordanian confederation. The U.S. government also mediated between Israel and Jordan on the possible structure of meetings and the nature of the representation at the meetings. These indirect negotiations were disrupted, not unusually in the Middle East, by violent attacks, including an Israeli air strike on the PLO headquarters in Tunis in October 1985—in retaliation for the killing of three Israelis in Cyprus—and the hijacking of the cruise ship Achille Lauro by the PLO faction headed by Mohammed Abbas.

More fundamentally, the apparent positions of the major negotiation partners continued to be far apart. None of them was able or willing to introduce enough resources to generate the conditions needed for direct negotiations, the Israeli government going so far as to challenge the PLO and others representing Palestinians seeking to end Israeli control over the West Bank.[62]

Explaining Effective Negotiations

The very diversity and complexity of the cases analyzed makes it impossible to answer simply why some negotiations succeed and others fail to conclude with agreements. But whatever can be based on the evidence will be presented as a partial answer and discussed in terms of ripeness, tactics, and strategies.

Ripeness

First, it is clear that a certain ripeness is necessary for negotiations to result in de-escalation agreements. What are the conditions of ripeness? The adversaries must believe that it is necessary or useful for them to enter negotiations and reach an agreement. In some circumstances adversaries enter into negotiations even when they prefer not to reach an agreement; the negotiations may serve to delay matters until conditions are considered improved. The need to *appear* willing to enter de-escalation conferences can arise from domestic conditions, adversary relations, or the international context.

Appearing to work for peace is politically popular in the contemporary world,[63] and sometimes the domestic pressure to act is felt as irresistible for a political leader. For example, in February 1971, Sadat had been president of Egypt for only five months when on 4 February 1971 he launched what he called a peace initiative: an offer to negotiate an interim agreement for the partial withdrawal of Israeli forces from the Sinai, extending the cease-fire for the War of Attrition and reopening the Suez canal.[64]

An adversary may seek to maintain the possibility of negotiations on the chance that the other party will change enough to make an agreement possible. An apparent readiness to enter negotiations is directed at opposition leaders or the public in the adversary countries. Soviet access to such elements in the United States partly explains the relative readiness of the Soviets to undertake peace efforts. The willingness to enter into negotiations is sometimes expressed only to appear reasonable and peace-loving to outside parties. In the Arab-Israeli conflict, negotiations were frequently entered into and pursued by both sides for the sake of relations with the United States, the United Nations, or others. Mediators initiated indirect negotiations, and adversaries—out of deference to mediators—were responsive to initiatives. The indirect negotiations mediated by Jarring and Rogers in the early 1970s are instances of this and were ultimately aborted.

Clearly, discussions undertaken solely for the above reasons are not likely to lead to treaties, no matter how skilled the negotiators are. The adversaries believe their positions to be too far apart for an agreement to be reached. As meetings are conducted, however, negotiators may discover that agreement is possible. This was nearly the case in the INF talks, when the heads of the Soviet and American delegations developed a proposed treaty. In rejecting the proposal, the Soviet and American governments demonstrated that each government's terms were rigid and ultimately unacceptable to the other; each thought they would do better than compromise.

Whether circumstances are ripe for an agreement is unequivocally clear only in extreme cases. Only sometimes is there no chance for an agreement or the pressure to reach a settlement so strong it is difficult to imagine failure, as when reaching a disengagement agreement between Egyptian and Israeli forces in 1973 was unequivocally necessary. I will review how the circumstances seem to compel an agreement, noting how even in those cases, failure is possible due to inadequate negotiation tactics or strategy. The circumstances compelling agreement must include factors that move primary actors to want the same understanding at the same time.

I have noted how domestic factors, relations between adversaries, and the international context contribute to reaching an accord. Conceivably, domestic pressures may be so great that the government is forced to accede to an adversary's terms. That was not true for any of the de-escalation efforts analyzed here. Domestic conditions were generally conducive to reaching an agreement, but not often compelling.

The aspect of the relation between adversaries most likely to bring about an agreement is the existence of a mutually hurtful or unacceptable condition that neither side believes it can improve unilaterally.[65] The ensuing settlement under such circumstances is an acknowledgment of an existing status quo. Usually one party has striven for recognition by the other of that reality, and at some point it is granted. This aspect is particularly apparent in the ABM and SALT I treaties, the Helsinki accords, and the Egyptian-Israeli peace treaty. But acceptance of the status quo in Central Europe and in the Middle East, as embodied in the Helsinki accords and the Egyptian-Israeli peace treaty, was very late in coming. Unalterable conditions are not self-apparent or necessarily openly accepted: witness the many years of PLO unwillingness to acknowledge the reality of the State of Israel and the Israeli refusal to accept the PLO as the effective representative of the Palestinians. Although acknowledgment of parity as indicated in the ABM and SALT I treaties was more rapid, it certainly was not prompt or complete. The clear prospect of mutual benefit or complementary benefits flowing from an agreement is also important. Benefits may arise not only from reduced damage but also from increased cooperation, including gains at the expense of players not party to the agreement.

The international context, including the relations each adversary has with other countries or with international actors, is important in several of the cases of negotiations examined here. The agreements reached in the beginning of détente were undoubtedly propelled by the Soviet-Chinese antagonism, the United States involvement in the Vietnam War, and the *Ostpolitik* of West Germany. Even in the case of earlier U.S.-USSR agreements, relations with other countries were motivating factors. In the case of the Austrian State Treaty, it was the actions of the Austrian government and Soviet relations with West Germany and the third world that were paramount.

Every negotiation sequence over a single set of issues is embedded in other disputes. If one of the negotiating parties becomes involved in another major conflict, it may be more ready to make concessions in what has become a secondary fight; conversely, it may seek to exploit the circumstances to increase its demands. Occasionally, a negotiating partner will express opposition to an adversary's conduct toward the third party by disrupting negotiations, as when Johnson postponed a planned meeting to continue discussions on ABM and SALT I when Warsaw Pact military forces moved into Czechoslovakia in August 1968.

External conditions are often dominant factors in the failure or success of negotiations. It is also clear that, except in the most extreme cases, there is room for maneuver: An appropriate strategy, skillfully executed, can discover an area of agreement even during inauspicious times.

Tactics

Skillful choices of negotiation tactics are especially significant in reaching agreements when external conditions neither compel an agreement nor make it impossible. Negotiation skills affect the outcome in two major ways. First, skillfully conducted meetings can speed the process of finding agreement; this can be critical since circumstances conducive to reaching an accord are never permanent. If negotiations are not completed in a timely fashion, the opportunity may not occur again for many years, if ever. Second, well-chosen and conducted negotiation tactics can produce combinations of benefits that are acceptable to the negotiating partners and to their constituencies. In the 1978 Camp David accords and in the 1972 U.S.-USSR Basic Principles Agreement,[66] when negotiating partners would not accept each other's language on a particular point, both wordings were used. The establishment of deadlines helped to conclude the 1978 Camp David accords and the 1971 seabed arms control agreement.[67]

Furthermore, it is possible to point to cases when tactics, rather than substantive disagreements, have hampered negotiations. In renewing SALT

II negotiations, Carter chose an opening position that called for major cuts in strategic nuclear weapons, thus altering the understanding earlier reached between the preceding U.S. administration and the Soviet government. In a 1974 interview, Prime Minister Rabin indicated what he thought would be the likely outcome of the second disengagement negotiations, which was mistakenly perceived by Egyptian officials as a bargaining position. In both cases, the actions delayed completing negotiations, though agreements were eventually reached; yet delay in the case of SALT II meant that the opportunity to gain Senate ratification had passed.

Even more relevant to arguments about the significance of negotiation skills are the instances of failure to use tactics that have been suggested as helpful. There are many such cases. The failure to conclude a Comprehensive Nuclear Test Ban Treaty might be interpreted as resulting from the U.S. and Soviet governments' rejection of the number of on-site inspections each would accept. The numbers were presented as positions, without exploring fully the characteristics of an inspection and thus without assessing the real interests of both sides.[68]

Another case is the collapse of Gunnar Jarring's 1971 mission. Jarring attempted an assertive mediation role and proposed an Egyptian-Israeli memorandum of agreement. The Egyptian government for the first time conveyed its readiness to conclude a peace agreement, conditional upon the withdrawal of Israel from the Sinai and the Gaza Strip. Israel said it would not withdraw to the pre–5 June 1967 line.[69] In retrospect, a response that said yes to the Jarring memorandum and offered reservations—as did the Egyptian response—might have sustained negotiations. The apparent lack of a responsive concession seemed to indicate that the overall positions were unalterable and thus too contrary for negotiations to proceed.

Despite these and other cases, the general pattern is that the use of particular negotiation tactics does not finally determine the success or failure of negotiations. It is not possible to say in principle that particular tactics are generally effective and others are not. Nevertheless, it is valuable to analyze tactics that are effective in reaching integrative, equitable, and long-lasting results.

Strategies

Strategic choices probably play the largest part in determining whether or not negotiations conclude with agreements. In the two conflicts studied here, the structure of the negotiations has varied greatly, substantively and over time. They differ in the parties to the negotiations, the issues that are the subject of negotiations, and the blend of inducements used. At the outset of this chapter, I gave arguments for the particular choices in these matters. No particular choice can be said always to be the correct one. Rather, different combinations are relatively effective for different sets of background conditions; indeed, that appropriateness is the essence of strategy.

The most critical skill is the ability to shape a strategy by choosing the most appropriate combination of negotiation partners, topics, and inducements. Finding a formula that reframes the conflict is often critical and involves a shift in conceptualization; this emphasis is consistent with the populist approach to international relations.

Negotiation Partners As suggested by the conflict resolution approach, a major circumstance in determining which strategy will be effective is the stage of the conflict. Conflicts have a course of development, and some strategies are appropriate during intense antagonism and others at reduced levels—evident when conflicts are considered over a period of forty years instead of four months or four years.

At the early stage of de-escalation, intermediaries are particularly important as parties in the negotiation. This is obviously the case in the Arab-Israeli conflict, where the State of Israel was not recognized by Arab governments and Israel recognized no Palestinian authority; hence, negotiations were usually indirect. Intermediaries can play a role in reframing a sequence of negotiations so that adversaries see significant mutual benefit in a settlement. This may be done, of course, by pointing out the costs of not reaching an agreement. Carter did this at the Camp David negotiations between Israel and Egypt. Another contribution intermediaries can make to negotiations is to add resources and positive inducements to the process. The United States has often been able to do this in Israeli-Arab negotiations, providing compensatory benefits to each adversary, which then enables each to make additional concessions.

In the U.S.-USSR conflict the role of intermediaries is less obvious. Intermediaries have played significant roles, however, particularly during the cold war. For example, the Austrian government waged a major effort to convince the Soviet government that Austrian neutrality was possible and desirable. The Antarctica Treaty was negotiated in a multilateral forum in which the U.S. and Soviet governments had to seek support from other countries. Even in the case of the partial nuclear test ban, the British government's encouragement and support of negotiations and its participation in the meetings were helpful.

The strategy of choosing to seek an agreement among those parties willing to do so, bypassing those who are not willing, is attractive. There is the risk, however, that those who are not at the table will try to overturn it. In many cases, groups that opposed any Israeli-Arab de-escalation moves have tried to disrupt them; often they succeeded. There is another risk—to be discussed in the next chapter—that the interests of parties not participating will be neglected and that those parties will try to subvert the settlement once reached.

Issues During the early stage of de-escalation, issues peripheral in significance and not linked to many other issues are more likely to be subjects of successful negotiations, which is clearly true in the U.S.-USSR conflict. Issues pertaining to major security and political matters were not successfully negotiated until late in the movement toward accommodation, in the early 1970s.

In the Arab-Israeli conflict efforts to negotiate matters of central and vital interests comprehensively have failed. Even dealing with matters not involving political and military security proved unsuccessful, as in the case of the U.S.-proposed Jordan Valley Authority. In the more limited realm of Egyptian-Israeli relations during the 1970s, de-escalation did move from narrower to more comprehensive matters in a series of negotiations and accords.

Inducements The evidence does not indicate that coercive inducements or noncoercive inducements always ensure expected outcomes, although some patterns can be observed. Once meetings are under way, offering benefits to an adversary is less fraught with the risk of being considered weak by the domestic constituency. Offers made after the initial stages, during ongoing negotiations, provide the assurance of some reciprocation. As negotiations proceed, more information is gathered by negotiators about equivalent values, and hence more accurate information about what mutually acceptable agreements may be possible.

Providing benefits or anticipating benefits concurrently with negotiations is associated with the successful completion of de-escalation negotiations, in part because benefits make it easier for a negotiating partner to reciprocate concessions and retain constituent support for doing so. Moreover, rewards granted by an adversary tend to increase interdependence, which facilitates integrative bargaining.

Concurrent fights sometimes escalate through the partly autonomous actions of groups that make up one or more of the adversary parties, as happened in the early 1950s in Israeli relations with Egypt with the "Lavon affair"[70] and with the disruption of the 1960 Paris summit when an American intelligence-gathering plane was shot down over the Soviet Union.

Concurrent coercion interferes with de-escalation, often interrupting negotiations before they have been completed. It will not, however, prevent completion if other conditions that contribute to de-escalation are strong, as was the case with the beginning of détente.

For negotiations to succeed, the salience of positive sanctions is always important. They must be recognized as based on self-interest but not stemming from weakness. The language surrounding actions is also important because it gives specific meaning to the actions. The presentation of interests and inducements in a problem-solving mode often provides an effective context, and the language used can provide a view of a settlement as mutually beneficial. In the mid-1950s, Soviet leaders sought to reframe the way officials viewed their relations by speaking of "peaceful coexistence"; in the early 1970s, U.S. and Soviet leaders used the word détente to characterize their relations; in the late 1980s, Gorbachev's used "new thinking."

Major de-escalation moves, when circumstances do not compel an accord, are significantly facilitated by gestures of reconciliation. This was the case with Kennedy's American University speech and Sadat's visit to Jerusalem. Such an action would have made agreements likely in Egyptian-Israeli negotiations even in the early 1970s. This insight, consistent with the populist approach, is underestimated in the statist approach.

The initiation of conciliatory gestures, however, does not in itself ensure significant de-escalation movement. For example, Khrushchev's gestures in the mid- and late 1950s did not produce any reciprocation that led to agreements. Instead, they were mixed with too many coercive gestures to be effective; the cold war required major and consistent positive sanctions in order to be thawed. In the early 1970s, when U.S.-USSR relations were in a context much more conducive to de-escalation, conciliatory gestures were not made and indeed were not necessary.

Once de-escalation has moved far enough, bilateral negotiations have a better chance. Agreements do have a cumulative character, but they do not necessarily constitute a steady progression; any agreement will produce disappointment and renewed antagonism.[71] In the next chapter, the quality of a settlement and its consequences are considered. In short, the analysis indicates how crucial strategic considerations are to negotiations. Although no strategic choice proves to be uniformly effective, analysis can indicate which combinations are more effective in particular circumstances.

7

The Consequences
of Agreements

aving considered the many de
escalation efforts that have led to agreements, we must ask whether the
agreements have endured. Have they actually contributed to further moves
toward peaceful accommodation, or did they result in reactions of disappointment and betrayal followed by renewed escalation of the conflict?
Have they been largely irrelevant to the moves toward or away from
accommodation, or have powerful domestic and international forces reduced agreements to insignificance?

In examining the developments following de-escalation agreements, I
focus on the relations between the parties after an accord and consider the

consequences to other actors in the general conflict within which the settlement is embedded, as, for example, the consequences of the Egyptian-Israeli peace treaty on Israeli and Egyptian relations with other Arab parties and later developments between the two primary parties.

Attributing changes in the relationship between adversaries to a formal de-escalation agreement ought not be done casually. Changes may actually be due to postagreement shifts in background conditions unrelated to the agreement itself. Cooperative and antagonistic interactions between the United States and the Soviet Union and between Israel and Egypt and other Arab nations have a dynamic of their own, only partly attributable to any agreements.

The possible consequences of agreements are nevertheless manifold. Not all can be examined here, but those that have policy and theoretical significance and for which adequate evidence is available receive the most attention in the following pages.

Explanatory Ideas

Most analyses of international de-escalation agreements examine the underlying bases for the agreements or the negotiation processes that lead to them. Less work has been done to explain the consequences of agreements. Theoretical perspectives already discussed, however, provide possible explanations for later developments. In addition, previous analyses of particular accords, such as those that were part of détente, include suggested explanations for specific consequences.

Conflict Mitigation

The conflict resolution approach contributes in several ways to understanding the consequences of settlements. One important idea is that agreements can be integrative, that is, mutually beneficial to the adversaries, and insofar as they are, they are likely to endure and foster further mutual accommodation.

Ascertaining what is and what is not an integrative settlement, however, is not always possible; I consider a variety of developments, including some that not everyone would consider integrative since many conflict settlements are mutually beneficial to the adversaries reaching the settlement but are costly to other actors in the conflict.

An important issue of this approach pertains to the distinction between conflict resolution and conflict settlement.[1] As discussed in chapter 1, the term conflict resolution is sometimes used to refer to the dissolution of the underlying conflict and the establishment of relatively harmonious relations. Settlement is often used to refer to ending a dispute by agreeing to terms that do not fundamentally alter the underlying conflict. Some analysts argue that resolution in this sense is possible and desirable; others do not believe that such resolutions are attainable but that settlements gradually create mutually accommodative relations whereby disputes are handled with a reduced risk of major escalations. Clearly, the agreements examined here do not constitute fundamental resolutions of conflict; they are all partial settlements of specific matters in dispute. Yet they may have had a cumulative effect that contributed to the transformation of the u.s.-ussr conflict after 1989.

The conflict resolution field has broadened to discuss issues of fairness and justness of an outcome and of the role of persisting power inequality among adversaries in preventing the attainment of a fair outcome.[2] Mediators are sometimes able to overcome that problem and to contribute to a just outcome; other observers argue that mediators often simply legitimate the acceptance of an outcome, without reducing or compensating for a power imbalance.

As many analysts apply the conflict resolution approach, each dispute has its own course of development and is embedded in other conflicts with their own ongoing histories. The consequences of an agreement to settle a particular dispute, therefore, depend on how the dispute figures within the context of the other conflicts.

Pluralism

The pluralist perspective fits well with the conflict resolution approach in helping to understand whether an agreement will survive or be extended. It emphasizes the variety of factions of every major global actor. As interests change, so does the interpretation of and likely adherence to an accord,[3] suggesting that groups will differ in their evaluations of an agreement and that the relative importance within each society is crucial.

Pluralist conceptualization and research raise expectations that international de-escalation agreements will generally foster the enhancement of peaceful accommodation. For example, David Mitrany argued that international organizations can be the basis for further international integration, reasoning that an international organization serving one function will tend to generate pressures for its expansion in order to serve related functions or even to create additional international structures.[4] International functionalism has been examined in several studies. The creation of an international organization has sometimes fostered vested interests in cooperation as well as new identities that encouraged additional organizations and further integration. The growth of the European Economic Community, beginning with the European Steel and Coal Community of the early 1950s, illustrates this process.[5]

Other observers of domestic policy note that bureaucratic organizations, once established, promote the expansion of their activities and related policies and that new agencies often support the expansion of related programs.[6] Organizations become bulwarks against the dismantling of policies that serve their interests. Agreements, however, sometimes generate opposite reactions that nullify their ostensible conciliatory thrust. This has been demonstrated in studies of specific cases, for example, the collapse of détente, which has been subjected to many examinations.[7] From such studies, one can understand several mechanisms that foster a return to hostility after conciliatory agreements have been formally concluded. In general, accommodation between adversaries, according to this approach, occurs in a step-by-step process. It grows gradually but does not preclude subsequent backward steps toward intense confrontations.

Another body of pluralist thought focuses attention on those characteristics of an agreement that lead to further reconciliation and those that lead away from it. Since an agreement entails different gains and losses at varying rates for the partners to it, one party may gain initially and then pay a severe cost later and vice versa.[8] Another possibility is that an accord will entail small benefits for a diffuse constituency while relatively heavy costs are borne by a small group; conversely, the agreement may entail small costs to many people and major benefits to a small group. Opposition is likely to be intense in the first case and minimal in the latter case. For example, arms reduction and even arms control agreements generally entail small diffuse benefits while the losses for elements of the military-industrial complex tend to be concentrated; new military expenditures, however, have diffused costs while significant benefits are concentrated among the companies that win new contracts,[9] which accounts for the effective resistance to arms reduction agreements. These arguments suggest that when a de-escalation agreement creates a vested interest, it will be perpetuated and extended; but if it is costly to a powerful group and those who benefit from it are few or the gains are small even if many benefit, the agreement will not usually foster additional accommodative moves.

The pluralist approach also suggests that attention needs to be given to the actors affected by a conflict but not parties to the agreement. If they find that their interests were ill-served by the settlement, they may seek to undermine it. An example of a successful undermining of an accord is the Syrian government's blocking of the 1983 peace treaty between Lebanon and Israel, mediated by the United States without Syrian participation.[10]

Populism

The populist approach stresses another set of considerations, including the importance of reframing adversarial relations as a result of an agreement. For negotiations to be undertaken and for an agreement to be concluded, a shift in perspective and a redefinition of a conflict is often necessary.[11] Populists ask to what extent an accord then leads to further redefinition of the conflict. The emphasis is on the transforming nature of the de-escalation agreement.

An agreement may be given major symbolic significance, for example, manifested in a grand public signing. Compliance is more likely to follow than if the agreement were downplayed. Like a public wedding versus a private ceremony, the social commitment and pressure for compliance is great when a treaty is proclaimed in a major public ritual.

In addition, the populist approach emphasizes the force of domestic factors, especially the role of the general populace. It suggests, for example, that if people expect a great deal from a treaty and are disappointed, they are likely to withdraw support from cooperative relations. This in turn weakens the coalitions that had worked to reach the accord. Another mechanism involves societal groups that have been relatively disadvantaged by an agreement and may mobilize support against it.[12]

The populist approach also directs attention to changes in the constituency that occur independently of an agreement insofar as shifts in popular moods have a dynamic of their own that may support or undermine further conciliatory movement. This dynamic may also result in changed leadership for reasons unrelated to the external conflict but which have great consequences for policies related to that conflict.

Statism

The statist approach focuses on changes in the international system and in the foreign policies of governments to explain changes in compliance to an agreement. The agreement itself is not perceived as having an inherent obligating significance.[13] An extreme viewpoint is to regard a treaty as a "scrap of paper." Even on ground of expediency, however, rulers may adhere to formal agreements in order to maintain their credibility in future commitments.

This approach also stresses the importance of an accord's balance for the progress of future relations between adversaries. A one-sided conciliatory accord, for example, may whet the appetite of an aggressor and lead to intensified hostility; this is the risk of appeasement measures. Another possibility is that an inequitable agreement will cause the "neglected" party to undermine or break the agreement.

The statist approach directs attention to the military security implications of any de-escalation agreement and stresses the calculations of government officials of the effects of an agreement on security and power.

Because my focus is on strategies for de-escalating international conflicts, the conflict resolution approach is especially relevant and fruitful. In this chapter, I examine how varying combinations of parties, issues, and inducements contribute to reaching agreements that are enduring and that contribute to building mutually beneficial relations among the adversaries.

Patterns of Consequences

Assessing the impact of de-escalation agreements on later developments might be attempted by several methods. One way entails quantifying relevant variables and carrying out a time-series analysis. But de-escalation agreements are not always discrete events occurring at clear intervals. Some are clearly isolated events, while others, like those in the context of détente, occur together or within a short period. Another method would be to carry out several case studies, selecting major de-escalation agreements and comparing their effects. But accords are not independent; all the actors are aware that every agreement follows past agreements. Hence, the consequences follow not only the most recent agreement, but all the previous agreements. We must therefore examine series of accords, as well as single de-escalation agreements for their possible relation to several developments, using qualitative and quantitative indicators.

Six areas of possible consequences are discussed for which relatively systematic data are available: (1) the implementation of agreements, (2) views of external adversaries, (3) economic trade and the exchange of persons, (4) military spending, (5) changes in conflictful and cooperative conduct, and (6) foreign and domestic policies not directed at an adversary. Each area is, of course, affected by many factors external to the agreements between the U.S. and Soviet governments or between Israel and an Arab government or another international actor. Our task is to assess the particular contribution of de-escalation agreements to variations in those areas of adversary relations.

U.S.-USSR Relations

First, the possible effects of u.s.-ussr agreements on developments within the United States and within the ussr and the ultimately transforming changes in their relationship are reviewed. Then a similar review will be made of possible consequences of the many fewer Arab-Israeli agreements.

Implementation of Agreements   The extent to which agreements between the U.S. and Soviet governments have resulted in greater cooperation must be affected at least by the degree to which agreements are implemented and their stated purposes are attained. To assess this, it is necessary to decide when to regard an agreement as concluded—whether it is when negotiators reach an understanding, when the heads of government sign a document, or when an accord is formally ratified by all signatories. Here, an agreement is regarded as reached when officials with authority to represent their governments (or other international actors) sign a written statement that commits them to specific future actions.

The controversy over the agreement to grant the Soviet Union most-favored-nation status illustrates the problems that exist in defining when an agreement has been reached.[14] The controversy also warrants review because it has substantive significance in assessing the consequences of the many agreements reached in the years of détente. In October 1972, the United States and the Soviet Union negotiated an agreement that the Soviets would repay a significant proportion of the lend-lease debt they incurred during World War II and the U.S. administration would seek congressional approval to grant the USSR most-favored-nation status for tariff treatment—that is, no higher tariffs would be imposed than those imposed on the most favored U.S. trading partner.

In August 1972, the Soviets "enacted a decree requiring would-be emigrants who had acquired higher education to pay a 'diploma tax.' "[15] The resulting outcry in the United States led Sen. Henry Jackson to propose an amendment to the Trade Reform Act, the legislation that included granting most-favored-nation status to the USSR. The amendment linked the granting of that trading status to emigration from the Soviet Union. Congressman Charles Vanik sponsored a similar amendment in the House of Representatives, which became known as the Jackson-Vanik amendment.[16]

For two years, a complex struggle was waged over the Trade Reform Act. The Soviets indicated their readiness to suspend the diploma tax and increase emigration but would not agree to any explicit linkage, expressing their objection to interference in their internal affairs. Nevertheless, the act was passed by Congress in December 1974 with the Jackson-Vanik amendment, which had become the major focus of the debate. In January 1975, the Soviet government canceled the American-Soviet trade agreement, which it considered had not been fulfilled by the U.S. government.

On the whole, most U.S.-USSR agreements have been implemented with little or no controversy, for example, the Austrian State Treaty and many cultural and scientific exchange agreements. Others have been the subject of considerable controversy, notably the final act of CSCE. A few quickly became dead letters, for example, the 1972 Basic Principles Agreement. Only a few, however, have been openly breached. For example, in May 1986 the U.S. government declared that in the future it would no longer be bound by limits of the SALT II treaty, which had been signed but not ratified by the United States. The limits were actually broken in November 1986 when the 131st modified B-52 to carry cruise missiles was put into service.[17]

Generally, agreements regarding nuclear weapon testing and strategic weapon limits have been adhered to—at least fundamentally. In the early 1980s, accusations of violations were raised by the U.S. government and then reciprocated by the Soviets. Even if true, the charges indicated that usually only marginal noncompliance had occurred. But in October 1989 a significant violation of the ABM treaty by the Soviets was admitted by Soviet Foreign Minister Eduard Shevardnaze—the construction of a radar station near Krasnoyarsk in Siberia; the Soviets agreed to dismantle it.[18]

The effectiveness of agreements also varies. As is widely recognized, the arms control agreements have not limited the growing capability of the Soviet and U.S. governments to wage annihilating nuclear wars.[19] They have, however, ended the extensive release of radioactivity into the atmosphere by U.S., Soviet, and British nuclear weapon testing. They have sometimes channeled expenditures away from weapon systems that might have been destabilizing and wasteful, as was the case for the ABM systems, until 1983 when Reagan undertook the Strategic Defense Initiative.

The purposes of arms control agreements have gone beyond trying to limit nuclear capabilities; they have had status-granting and political significance. Thus, they have served to acknowledge superpower parity between the United States and the USSR, a recognition persistently sought by the Soviets.[20] At the same time, initial arms control agreements have also demonstrated that settlements were possible and hence have made it easier to conclude additional agreements.

Agreements in areas not pertaining to arms control have varied greatly in effectiveness. The Austrian State Treaty has been complied with fully by the signatory powers. The October 1973 surprise Egyptian-Syrian attack on Israel, however, led many officials in the United States to believe that the Soviets had not complied with the Basic Principles Agreement while leading Soviet officials to believe that the U.S. government had not complied.[21]

Generally, agreements have been implemented and rarely have been overtly repudiated. A significant exception were the embargoes, the suspension of licensing, and other limitations on economic relations announced by Carter in early 1980 in reaction to the Soviet invasion of Afghanistan.

Views of Each Other Data about the ways people in the Soviet Union and in the United States view each other are not equally available for the two societies. For the United States, but not the USSR, there has long been extensive survey data on public and elite opinions. American public opinion surveys document that antagonism toward the Soviet Union was intense and widespread in the 1950s. Beginning in the mid-1950s, however, and lasting until the early 1970s, public disapproval of the USSR declined.[22] This was partly a result of general trends toward tolerance and away from conservatism—trends that had many domestic sources, but Soviet conduct was relevant too. The Soviet campaign for peaceful coexistence and the reaching of agreements in 1955 and 1963 probably fostered the growing view that the Soviet Union was not wholly evil nor always wrong.

During the 1960s, anti-Soviet sentiment declined greatly and in the early 1970s, it dropped further. Then, in the mid-1970s, antagonism began to rise again. Increased anti-Soviet sentiment when détente was just getting under way is surprising. After all, Soviet conduct had improved—according to American standards—and the U.S. government was less critical of the Soviet Union. Increased anti-Sovietism was partly due to raised expectations about the Soviet Union and a consequent disappointment. But there were also significant domestic changes, including a resurgence of conservatism, probably in reaction to the liberalism of the 1960s.[23] By the end of the decade many events, notably the Soviet invasion of Afghanistan, could account for the upsurge in anti-Soviet feeling. Nevertheless, although there was a sharp increase in anti-Soviet opinions around 1980, they did not reach the widespread high levels of hostility that had prevailed during the cold war of the 1950s.

Beginning in the mid-1980s, negative evaluations of the Soviet Union declined sharply and positive evaluations rose steeply. On a scale of +5 to −5, in 1983, only 22 percent of Americans gave a positive rating (+1 to +5) to Russia; by 1988 this had risen to 47 percent.[24]

In 1985 a national sample was asked, "Generally, would you describe the Soviet Union as a peace-loving nation . . . or as an aggressive nation?" Seventeen percent said peace-loving, and 69 percent responded aggressive; but in November 1989, 36 percent said peace-loving and only 42 percent said aggressive.[25] This radical change was undoubtedly largely the result of new Soviet domestic and foreign policy initiatives. The response of the American public is partly explained by the previous experience of détente and the anxieties generated by the renewed antagonism of the early 1980s. The shifting opinion was reinforced by the summit meetings and then the signing of the INF treaty in December 1987.

Opinions about military spending is another indicator of antagonism toward the Soviet Union, since the Soviet threat is the usual justification for U.S. defense expenditures. Public opposition to increased military spending was generally low in the 1950s and into the mid-1960s; only about 20 percent of national samples believed that too much was being spent. Opposition rose sharply in the late 1960s; between December 1968 and March 1971, more than half of the respondents with opinions thought the U.S. government was spending too much.[26] Then support began to rise, and at the end of the decade public support for increased arms spending climbed sharply following the Soviet invasion of Afghanistan, reaching 60 percent in 1980 with only 12 percent saying the United States was spending too much. Ronald Reagan became president and spurred a great increase in military spending, but public support for increased military expenditures quickly declined. By early 1982, 32 percent said the United States was spending too much and 31 percent too little.

With the Soviet emphasis on new thinking and proposals for arms reduction, support for increased military spending further declined. In 1988, only 17 percent of a national sample thought the United States was spending too little for the military, armaments, and defense, and 41 percent thought too much was being spent.

Studies of business, military, educational, religious, political, and trade union leaders provide comparable information for a few periods since the end of World War II. At the beginning of the 1950s, business and other elite groups generally shared anti-Communist sentiments, but there was not a complete consensus for international interventionism supported by a military buildup.[27] Some conservative groups favored a relatively isolationist strategy with more attention to Asia and less to Europe.

Anti-communism expressed in support of a strategy of militant containment was widespread in the 1950s and early 1960s. By the later 1960s and early 1970s, however, largely as a result of the Vietnam War, the consensus among the elite elements weakened again.[28] Although internationalism was now widely shared, a split emerged between those emphasizing military confrontation and those stressing management of the rivalry with the USSR, partly through trade and partly through other kinds of exchanges. This split was reflected in a division of public opinion that emerged in the late 1960s and persisted.[29]

It is obviously impossible to describe trends in Soviet opinions as has been done for American opinions. Some characterizations, however, can be made. Until Stalin's death in 1953, Soviet leaders and the masses probably shared a basic vision of the Soviet relationship to the capitalist world. That vision was shared because alternatives were not allowed to be expressed. In that view, the capitalist world encircled the Soviet Union and socialist camp, seeking their destruction; at the same time, the socialist system was gaining strength and would ultimately triumph.

With Khrushchev's rise to power in the mid-1950s, Soviet elite groups stressed the possibility of peaceful coexistence between the socialist and capitalist worlds.[30] The U.S. ruling class was viewed as including both aggressive and sober-minded circles.

When détente emerged in the early 1970s, it was universally supported and continued to be stressed as the correct relationship between the Soviet and American governments. The United States' receptiveness to détente was seen as its accommodation to the new correlation of world forces, recognized by sober realists in the United States. Although some nuances of differences have been noted among elite groups in the Soviet Union during the 1970s, consensus was certainly much greater than in the United States,[31] which was both a cause and a consequence of a foreign policy less frequently marked by major changes than that of the United States.

In 1985, all this quickly began to change when a new generation assumed leadership in the Soviet Union. Gorbachev's new thinking was accompanied by an openness of discussion unparalleled since the first years of the October 1917 revolution. Such openness, characterizing glasnost, revealed disagreements over past and future policies. This increasingly open discussion, however, has not revealed major divisions among elite groups regarding a policy of peaceful accommodation with the West.

Bilateral Trade and Exchanges   The United States and the Soviet Union have not been major trading partners. There are relatively few products that the Soviets might export that would have large markets in the United States. The Soviet market for U.S. products is much larger; it includes grain and a wide variety of manufactured goods. The limited export market for the Soviet Union to the United States constrains imports from the United States, because the Soviets have to pay for the products in hard currency.

Whatever the limits are, changes in trade between the two countries indicate changes in the tension between them and varying degrees of common interest. American analysts have presumed that the Soviets are anxious to import goods from the United States, particularly high-technology products.[32] Yet in the past Soviet analysts have argued that capitalist economies need markets in socialist countries, especially in periods of economic recession. Relating variations in trade between the two countries to the de-escalation agreements provides a basis for assessing whether or not agreements have contributed to further accommodation.

Soviet exports to the United States as a percentage of total exports, beginning in 1954, generally declined until the mid-1960s.[33] They then increased slightly and fluctuated until they rose sharply in the early years of détente. They declined markedly in 1975 following the passage of the Jackson-Vanik amendment. Soviet exports began to rise again in the later 1970s, although not to 1973 and 1974 heights. They dropped greatly in 1980 and 1981, following the Soviet invasion of Afghanistan and the imposition of U.S. sanctions, but stabilized at levels above those of the cold war. Since the mid-1980s, new and expanded trade and investment opportunities have developed.

Soviet imports from the United States, as a percentage of all Soviet imports, are larger than USSR exports to the United States as a proportion of USSR exports. From 1954, Soviet imports from the United States fell and remained low except for a small increase in 1960 and then a larger increase in 1964, following the 1963 grain agreement. They returned to their relatively low levels throughout the rest of the 1960s and rose sharply in 1972 and 1973, and fluctuated during the remainder of the 1970s. Soviet imports rose in 1979 but fell again in 1980 and 1981, after the Soviet invasion of Afghanistan. They declined, however, only to 1974 levels, about three times as high as the levels of the 1960s. In the end of the 1980s, they began to rise more sharply.

The interest of American farmers and manufacturers in selling goods to the Soviet Union was strengthened by the experience of détente. One of the first acts of the Reagan administration in 1981 was to seek to renew grain sales to the Soviet Union. Later, many manufacturers, wanting to expand sales to the Soviet Union, tried to reduce the constraints on trade imposed at the urging of the Defense Department. Some U.S. business leaders participated in associations working within the United States or in cooperation with the Soviet Union to foster trade. The U.S.-USSR Trade and Economic Council, for example, was organized in 1973 and includes American companies and Soviet foreign-trade enterprises. At a news conference after a council meeting in 1984, C. William Verity, chairman of the executive committee of Armco and co-chairman of the council, pointed out that U.S. government restrictions were costing American companies at least $10 billion a year in lost sales to the Soviet Union. He argued that trade should be separated from political issues.[34]

The patterns of U.S. imports from and exports to the Soviet Union generally paralleled Soviet changes, but the overall level was lower and imports from the USSR were always a very small fraction of imports from all countries, from .1 percent to a little over .3 percent in 1974.

There is obviously substantial Soviet interest in importing goods from the United States and an interest among many U.S. groups in exporting to the USSR. Hence, once a higher level of trade was attained, it was maintained. Soviet exports to the United States, however, continue to have a smaller market.

The movement of people between adversary countries is an important basis for constructing peace between them. Official cultural and scientific exchange agreements began in the 1950s and resulted in many cultural, scientific, and research projects in the 1960s. The movement of people in such projects increased in the early and mid-1970s with the rise of détente; interestingly, they continued to rise into the late 1970s, even as détente broke down. After Ronald Reagan became president, official exchanges were reduced; they did not, however, return to the low levels of the 1950s. During the years 1958–70, for example, 1,370 American and Soviet scholars exchanged places. On the average, 114 persons exchanged places each academic year; in 1970/71, the number was 193. The numbers rose steadily, reaching 336 in 1977/78, declining then to between 295 in 1979/80 to 138 in 1983/84.[35] The momentum of the agreements and the relations that had been established helped to sustain the exchanges even in the early 1980s.

Private, nongovernmental exchanges have also grown since 1948. They were limited during the cold war, beginning officially with the cultural exchange agreement of 1958. They increased slowly until the 1970s when they grew in the détente years. But during the late 1970s, as détente crumbled, the exchange also stagnated.

Renewed antagonism of the early 1980s between the United States and the Soviet Union, however, was not accompanied by a steady decline in nonofficial exchanges. Indeed, many private groups were formed to organize visits by Americans to the Soviet Union and by Soviets to the United States. For example, U.S. universities, colleges, and even high schools organized study trips to the Soviet Union.[36] At the high point of tourism during the 1970s, about one hundred thousand U.S. travelers visited the USSR in one year. The number fell sharply at the beginning of the 1980s, but by 1985 there were more than eighty thousand U.S. visitors. The number of Soviet visitors to the United States was far smaller but did not fluctuate as greatly as did the U.S. numbers. The détente years provided a base of experience for these exchanges, even when the governments were not disposed to organize or even encourage the exchanges.

Military Expenditures   In considering changes in military expenditures and the level of military forces as possible consequences of de-escalation agreements, all de-escalation agreements, not only arms control measures, should be examined. I do not compare Soviet and American military expenditures but the changes of each over time. Of course, to assess how they may have been affected by de-escalation agreements, other factors that influence military spending must be considered. These factors include the military conflicts of each government with other countries and domestic forces in each country that constitute an arms dynamic.

Assessing trends in military expenditures, particularly for the USSR, is not easy.[37] The estimates of Soviet military spending presented in table 10 suggest that in constant prices, Soviet expenditures declined slightly in the late 1950s. The decline also occurred as a percentage of the GNP and is consistent with the Soviet de-escalation efforts at that time.

Soviet expenditures in constant prices generally increased in the 1960s and 1970s. The Soviet response to the 1962 Cuban missile crisis could be expected to be an increase in military spending, and the evidence indicates that Soviet military spending began to increase each year; the steady increases continued through and beyond the period of détente and arms control agreements. They constituted a significant proportion of the Soviet economy; Central Intelligence Agency estimates put them at about 12–15 percent of the GNP (or about twice the usual U.S. percentage). Recent Soviet estimates have been much higher, in the 25–30 percent range.

In the mid-1980s, after the ascension of Gorbachev to power, a reduction of offensive military forces began to be proposed and unilateral reductions implemented. In December 1988, Gorbachev announced to the UN General Assembly that within two years Soviet armed forces would be reduced by five hundred thousand and that, among other actions, six tank divisions would be withdrawn and disbanded from Czechoslovakia, East Germany, and Hungary.[38]

U.S. military spending has varied more widely than Soviet spending. In constant dollars, U.S. military expenditures went up sharply in the early 1950s in conjunction with the Korean War and the early years of the cold war. They declined in 1954 after the Korean War but remained much higher than pre–Korean War levels. There is no indication that they declined subsequent to de-escalation agreements in the 1950s.

U.S. military spending increased a little in 1962 and 1963 and then declined slightly in 1964 and 1965 but remained above pre-1962 figures. Probably, the de-escalation agreements of 1963 facilitated a slight decrease in military spending. In 1966, however, military spending began to rise again as the Vietnam war escalated; spending increased again in 1967 and yet again in 1968. After 1968, expenditures began to decline (except for a slight increase in 1972) through 1976, when they began to rise—first slowly

Table 10. Soviet Military Expenditures, 1955–1989

Year	Soviet Official Defense (current prices)	CIA (1970 prices)	Steinberg (1982 prices)	SIPRI (1979[d])	SIPRI (1982–83[e])	CIA (1970 factor cost[f])
	Billion rubles			Defense to GNP ratio (%)		
1955	10.7	30	—	—	—	17
1956	9.7	29	—	—	—	15
1957	9.1	26	—	11.0	—	13
1958	9.4	26	—	11.2	—	12
1959	9.4	26	—	10.4	—	11
1960	9.3	27	—	12.3	—	12
1961	11.6	30	—	12.5	—	12
1962	12.6	34	—	13.4	—	13
1963	13.9	35	—	11.9	—	14
1964	13.3	38	—	10.7	—	14
1965	12.8	39	55.1	10.5	—	13
1966	13.4	40	—	10.5	—	13
1967	14.5	43	—	11.0	—	13
1968	16.7	46	—	10.9	—	13
1969	17.7	48	—	10.0	—	13
1970	17.9	49	65.3	9.7	—	13
1971	17.9	50	69.5	9.6	—	12
1972	17.9	51	69.2	9.0	11.4	13
1973	17.9	53	72.5	8.7	10.8	12
1974	17.7	57	74.6	8.6	10.4	13
1975	17.4	59	77.2	8.3	10.3	13
1976	17.4	63	79.3	8.0	9.9	13
1977	17.2	63	79.2	—	9.5	13
1978	17.2	65(64)	81.9	—	9.2	13
1979	17.2	67(66)	81.3	—	9.0	13
1980	17.1	71(67)	86.9	—	8.8	14(13)
1981	17.1	—(68)	88.5	—	8.7	13–14
1982	17.1	—(70)	94.3	—	—	13–14
1983	17.1	—	95.8	—	—	—
1984		—	97.3	—	—	—
1985		—	101.0	—	—	—
1986		—	102.9	—	—	—
1987		—	105.3	—	—	—
1988		—	105.9	—	—	—
1989		—	100.0	—	—	—

[a]Abraham S. Becker, *Sitting on Bayonets: The Soviet Defense Burden and the Slowdown of Soviet Defense Spending,* Center for the Study of Soviet International Behavior, RAND/UCLA (December 1985), table 1.

[b]Ibid., table 2. Figures are midpoints of CIA ranges; those in parentheses are Becker's estimates.

[c]Dmitri Steinberg, "Trends in Soviet Military Expenditures," *Soviet Studies* 42 (October 1990): 675–99, tables 2 and 3.

[d,e,f]*Sitting on Bayonets.* Denominator = Western estimates of Soviet GNP, table 2.

and then rapidly. The general decline was related to the winding down of the Vietnam War, but its persistence and degree may be partly attributed to détente.

In the late 1970s and early 1980s, U.S. military expenditures increased greatly. Many new weapon systems were developed and deployed in an immense expansion. Coupled with the Reagan administration's failure to raise additional revenues, the federal debt rose sharply to unparalleled heights. Public and congressional resistance to this vast military buildup grew. The new Soviet foreign policy undertaken in the late 1980s provided the opportunity to reign in military spending, and this trend began to take place even while Reagan was president.

U.S. and Soviet military spending often have not been coordinated.[39] Various evidence indicates that domestic factors strongly influence the level and changes in level of such spending. For example, there is evidence of weapon systems being introduced in part to accommodate the rivalry between military branches and in order to maintain the production activities of major corporate producers of military hardware. In the United States, fluctuations in military spending have been associated with presidential terms of office, generally rising at the end of the term, and perhaps related to efforts to stimulate the economy before elections.[40] There is even evidence that fluctuations in Soviet military spending have been related to the Soviet national economic planning cycle, peaking in the middle of the five-year cycle.[41]

Since domestic factors significantly influence changes in the levels of each country's military spending, they are not responsive to de-escalation efforts by the other government. Reductions by one side have not always been responded to with reductions on the other side; nor is there evidence that one party has sought to gain unilateral advantage through a military buildup after a major de-escalation agreement.

The evidence suggests that disgruntled adversaries of de-escalation in each country generally have failed to rally opposition and to support increased military spending—at least immediately. Soviet increases in the late 1960s and U.S. increases in the late 1970s and early 1980s, however, appear to have had such causes. For example, in the United States, the Committee on the Present Danger was formed to mobilize support for a more militant posture against the Soviets.[42]

An increase in U.S. military spending beginning in the late 1970s resulted from the convergence of many domestic trends and some external events. The taking of U.S. embassy personnel as hostages in Iran aroused in many a sense of humiliation and a great deal of anger. Those feelings were often given voice by demonstrations of patriotic solidarity; support for increased military expenditures was one way of expressing such sentiments.

On the whole, the de-escalation agreements were at least initially associated with small reductions or slowed increases in military spending, suggesting a vested interest in groups pursuing the de-escalation policy to enhance reductions.

Conflictful and Cooperative Conduct Three indicators of conflictful and cooperative conduct will serve to assess possible consequences of de-escalation agreements: the frequency of additional significant de-escalation agreements, quantitative indicators of interaction, and the eruption of additional disputes.

As indicated in table 11, although some de-escalation agreements were followed by bilateral agreements, others remained isolated for at least a few years. The Austrian State Treaty, for example, was followed by only three limited bilateral agreements, yet it contributed to the atmosphere that led to the Geneva Conference of 1956.[43] Nevertheless, it did not create any vested interests for continued de-escalation moves by the U.S. government, particularly since some American leaders believed that the Soviets had agreed to the treaty only because the U.S. government had been firm.[44] In the Soviet Union, however, Khrushchev and others initiating the change in policy that led to the treaty may have been committed to take other actions consistent with it.

The Partial Nuclear Test Ban Agreement signed in August 1963 was followed by a few other agreements. Although some groups within and outside the U.S. government may have developed a vested interest in additional de-escalation actions, opposition had also intensified. The assassination of Kennedy in November 1963 and the ousting of Khrushchev in October 1964 further interrupted any momentum that might have been developing.

Even nonmajor agreements can lead to additional accords. As noted in the preceding chapter, several agreements between the U.S. and Soviet governments have been reached on fishing operations. The first postwar agreement was for the northeastern Pacific Ocean and was signed in December 1964, followed by an agreement on king crabs in February 1965, then three other agreements in 1967, 1968, and 1969, and several others in later years. Yet, they have received little public attention and are rarely mentioned in discussions of u.s.-ussr relations.

The efforts to reach arms control agreements in 1967 and 1968 fostered groups of people in the United States and the Soviet Union who had an

Table 11. Bilateral U.S.-Soviet Treaties and Agreements by Year

Year	Major Agreement Signed	Number of Bilateral Agreements
1945		2
1946		—
1947		—
1948		—
1949		—
1950		—
1951		—
1952		—
1953		—
1954		2
1955	Austrian State Treaty	3
1956		—
1957		—
1958		2
1959		1
1960		—
1961		—
1962		1
1963	Partial Test Ban Treaty	1
1964		3
1965		1
1966		3
1967		5
1968	Non-Proliferation Treaty	7
1969		6
1970		4
1971		5
1972	ABM and SALT I	18
1973		23
1974		9
1975	Helsinki Accords	12
1976		5
1977		6
1978		7
1979	SALT II	4
1980		—
1981		2
1982		3
1983		2
1984		—

interest in advancing arms control. Informal ties, such as those developed in the Pugwash meetings, as well as the creation within each government of groups devoted to developing proposals and anticipating responses, helped to create a momentum for continued negotiation.[45] Then, when the major agreements were signed in 1972, additional agreements readily followed. The momentum was such that even with the deterioration of détente, SALT II was negotiated and then signed in 1979.[46]

Published accounts of international events can be used to assess trends in hostile and cooperative actions. The discussion here is based primarily on two such data sets: the Conflict and Peace Data Bank (COPDAB), developed by Edward Azar, and the World Events Interaction Survey (WEIS), developed by Charles A. McClelland. Actions by each country directed at another and reported in major newspapers were categorized as conflicting or cooperating, and each was also rated in terms of magnitude. The event data can be aggregated by month or year, multiplying the frequency of each type of event by a score for its magnitude. The difference between the negative conflict scores and the positive cooperation scores yields a net cooperation score. The data reported in figures 3 and 4 are derived from the work of Joshua S. Goldstein and John R. Freeman, who extended the data sets and adapted them so that they would be more comparable.[47]

In figure 3, the net cooperation score of actions from the Soviet Union toward the United States is summarized for six-month intervals. Clearly, the second halves of 1948 and 1962 were periods of intense conflict behavior. The early 1970s, the years of détente, showed relatively high cooperation. There are also indications of a general trend, marked by wide fluctuations, toward increased cooperation. The high points of cooperation are generally associated with the reaching of de-escalation agreements.

Soviet support for national liberation and Marxist movements against some third world governments and the extension of Soviet military aid to other third world governments have often been regarded as hostile acts by most Americans. Such actions are not usually so categorized by international interaction event data. The U.S.-USSR rivalry in the third world, however, was an increasingly important arena of confrontation in the 1970s and early 1980s.[48] The Soviet Union gave support to governments in Angola, Ethiopia, and Nicaragua that were opposed by challengers in those countries and supported by the U.S. government.

The event data indicate that U.S. action directed at the USSR has generally paralleled Soviet action toward the United States (see figure 4). U.S. conflict behavior was also high in 1948 and then declined sharply in 1949. U.S. net cooperation was extremely low in the latter half of 1948, but conflict behavior declined sharply and net cooperation scores rose and then

Figure 3   Net Conflict Interaction: U.S.S.R. toward the United States, 1948–1988

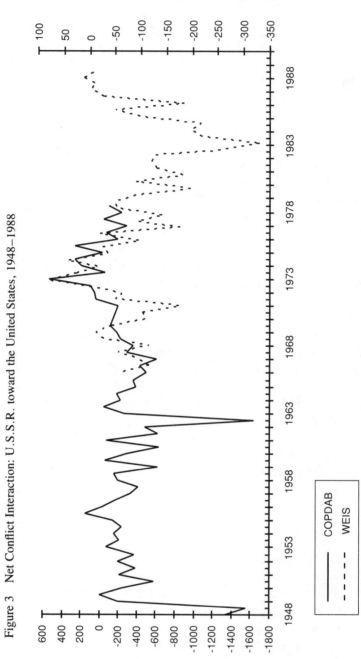

Source: Adapted from Goldstein and Freeman, *Three-Way Street*, appendix A.

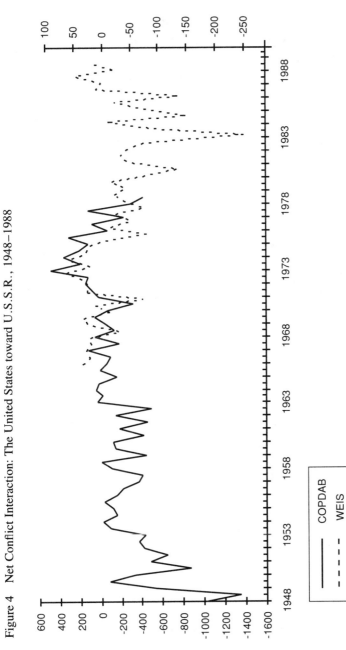

Figure 4   Net Conflict Interaction: The United States toward U.S.S.R., 1948–1988

COPDAB

WEIS

Source: Adapted from Goldstein and Freeman, *Three-Way Street*, appendix A.

fluctuated along a general upward trend. Net cooperation scores were higher for the United States in the second half of 1962 than for the Soviet Union. As was the case for Soviet actions toward the United States, net cooperation scores tend to rise in association with de-escalation agreements.

In addition to actions directed at each other, much superpower interaction occurred through proxies. Attacks at governments or movements allied with the other side were important ways for each power to struggle against the other. Such fights constituted major components of the cold war and continued to some extent during the years of détente. The end of the cold war has meant the liquidation of most aspects of these indirect confrontations.

Domestic Policies   According to the doctrine of national sovereignty, the United States and the USSR would not seek changes within the other's country. Yet both have attempted to do so. Interestingly, the supposedly revolutionary Soviet government has been less prone to do this since World War II than the status quo government of the United States. The U.S. government has sought a democratization of the Soviet Union and in particular has acted as if the rights of Soviet citizens were a major foreign policy concern.[49] The right of Soviet citizens, particularly of Jews, to emigrate, for example, has been a matter of considerable contention in the 1970s and early 1980s.

During the early 1970s, the number of Jews who were allowed to leave the Soviet Union began to rise.[50] In 1968 only 229 Jews left the USSR; the next year the number increased to 2,979, and in 1971 it rose to 13,022; the number continued to rise in 1972 to 31,681, and in 1973 to 34,733. The numbers then declined, falling to 13,221 in 1975 and fluctuating until they dramatically increased in 1979 to 51,333. They then went into a steep decline, falling to 866 in 1984. Note that even this decline did not fall to the low levels preceding détente. Under Gorbachev, the emigration of Jews began to rise sharply again: to 1,140 in 1985, 914 in 1986, 8,155 in 1987, 18,965 in 1988, 71,217 in 1989, and 186,815 in 1990.

Human rights has been another important issue of contention in U.S.-USSR relations. For many years, the U.S. government charged that violations of human rights within the Soviet Union were an obstacle to peace. The Soviets replied that, on the one hand, this was unacceptable interference in internal affairs and, on the other hand, the USSR provided fundamental human rights in the social and economic spheres (guaranteeing work and housing) *not* provided in the United States. Soviet officials waged an intense ideological struggle within the USSR to counter Western influence.

This situation has dramatically changed with the coming to power of Gorbachev and his associates. Many aspects of democratic goals in human rights are increasingly accepted as worthy in the Soviet Union. Constraints on the emigration of Jews, Germans, and other ethnic groups have increasingly been eased. The rights of religious as well as ethnic groups to pursue their own practices are expanding, including those for Soviet Jews.

Many Soviet officials, academics, journalists, and other intellectuals have supported these developments, not as concessions to the West, but as rights for themselves. To establish a Soviet state bound by laws, some Soviets have urged that Soviet individuals should be able to appeal to outside tribunals to protect their rights. Ernest Ametistov, a member of the Public Commission for International Humanitarian Cooperation and Human Rights under the Soviet Committee for European Security and Cooperation, wrote in *Moscow News,* December 1988: "Our country is in dire need of an effective and diverse system of legal defense which to the maximum draws upon world experience."[51] He urged that the Soviet Union participate in the Optional Protocol to the International Covenant on Civil and Political Rights, which enables citizens of signatory states to file complaints with the international Committee on Human Rights when domestic means of defense have been exhausted.

Finally, and perhaps most significantly, the Soviet economy began to move away from the centrally planned system, which was the Soviet version of socialism. By the end of the 1990s, the fundamental change to a market system, to the private ownership of many forms of property, and to a system allowing foreign investment was well under way. The integration of the Soviet Union and its constituent republics into the global capitalist market was moving forward.

Arab-Israeli Relations

Agreements between the Israel and any Arab government or the PLO have been relatively few. I will first consider the extent to which agreements have been implemented and, insofar as the data permit, the views of adversaries toward each other, military expenditures, trade and exchanges, conflicting and cooperative conduct, and domestic policies.

Implementation of Agreements De-escalation agreements are central to this book—those moving toward increased accommodation from high levels of antagonism—and not simply cease-fires or armistices that end wars or violent engagements. The negotiations and the agreements reached between Egypt and Israel between 1974 and 1979 are the only ones that clearly meet these criteria. Although concentrating on the consequences of the agreements, I also consider Israeli agreements with other Arab adversaries.

The Egyptian-Israeli agreements before 1974 were cease-fires and armistices that followed wars between them. The 1970 cease-fire agreement ending the War of Attrition was immediately violated by Egypt, which installed surface-to-air missiles along the Suez canal in violation of the agreement.[52] The accords reached after the October 1973 war, however, were more than cease-fires. The agreements, Sinai I and Sinai II, involved partial withdrawals by the Israelis from the Sinai and increased commitments by both governments not to engage in military actions. The Sinai disengagement agreements of 1974 and 1975 were carried out fully by the signatories.

The extent to which the Egyptian-Israeli Camp David accords and the resulting peace treaty were implemented is a matter of continuing controversy. The treaty was signed in March 1979 and included a series of interdependent steps to be completed in three years. The Israeli withdrawal from the entire Sinai and the implementation of full diplomatic relations was to be carried out in stages. On the whole, it was conducted expeditiously, being completed in April 1982.

Although the two agreements constituting the Camp David accords were not formally linked, they were not independent of each other. The first led to the 1979 peace treaty, and the second was followed by fruitless Egyptian-Israeli negotiations to reach a comprehensive settlement on the national rights of Palestinians and control over the West Bank and Gaza Strip.[53]

Yet, the peace treaty itself proved durable. Sadat was assassinated in October 1981, but Mubarak, upon succeeding him as president of Egypt, asserted Egypt's continuing adherence to the peace treaty. After the Israelis completed their withdrawal from the Sinai in April 1982, however, they invaded Lebanon in June 1982. The Egyptian government withdrew its ambassador in protest but did not abrogate the treaty. Sadat was vehemently condemned by other Arab governments for signing a separate peace with Israel and thereby betraying other Arabs who would continue the struggle against Israel. The Israeli invasion of Lebanon added to the strain on Egyptian-Israeli relations, and many Egyptian intellectuals expressed shame that this separate peace had allowed the Israelis to attack another Arab country (based on personal interviews in Cairo, November 1983, with Saad Eddin Ibrahim and other Egyptian academics and observers). Negotiations on the future of the West Bank and Gaza and on the future of the Palestinian people ground to a halt and failed.

Other agreements between Israel and Arab governments or with the PLO were informal and sometimes only tacit. Jordan and Israel after 1967, for example, generally cooperated in the administration of the West Bank.[54] Jordan helped to pay the salaries of local Palestinian officials and school teachers. In 1974, when the Arab League recognized the PLO as the sole legitimate representative of the Palestinians, Jordan ended its active involvement. Later, it gradually restored its role and in 1985 and 1986 worked with Arafat in developing a joint policy for an international conference that would include Israel. As this effort broke down, relations between Jordan and the PLO were also disrupted.

The Palestinian uprising strengthened the hand and the demands of the PLO relative to Jordan, which again withdrew active support for the Palestinians in the West Bank and efforts to represent them.[55]

Views of the Adversaries   In Israel, beginning in 1967, a national sample has been frequently asked, "Do you believe the Arab countries are ready to talk about *real peace* with Israel?"[56] Responses were increasingly pessimistic after the 1967 war, reaching a low point during the War of Attrition, when less than 10 percent of the respondents believed the Arab countries were ready to talk about real peace. When the War of Attrition ended in 1970, the proportion rose sharply to a little over 30 percent and fluctuated between 20 and 35 percent until the October 1973 war, when it actually rose. It fluctuated at somewhat higher levels during negotiations on the separation of forces in the Sinai and the Golan Heights. After the separation of forces agreements were signed, the proportion declined to the levels of the early 1970s. When Sadat went to Jerusalem in 1977, the proportion soared. Having become a widely held belief, ensuing negotiations and even the peace treaty were accompanied by a decline, the proportion falling to the previously high levels of 1974.[57]

Military Expenditures   Before the Sinai disengagement agreements, the military confrontations and recurrent wars between Israel and Egypt resulted in large proportions of each country's GNP being spent on armed forces. For example, in 1973, Egypt spent a third of its GNP on its military services;[58] in 1970, it spent 13 percent. Israel's expenditures constituted an even greater share of its much larger GNP in 1970 and 1973. Reducing the threat of another war between Israel and Egypt enabled both to reduce substantially their military costs. In the mid-1970s, after the war with Israel, Egyptian military expenditures declined sharply from almost a third of the gross domestic product and continued to decline after the 1979 peace treaty; they fell from around 10 percent in 1979 to about 6 percent of GNP in 1987.[59] The reduction in military expenditures in Egypt was accompanied by an increase in GNP per person.

Israel, however, still faced the possibility of warfare with Syria and other Arab countries. Its military expenditures declined somewhat after the 1973 war and fluctuated between 20 to 25 percent of its GNP, except for a marked increase in 1982, when Israel invaded Lebanon. The peace treaty did not affect Israeli military spending as it did Egyptian military spending.

Jordan's military expenditures can be usefully compared since Jordan did not sign a peace treaty with Israel. They fluctuated between 13 and 23 percent of the GNP between 1959 and 1988. There was no clear and consistent pattern, however, except that spending tended to stay at the lower end of the range during the late 1980s.

Trade and Exchanges From the birth of Israel, the Arab governments did not trade or conduct official relations with it and even boycotted companies that conducted business with Israel. These practices continued, with two major exceptions. First, when Egypt signed a peace treaty with Israel in 1979, it brought the possibility of trade and the free movement of persons between the two countries. Second, the kings of Jordan conducted several secret meetings with Israeli officials about possible accommodations.[60] Jordan also cooperated with Israel after the 1967 war over the West Bank, and the border between Jordan and the West Bank occupied by Israel was open for trade and visitors.

After the peace treaty with Egypt, Israelis began to visit Egypt as tourists, especially valued by Israelis, long isolated from their neighbors. Sixty thousand Israelis visited Egypt in 1988. Tourists from Egypt to Israel, however, have required permits from the Egyptian government and have been relatively few. This is taken by Israeli Jews as another sign that there is only a cold peace between them.

Before 1980, trade between Egypt and Israel was virtually nonexistent. After the treaty, trade began, particularly Egyptian exports to Israel. Israeli exports to Egypt also increased but then fell sharply following the 1982 Israeli invasion of Lebanon. They then remained relatively small but did rise in the mid-1980s with the conciliatory efforts of the Israeli government headed by Shimon Peres.[61]

Conflictful and Cooperative Conduct The patterns of cooperative and conflictful interactions between Israel and Egypt are unlike those between the United States and the Soviet Union. Hardly any cooperative actions were taken before 1974, and only after the 1973 war did either country cooperate significantly. The low and noncumulative character of cooperative action is consistent with the absence of major agreements before the 1979 peace treaty. Cooperation, however, did begin to increase after the

1974–75 agreements over Sinai. Conflict behavior was high at the time of the wars but was low otherwise. The Israeli-Egyptian peace treaty marked a fundamental shift in the way the two governments dealt with each other. Cooperative relations and agreements were now possible, and some were realized.

Conflictful interactions did not stop, however, after the treaty was signed. The major contentious issue concerned implementing the other agreement reached at Camp David, namely, to reach a comprehensive Middle East settlement. The critical component of that agreement was to reconcile the interests of the Palestinians with those of the other peoples in the region. The negotiations centered on the Israeli proposal for an interim arrangement, granting autonomy to the Palestinians living in the West Bank and Gaza, the final status of the West Bank and Gaza to be resolved in five years.

Taba emerged as a controversial issue between Egypt and Israel as the Israelis completed their withdrawal from the Sinai in April 1982. Taba is a 250-acre piece of land on the Gulf of Aqaba, twelve miles southwest of Elath. The Israelis had allowed a private resort to be developed there and claimed the area, while the Egyptians insisted it belonged to Sinai.[62] After considerable acrimony, the controversy began to move toward settlement only in September 1984 when Peres became prime minister and agreed to arbitrate the issue.

Since the conflicts in the Middle East are interconnected in many ways, it is difficult for analysts (and partisans) to look at changes in the level of antagonism for a particular conflict isolated from others. For example, Syria has long had ambitions to be the dominant influence in Palestine and Lebanon, former Syrian nationalists having claimed them (with Jordan) to be part of greater Syria. Syria and Iraq have continued an intense rivalry and antagonism for many years, so that when Iraqi armed forces invaded Iran, Syria was the only Arab country to support Iran. Syrian relations with Israel are affected by the intensity of Syrian confrontations with other Arab governments, leaders, and peoples.[63]

Domestic Policies For the Israelis, the treatment of Jews and the teachings about Israel in Arab countries are the most salient domestic policies of Arab governments. Israeli scholars and officials monitor the Arab press and the content of school lessons. They point to cartoons attacking Israelis and Jews. Egyptian newspaper and mass media presentations of Jews and Jewish Israelis have improved.[64]

For the Arabs, the Israeli treatment of Arabs in Israel and the occupied territories is a fundamental matter in Israeli domestic policies. Since the establishment of the State of Israel, Arabs have sought Israeli recognition of the right of Palestinian Arabs to return to the land they left behind when they fled during the fighting. Israel did not recognize that right, and there was no change in Israeli policy after the peace treaty with Egypt.

A fundamental objection of many Arabs against Israel is its Zionist character—specifically, the law of return, which refers to the right of Jews anywhere to come to Israel and immediately become citizens. Arab residents of Israel are also citizens, but non-Jewish immigrants are not automatically granted citizenship. Palestinians and other Arabs reject this policy, calling it racist. Israelis hear the Arab charges as demands to alter the premise of Zionism and undermine the State of Israel. This issue was not a part of negotiations for the Israeli-Egyptian peace treaty. The Israeli policy on the law of return did not change after the treaty and has never been regarded as negotiable.

Accounting for the Patterns

Several patterns can be discerned on the basis of the cases reviewed. First, agreements are generally implemented and endure. Formal accords are few, but those that exist are more than scraps of paper. Second, the consequences of agreements vary, and the ideas outlined at the beginning of the chapter should clarify the few commonalities and many variations in consequences.

Commonalities

The almost universal survival of formal agreements is in many ways surprising. The heads of governments who signed agreements have died or been forced from office and the convergence of circumstances that enabled adversaries to reach an agreement have broken apart, yet the agreements survive.

The realist approach has the most difficulty in accounting for the endurance of agreements. It does suggest that the agreements themselves are essentially irrelevant; there is no need to abrogate them since they do not inhibit the actions of governments anyway. Although there may be some truth to this explanation for some treaties, it is not adequate. Since opposition to most agreements can be found in each constituency, adherence to them has usually not been cost free. This approach also maintains that the external conditions that led to the agreement in the first place usually do not fundamentally change. This is an important insight, and for many treaties it is certainly critical; external conditions do set limits on the survival of an agreement, but a further explanation is needed.

The pluralist approach suggests that concluding an agreement helps to create vested interests in its survival. This is undoubtedly true for the signatories, their supporters, and those identified with them. They constitute a core of defenders of the agreement. Furthermore, insofar as the agreement generates changed conditions, some people will benefit from the change, and others will search for ways to do so.

There are many parties involved in a conflict and in its settlement. Even if the agreement is a bilateral one, nonsignatory parties have a stake in the agreement. Some parties may play a role in reaching the settlement, serving as a mediator, and some may find that their relation to one or more of the signatories changes with the agreement. Thus, the survival of the Egyptian-Israeli peace treaty owes much to the role that the U.S. government played in its achievement and maintenance. Egyptian dependence on U.S. economic and military aid makes it difficult for it to renounce the treaty.

The populist approach and its emphasis on subjective factors provide additional insights. The signing of an agreement is often made a ritual. The public nature of the ritual and the appearance of senior representatives of adversary governments in an exchange of friendly gestures constitute an expression of mutual trust, which creates additional obligations of trust, increased according to the magnitude of the ritual. Ratification is often important in establishing further obligations and has symbolic significance.

Perhaps, more ceremonial attention to the U.S.-Soviet fishing agreements would have enhanced their impact on U.S.-Soviet relations generally. Perhaps, too, if the PLO had given more publicity to the cease-fire on Israel's northern border in 1982, it would have contributed to inhibition or restraint in the Israeli decision to attack the PLO in Lebanon in June 1982. The support of constituents for their leaders to honor commitments is widespread. It is possible, however, for leaders to accuse adversaries of violating an agreement, thus freeing them to renounce or violate it themselves.

The conflict resolution approach suggests that settlements are enduring because they are often actual solutions to problems. A settlement is reached because a formula—with an acceptable combination of parties, issues, and inducements—was found. For adversaries, settlement seems better than no settlement. A conflict, however, is not likely ever to be fundamentally resolved, and certainly not on the basis of a single agreement. The transformation of an intractable international conflict into a tractable one takes time; further transformation into a relationship characterized as peaceful or at least nonadversarial takes more time.[65]

Variations

Whether or not de-escalation agreements have generally fostered further accommodative moves between adversaries varies with the indicator of the relationship being considered. Variations in the form and content of agreements also affect different consequences to different degrees. Both the form and content of agreements can affect their survival and expansion. Of those agreements reviewed, the relatively imprecise and uncircumscribed ones have been the least likely to survive, such as the Basic Principles Agreement of 1972. Written agreements have been more enduring than unwritten understandings.

Parties Having many governments as signatories to an agreement contributes to its survival and to its extension, leading to further accommodation. As noted in the preceding chapter, the participation of obdurate parties in negotiations may hamper reaching an agreement; excluding the more intransigent parties enhances the chances of finding a mutually acceptable settlement. Such exclusion, however, endangers its survival. Excluded parties with a great stake in the matter may wish to and succeed in undermining an agreement. This has happened in the Middle East in the 1983 Israeli-Lebanese treaty mediated by the U.S. government when the Syrian government was able to prevent the Lebanese government, dominated by the Phalangie, from ratifying and implementing the treaty.

If many governments sign an agreement, the likelihood of creating vested interests in the agreement is enhanced. One or two governments that derive benefits from an agreement can help to sustain it, even if other signatories have little interest in doing so. The survival of the CSCE agreement and its progress, even during the intense U.S.-USSR antagonism of the early 1980s, bears witness to this.

Inducements What is significant about the content of an agreement is the cost-benefit balance. As pluralists emphasize, many groups in each country derive various benefits and costs from every agreement. Moreover, the timing of those benefits may not coincide with the time schedule of the costs, which might cause a group to feel relatively disadvantaged.

The Austrian State Treaty brought great gains to the Austrians, but the costs and benefits to the Soviets and the United States were not great. Each side could claim that it had vindicated holding out for a better settlement and provided useful gains at relatively little cost. Although some in the United States might feel that the Soviets had gained more than the United States, there has been no agitation against the agreement having been made.[66]

The 1963 Partial Test Ban Agreement and associated agreements have also been regarded as mutually beneficial by Soviet and American officials and elite groups, probably because the costs for all groups have been minimal and because there were initial benefits and even continuing benefits, at least in the form of reduced radioactive pollution of the world.

The agreements reached in the early 1970s during détente are more complex. The ABM Treaty was relatively symmetrical and had immediate as well as long-lasting mutual benefits. There were also asymmetric gains for each side: U.S. officials felt that the treaty indicated a newly achieved acceptance by Soviet officials of American nuclear strategic thinking, and the Soviets saw American acceptance of Soviet strategic parity. SALT I, as an interim agreement and in the context of the other agreements and trade-offs, was balanced. The time schedule for the payoffs, however, was not symmetrical. The Soviets assumed that they had gained recognition as an equal global super power, something not fully accorded by the U.S. government. Soviet conduct based on that assumption was viewed by many Americans as provocative. Furthermore, the value to the United States of trade-offs— such as assistance in gaining North Vietnamese agreement to an honorable U.S. withdrawal from South Vietnam—became of little value when that war was liquidated.

The final act of the CSCE also led to asymmetrical trade-offs over time. The Soviets immediately gained recognition of the permanence of the borders of Eastern Europe. But in the 1970s and early 1980s, they had to pay by being subjected to recurring recriminations over their violations of human rights. Only with a change in Soviet policies in the late 1980s did many of these costs disappear, as the Soviets themselves supported human rights, even as defined in the West.

Agreements sometimes incorporate carefully planned schedules for the exchange of costs and benefits. This was the case, for example, in the Israeli-Egyptian peace treaty when moves between Israeli withdrawals from the Sinai were linked to the normalization of Israeli-Egyptian relations over three years. That plan worked. The peace treaty was not linked, however, with autonomy talks (with good reason, as far as the Israeli government was concerned); the failure of those talks endangered the durability of the peace treaty.[67]

The movement toward or away from accommodation between the Soviet and American governments is largely affected by developments within each country and by the world context. Within the United States, swings of public and elite group opinion between liberalism and conservatism affect evaluations of the Soviet Union and policies toward it. For example, the American mistrust of the military and acceptance of diversity in the late 1960s was part of the movement that facilitated détente; the reaction against those developments and the increased support for many conservative policies helped to turn U.S. policy away from détente.[68] In the Soviet Union, economic difficulties and an increase in the priority given to consumer benefits encouraged de-escalation efforts.[69] There is also much evidence that particular trends have their own dynamic. In military spending, there is evidence of a domestic dynamic in both the Soviet Union and the United States that has generated pressure for additional expenditures and resisted reductions in military spending.[70]

The international context obviously has been a major factor in reaching, sustaining, and extending de-escalation agreements. Soviet relations with the two German states and with China have been particularly important. Similarly, U.S. relations with West Germany, Vietnam, Israel, and national liberation movements have all affected accommodations with the Soviet Union. The convergence of many domestic and international developments supported the de-escalation known as détente. Those conditions changed in the course of the 1970s; the high level of accommodation that had been attained could not survive new conditions.

In the years since 1948, considerable movement toward accommodation between the United States and the Soviet Union, and even between Egypt and Israel, has been evident. De-escalation settlements are often long in coming, but once made they have usually contributed to additional de-escalation agreements and mutual accommodation. The magnitude of that contribution varies with different measures of de-escalation as well as with different agreements.

First, whether an agreement is isolated or is followed by additional agreements has varied over the course of the conflict. In U.S.-USSR relations generally, earlier agreements were more isolated than later ones, suggesting a cumulative movement but not an evenly paced progression. For example, détente ended in the late 1970s, and accommodative movements began tentatively, gained momentum, and regressed when interrupted until later renewed. This pattern also can be discerned in Israeli-Egyptian relations in the 1970s.

Second, approval of an adversary rises with de-escalation efforts and agreements but usually falls again once a major de-escalation achievement has been made. Presumably, the high expectations aroused by the move are not fully satisfied and disappointment follows. The decline, however, is usually not to the low levels prior to de-escalation, as is clear in both U.S.-USSR and Israeli-Egyptian relations.

Third, trade relations and exchanges of people may have fluctuated, yet there has been a general upward trend fostered by major de-escalation agreements. Soviet imports from the United States after a period of fluctuation in conjunction with de-escalation efforts have remained at a higher level than before the de-escalation efforts. Furthermore, there is evidence that trade between the United States and Warsaw Pact members resulted in reduced conflict interaction.[71] Comparatively, Egyptian and Israeli trade and cultural exchanges have been smaller thus far and have had relatively little impact. The Egyptian-Israeli conflict, more fundamentally, remains linked to the ongoing struggle between the Jews of Israel and the Arab Palestinians and other Arab antagonists.

Fourth, event data indicate that conflict actions by the Soviet Union toward the United States and vice versa are not simply inversely related to cooperative actions. Soviet conflict actions and U.S. conflict actions have more likely been constrained than provocative following de-escalation agreements. The pattern in Egyptian-Israeli transactions is quite different. Lacking any major de-escalation agreement before 1974, there was little interaction except for conflict behavior during wars. However, in the late 1970s, following the 1974 and 1975 Egyptian-Israeli agreements on the Sinai, cooperative actions increased.

Fifth, both U.S. and Soviet military expenditures have fluctuated but tended to increase in absolute amounts since 1948. The expenditures of the United States rose greatly in conjunction with wars and then again in the late 1970s. Soviet expenditures, after rising in the early 1950s, exhibited small fluctuations during the 1950s. They then rose in the early 1960s and again flattened until they began to rise steadily in the late 1960s. In the mid-1980s, there was again a slowing and even reduction in military spending. Domestic factors have been important in each country in affecting these trends, but some constraint in arms spending appears to have been related to a few de-escalation agreements.

Egyptian military expenditures greatly declined after the signing of the peace treaty with Israel. Israeli military expenditures did not decline as markedly, since peace with Egypt did not end Israel's state of war with other Arab governments or its struggle against the PLO. The peace with Egypt led to a restructuring of the Arab-Israeli conflict, to focus on the Israeli-Palestinian relationship. The Israeli invasion of Lebanon in June 1982 was a manifestation of that new focus.

Certainly, the various measures of accommodation have been shaped by many forces in addition to de-escalation agreements. Each has been the result of the convergence of many changing conditions. Nevertheless, the evidence also indicates that major peace accords have diffuse and lasting consequences. Agreements generally survive and within their narrow domain are fulfilled. Furthermore, they have usually had a general de-escalation effect, at least in the short term. Most significantly, looked at from the perspective of more than forty years, U.S.-USSR de-escalation agreements have had a cumulative effect. Despite a general increase in military capability, the public and elite groups in each country have developed a more differentiated view of one another.

In the United States, even in the years of antagonism in the early 1980s, there was no cold war consensus. There was not the widespread dislike of the Soviet Union and readiness to rely on military means that there was in the early years of the cold war. In trade, before the efforts to transform the Soviet economy beginning in the late 1980s, Soviet imports from the United States had fallen from the détente years but remained above the levels of the 1950s cold war.

The major de-escalation periods have become more significant: mutual, broader, and longer. Knowledge about managing de-escalation and vested interests in pursuing it have grown with each period. Not surprisingly, there have been reactions to each period that in some ways have meant renewed escalation. With the exception of military spending, however, these reactions have not meant moving back to levels of accommodation below what they had been before the de-escalation agreement.

Even in the Arab-Israeli conflict, the agreements reached in the mid-1970s between Egypt and Israel were steps toward the peace treaty between them. However, the very limited understandings or agreements between Israel and Syria or Israel and the PLO have not led to any general accommodation. Clearly, agreements contribute to an accommodating movement between adversaries, but the international context and domestic developments in each society are major constraints.

8

Transformations
and Continuities

Clearly, the years since 1948 are part of the continuum that is history. Although particular de-escalation efforts have generally been treated in this book as isolated episodes for purposes of comparison, they represent a historical continuum. The linkages and cumulative effects of the peacemaking episodes analyzed in previous chapters are examined here. I will assess the role of de-escalation efforts in the transformation of the U.S.-USSR conflict from the frigidity of the cold war to the contemporary warm accommodation between rivals and examine the failure of de-escalation efforts to resolve the Arab-Israeli conflict while contributing to its partial transformation.[1]

The U.S.-USSR Conflict
The Cold War

Shortly after the allies defeated Germany, Italy, and Japan, the rift between the Soviet Union and the United States emerged.[2] In 1948, the enmity between the Soviets and their former allies was everywhere manifest; the cold war was waged with great intensity. The struggle was ideological, with each side making universal claims. It was also traditional: a great power rivalry for dominance and influence in the same areas of the world. More specifically, the Soviets had shifted the borders of the USSR and Poland to the west, generating grievances from many Germans and the fears of others that the Germans would seek to regain lost territories. In West European countries, government coalitions soon excluded Communist parties; in East European countries, Communist parties increasingly dominated governments, culminating in the Communist assumption of power in Czechoslovakia in 1948.

In 1948, too, the Western allies, seeking to reconstruct the West German economy, proposed a currency reform to include West Berlin. To prevent this inclusion, the Soviets instituted a blockade of West Berlin. A Western airlift sustained the people of West Berlin until the blockade was lifted a year later. Then in June 1950, North Korean forces invaded South Korea. In the resulting war, U.S. military forces fought not only the North Koreans but also the army of the People's Republic of China, at that time closely allied with the USSR.

Within American society, anti-Communist sentiments were widely and deeply held; McCarthyism reinforced the general consensus by threatening and punishing dissent. Liberals and conservatives competed in their anti-Communist militancy and opposition to Soviet expansionism. In the Soviet Union, the domination of the people and the elite groups by Joseph Stalin intensified the doctrinaire view that the socialist camp was threatened by an imperialist-capitalist camp, striving for the overthrow of the socialist system.

In this context, peace initiatives by an adversary's officials were likely to be dismissed as self-serving devices to rally constituent support. Not without reason. For example, U.S. and Soviet disarmament proposals were usually formulated to advance self-interests. Consider even the U.S. proposal presented by Bernard Baruch to the United Nations in June 1946, put forward as an offer to surrender the American monopoly of nuclear weapons.[3] This surrender would follow the establishment of an international authority to control all activities leading to nuclear weapons. The authority would have the right to sanction violations, unlimited by any veto power. The Soviets counterproposed that all nuclear weapons should be destroyed before instituting international controls. Variations on such proposals were made for many years: the West proposing inspections and controls before arms reduction and the Soviets proposing that reductions occur first.

Mid- and Late 1950s

In 1953, several changes occurred that produced a slight thaw in the cold war. In the United States, Dwight D. Eisenhower, elected on the Republican ticket, became president. He was more able than a Democratic president to consider conciliatory moves with the Soviets, being less likely to be attacked as soft on communism. In addition, Sen. Joseph McCarthy soon overreached himself and anti-Communist hysteria diminished.

In 1953 in the Soviet Union, Joseph Stalin died, and his successors began to allow fresher ways of thinking about relations with the capitalist world. The improvement of domestic, social, and economic conditions was acknowledged to have high priority. When Khrushchev became the preeminent Soviet leader, he launched several broad changes in domestic and foreign policy. In foreign affairs, he stressed a policy of peaceful coexistence between the capitalist and socialist systems: War between them was no longer inevitable and indeed had to be avoided. Other governments need not be subordinated within the socialist camp or be regarded as members of the enemy camp; nonalignment was possible.

Few de-escalation agreements, however, were reached. Most significantly, the Austrian State Treaty was signed early in 1955, ending the military occupation of Austria by the United States, Great Britain, France, and the USSR. The USSR took some unilateral initiatives, reducing the size of its army and withdrawing from military bases in Finland. Mutual de-escalation efforts were made, without reaching formal agreements. Most notably, Khrushchev visited the United States in 1959 and was invited to Camp David. The visit helped to provide more realistic, differentiated, and humanizing perceptions among Soviet and American leaders and their compatriots. For example, Khrushchev admits in his memoirs, in fact, how ignorant he and his advisers had been about Camp David, thinking they were being invited to go to a place they thought similar to a leper colony![4]

Early 1960s

The thaw of the mid- and late 1950s did not melt the cold war. Several developments had made the antagonism evident and interrupted any enduring movement of mutual accommodation. For example, in the fall of 1956, the Hungarian uprising was ruthlessly suppressed. Then in 1958, Soviet pressure over the status of Berlin resulted in another crisis. The May 1960

Big-Four summit to be held in Paris was aborted when the American U-2 was shot down over the USSR. The cold war culminated in October 1962 in what the Americans call the Cuban missile crisis and what the Soviets identify as the Caribbean crisis, beginning with U.S. attempts to overthrow the Cuban government.[5] Paradoxically, in 1963 another thawing of the cold war occurred, despite and *because* of the missile crisis. After many years of negotiations on a comprehensive nuclear test ban agreement, a partial test ban was signed and ratified. A few other de-escalation agreements were signed that year, before Kennedy was assassinated.

No formal agreements were reached that settled major political issues on, for example, the status of Berlin or the borders of Eastern Europe. The thaw, however, reflected the emerging recognition that the cold war was beginning to end, as a result of changed conditions within many countries and in the international system as a whole. It also was fostered by many previous small accommodative efforts.

The agreements of 1963 provided a basis for additional peacemaking moves. Many Americans had come to believe that mutually beneficial agreements could be reached with dominant groups in the USSR, where, similarly, many of the elite had come to believe it was possible to reach satisfactory agreements with the realistic factions of the American ruling class, isolating extreme imperialistic factions. After this thaw, Kennedy was represented to the people of the Soviet Union with respect and admiration.[6]

Early 1970s

The warming in U.S.-USSR relations in 1963 did not continue steadily and cumulatively. Under the leadership of Johnson and Brezhnev, small accommodative actions were taken, but they did not capture popular attention. Intensification of U.S. involvement in the Vietnam War was the center of growing concern in the United States and many other parts of the world. The Soviets sought to create a global military capability that would at least equal that of the United States. These two consuming agendas precluded major de-escalation moves.

By the early 1970s, nevertheless, domestic conditions, the international context, and the structure of U.S.-USSR relations had changed sufficiently so that many fundamental East–West issues could be settled. The resulting decrease in tension known as détente, incorporated an extraordinarily broad range of agreements, as many issues were linked. These agreements included bilateral accords not only between the United States and the Soviet Union, but also between West Germany and its eastern neighbors as well as several multilateral European agreements.

The period of détente had its roots not only in changed domestic, international, and relational conditions, but also in the experience of earlier thaws and limited agreements, which provided models of what might and might not work in the future. They helped to build the interpersonal connections that facilitated and supported the accommodations of détente.

Late 1970s and Early 1980s

Détente was followed by such a deterioration of u.s.-ussr relations that many observers and elite groups from both sides spoke about a renewed cold war. The anti-Soviet rhetoric of Reagan's first term was certainly reminiscent of the early 1950s but lacked consensual support. Large increases in military spending were made, building on the increases already begun in the waning years of Carter's presidency. The uses of the military in actual combat and in confrontations, however, were limited compared to the Korean and Vietnam wars. The Soviets, enduring their stagnation, persisted in their ongoing production of military weapons and marched into Afghanistan.

The revived antagonism in u.s.-ussr relations has been described by some as a failure of détente.[7] It is alleged that the expectations of peaceful relations were doomed to disappointment, frustration, and therefore to a reversal. Others believe that either the ussr or the United States or both sought unilateral advantage and exploited détente until the other was forced to respond. These are inadequate explanations. Undoubtedly, détente did raise expectations too high to be realized, and some were disappointed by the reality of the experience each side had with the conduct of the other. Furthermore, there were differences in the interpretation of détente that led to misunderstandings and sometimes a sense of betrayal. For example, Soviet officials may have thought détente meant that the U.S. government had acknowledged the ussr as a superpower of equal status throughout the world. The global role of the United States, however, remained preeminent and was so regarded by the American leaders. Détente did not mean that either government had renounced its interests in other parts of the world; each would and did seek to advance them.

Nevertheless, these alleged failures of détente do not adequately account for the changes in u.s.-ussr relations during this period. Most importantly, the background conditions that shaped détente had changed greatly by the end of the 1970s, so that much of its support was undermined. The American need for Soviet help, for example, in ending the Vietnam War was no longer important after the United States was out of Vietnam.

Despite deterioration, détente made significant and lasting contributions to an accommodation between the Soviets and Americans. The increased antagonism in U.S.-USSR relations was checked from reaching the extremes of the original cold war. Of course, to some extent this was because the conditions that supported the intense cold war of the early 1950s no longer existed. The world was no longer monolithically bipolar, the United States no longer had a monopoly of nuclear weapons; and the cold war consensus in the United States had disintegrated and was not restored. Détente itself, however, was crucial in creating conditions that limited the deterioration of U.S.-USSR relations in the late 1970s and early 1980s.

Détente had shown the value of interdependency and the mutual gain that could be derived from it. Segments of the elite groups in the West and the East had their belief in these possibilities reinforced. This was particularly true for many groups and organizations in Western Europe, especially West Germany, and in Eastern Europe and the USSR. Even wider segments of the populations in the East and West had had some experience in cultural, educational, scientific, and other exchanges, so that their views of each other were more differentiated and less stereotypical. In some cases, interpersonal networks were established.

Mid-1980s

In 1985, a new generation led by Gorbachev came to power in the Soviet Union, and a fundamental transformation in U.S.-USSR relations began. Through a series of Soviet statements and unilateral moves, the sense of threat from the USSR was greatly diminished in Europe and later in the United States. Several American-Soviet summit meetings were held and agreements signed, most notably the INF treaty. By the end of the 1980s, the cold war had ended, and the U.S.-USSR conflict was transformed into an increasingly cooperative relationship. My analysis suggests that the transformation is in part attributable to the preceding years of de-escalation. To assess how large a role that movement played, other explanations are discussed first.

An interpretation, popular in the United States among advocates of a hard-line posture, is that the U.S. militancy of the early 1980s forced the Soviets back to the negotiating table and to acceptance of many U.S. policies.[8] The U.S. military build-up and increased anti-Soviet militancy raised the costs of Soviet superpower pretensions to unsupportable heights. A more benign version of this view is that the transformation was a consequence of the firm containment policy pursued by the United States and NATO. Another interpretation is that the transformation was primarily due to economic troubles within the Soviet Union. The failure of the Soviet economy required improved economic relations with the West and reductions in the allocation of resources to the military services. An accommodation with the West was a requirement for these changes. A third explanation is less often noted, but worthy of consideration. Changes in the international economic system and the military overextension of both the Soviet Union and the United States had produced a relative decline of both in the world system. The weaker Soviet economy led Soviet leaders to recognize the need for change before U.S. leaders did, but the United States would continue to decline relative to Japan and Western Europe unless its leaders also recognized the need for fundamental change.

These explanations do not fully account for Soviet decisions to undertake glasnost and perestroika and to seek cooperative relations with the West. Nor do they adequately explain the speed, extent, and direction of unplanned developments in Eastern Europe and the Soviet Union. The Soviet economy was stagnating but had not yet reached such a crisis that a fundamental change was immediately needed. A policy of stringent discipline might have been tried and even spurred by a mobilization of energy to counter the anti-Soviet policies of the Reagan administration. The Soviet control of Eastern Europe could have been maintained a while longer. Additional factors must be taken into account to explain the direction chosen to meet the challenges posed by external military pressure, domestic economic problems, and rising international pressures.

The cumulative effects of the de-escalation agreements reached in preceding decades greatly influenced initial decisions on the direction of change and the resulting transformation within the Soviet Union and in Eastern Europe. Seven developments arising from previous agreements are particularly important. First, the increased exchange of students, scientists, artists, and other intellectuals and the freer movement of people generally expanded the knowledge and tolerance in the Soviet Union of attractive alternatives to many aspects of Soviet life. Such developments diminished the ideological fervor that had helped to sustain the cold war.[9] Increased attention to the West as a relevant model was particularly true for Soviet intellectuals and other elements of elite groups. They, more than the masses, were strong supporters of the restructuring policies of Gorbachev.

Second, increased familiarity with the West also enhanced the desire of many in the Soviet Union for civil liberties and higher standards in consumer goods and services. The new generation of Soviet elite was especially likely to be affected. These views were coupled with a growing belief that better access to Western consumer goods, advanced technology, and other materials and information would bring beneficial improvements to Soviet society.

Third, although actual economic benefits were disappointing in relations with the United States, trade with Western Europe and especially Germany was extensive and sustained even when U.S.-USSR political relations deteriorated in the late 1970s and early 1980s. The prospect of improved economic conditions in the Soviet Union resulting from expanded economic relations with the West was not destroyed with the ending of détente.

Fourth, agreements reached during détente and before convinced many of the Soviet elite that major elements in the U.S. ruling class had accepted the USSR as a superpower. There was also evidence of popular opposition to what the Soviets considered American imperialism, made manifest and sometimes effective again, even during Reagan's first term.

Fifth, the period of détente contributed to the "normalization" of the Soviet Union in U.S. public opinion, which in turn contributed to the resistance of the U.S. Congress to the Reagan administration's military buildup and anti-Soviet pressure and to the public's profound division over these policies. These developments signified that a more accommodative policy by the Soviets would be reciprocated. Moreover, the strength of the peace movements in Western Europe also served as a warranty that unilateral advantage would not be taken of Soviet accommodation.

Sixth, changes in Europe, particularly between the two Germanys and between West Germany and the Soviet Union and Poland had great importance. They were initiated in 1969 with the Social Democratic Party's *Ostpolitik* and institutionalized with CSCE following the Helsinki accords in 1975. These changes reduced fears in Eastern Europe of a German threat to regain lost territories, reducing the need for Soviet protection. They helped to open up the East to Western influence and mutual dependence. The basis for the rapid unification of the two Germanys was laid down during this period. The absence of such prior agreements and experiences between the two Koreas partially explains the continuing rigidity in their relations, despite the end of the cold war.

Finally, important new ideas about security were developed by peace researchers and activists, particularly in Denmark, Great Britain, and West Germany. Ideas of nonprovocative defense, common security, and security broadly conceived to include welfare and environmental concerns provided a conceptual alternative to the mutual-threat strategies of NATO and the Warsaw Pact. The Soviets discussed these ideas with Western specialists while developing their own new thinking.[10] These Soviet and East European experiences combined to make the construction of a stable East–West accommodation seem worthwhile and possible. Without decades of experience and observation, Soviet domestic troubles could readily have become the basis for accusations against foreign enemies and the mobilization of the home front to fight external threats.

In turn, the experiences of reaching many de-escalation agreements contributed to developments within the United States that fostered the accommodation emerging in the mid-1980s between the United States and the USSR. First, de-escalation moves achieved earlier created a vested interest in further accommodation, which included companies engaged in foreign trade, research institutes, government agencies, and nonofficial organizations.

Second, exchanges and increased contact in the context of de-escalation moves produced a more differentiated view of the Soviet peoples and leaders, which created a momentum so that even when official relations deteriorated in the early 1980s, private groups carried on various exchanges, engaging in what came to be called citizen diplomacy.[11] These and related developments contributed to a readiness to downgrade anti-Soviet ideology when Gorbachev and his colleagues began to change domestic and foreign policies.

Third, for many Americans, the new content of Soviet thinking was irresistible. It seemed to express what Americans had long wished the Soviets would say. Soviet officials began to acknowledge the legitimacy of religious, ethnic, artistic, and other claims to human rights. In military matters, they acknowledged that Westerners may have had reason to fear that the Soviets were preparing for a military attack. The officials began to write and speak about the need for common security, security that each side could have only if the other had it as well. Furthermore, the basic tenets of Marxism seemed to be repudiated as the economy began to shift toward a market system.

Finally, and fundamentally, many Americans came to believe in the mid-1980s that a stable accommodation with the Soviets was desirable and had now become possible. The changes in the Soviet Union were viewed as profound and worth supporting by reciprocating the de-escalation moves undertaken by the Soviets. The construction of peaceful relations was under way.

The Arab-Israeli Conflict

Periods in the Arab-Israeli conflict are usually designated by wars. Indeed, wars generally mark important changes in the structure of an ongoing conflict and so serve as significant demarcations. The years of struggle since 1948 may be regarded as a series of failed efforts to find a solution to the conflict between Israeli Jews and their Arab neighbors. Many aspects of the struggle became increasingly institutionalized and irreconcilable. Within that context, substantial de-escalation efforts were rarely attempted. Nevertheless, some efforts resulted in partial solutions, and elements of peaceful relations were constructed. An assessment of the effect of de-escalation efforts must be made in the context of the history of the Arab-Israeli struggle.

1948–1956

In an effort to resolve the conflict between Jews and Arabs over the future of Palestine, in November 1947 the UN General Assembly passed a resolution for the partition of the territory, then controlled under a UN mandate by Great Britain.[12] Although the partition plan was not accepted by the Arab states, British military forces were withdrawn in May 1948. The Jews in Palestine declared the establishment of Israel, and the Arab governments launched a war to prevent and nullify that event. When the fighting stopped, Israel controlled territory beyond the previously proposed partition lines. The Kingdom of Jordan controlled most of the land along the west bank of the Jordan River and East Jerusalem; Egypt controlled the Gaza Strip.

At the outset of this period, the international context in many ways was conducive to settlement. The U.S. and Soviet governments had quickly recognized the State of Israel. The United States had good official relations with all Arab states, ruled by conservative groups long tied to the former colonial powers in the region. The United Nations was actively engaged in efforts to resolve the conflict and, under U.S. leadership, could muster working majorities for action. By the mid-1950s, however, the international context was much less conducive to settlement. The Soviet Union had become a supporter of the new Egyptian government, and the cold war rivalry had become superimposed on the Arab-Israeli conflict.

The conditions within Arab countries relative to relations with Israel varied greatly. For the king of Jordan a settlement with Israel, dividing Palestine at the armistice lines, might appear as a realization of his ambition for a greater Jordan.[13] This was not compatible, however, with the interests of the many Palestinian refugees in Jordan who wanted to return to their homes in what was now called Israel to live in an Arab Palestinian country, not a Jewish state.

In Egypt, the defeat of Arab forces in 1948–49 prompted the overthrow of the old regime by a modernizing military group led by Nasser.[14] An initial goal of the new leaders was the removal of British military forces stationed at the Suez canal. After Great Britain agreed in 1954 to evacuate its forces, foreign policy attention shifted to relations with Israel. Nasser increasingly acted as the leader of the Arab world. For many Arabs and

Arab leaders, the imposition of a Jewish state by Western imperialist powers was categorically unacceptable, and the Jews who had recently come to settle in Palestine would have to leave and the Jewish state abolished.

Within Israel, the creation of a Jewish state meant that priority was given to the gathering of Jews, survivors of the Holocaust in Europe, refugees from many Arab countries, and Jews from all over the world who wished to fulfill their Zionist dream to live in Israel. There was high consensus that peace with the Arab governments should be based on the new reality created by the war of independence. The need for maintaining a Jewish political entity was categorical.

In the context of these fundamentally opposed commitments, most of the de-escalation efforts were initiated and pursued by intermediaries. At the outset, these were efforts by the United Nations seeking armistice agreements; then efforts to reach political settlements or agreements on Palestinian refugees were made. Also, official and unofficial emissaries sought to facilitate de-escalation negotiations, usually between Egypt and Israel. There were secret bilateral negotiations between the King of Jordan and Israeli government officials.

The failure of all these efforts to produce a peace agreement or even the settlement of a significant matter laid the basis for the increasingly intractable nature of the conflict. Without significant agreements, relations achieved with the armistice agreements of 1949 deteriorated. Raids and counterraids between Israel and Egypt escalated. In October 1956, when the conflict between Egypt and France and Great Britain over the Suez canal erupted, Israel colluded with France and Great Britain in attacking Egypt. The failure to make progress toward an accommodation afterward was evidence to each of the other's intransigence. Aborted peacemaking efforts often confirmed their mistrust of one another.

1956–1967

The 1956 war exacerbated the difficulty in reaching a settlement of the conflict. The sale of East bloc weapons to Egypt was a source of the war, and the introduction of the cold war into the region perpetuated the Arab-Israeli conflict, which became embedded within the East–West conflict.[15] Egypt became even more dependent on the Soviet bloc, although the United States acted forcefully to stop the war and to insist that Israel withdraw from the Sinai, which it had occupied in the war. Despite the Egyptian military defeat, its political victory raised Nasser to high standing in the Arab world. From the perspective of many Arabs, the war demonstrated that Israel was an instrument of Western imperialism and an alien agent in its world.

The Israelis might have concluded that military force could not realize their goals. Some concluded, however, that a military confrontation would persist for a very long time. Eventually, the Arabs would accept the new reality and meanwhile a policy of military vigilance and retaliation for attacks was necessary.

The October 1956 war ended with an agreement to place UN peacekeeping forces along the Egyptian side of its border with Israel to prevent cross-border raids; UN forces were also stationed in Sharm el Sheikh, at the southern tip of the Sinai peninsula to prevent the Gulf of Aqaba from being closed to Israeli shipping by Egypt. Among Arab countries, domestic social and economic changes spurred a desire for modernization and more rapid development. In many countries the result was political turmoil, notably in Syria. After three irregular changes of government in 1949, other coups and struggles for power ensued. In 1954, a coalition helped to install the Ba'th party. Continuing instability led to an effort at union with Egypt in February 1958, but this union was terminated after a Syrian military coup in September 1961. Iraq also had several military coups. In 1958 the monarchy was overthrown, and the new government moved from its pro-Western policy and accepted aid from Communist countries. In 1963, military officers and Ba'th party members seized control of the government.

The Palestinians, on the whole, lacked an effective independent voice. Those living in the West Bank had become Jordanian citizens, as Jordan incorporated the territory it controlled. Palestinians elsewhere in the Arab world were generally not allowed to become citizens of the country in which they lived. Many lived in refugee camps, supported by the United Nations. As a result, Palestinian nationalism was becoming more intense and salient as it became more frustrated.

Nasser became more and more clearly the dominant leader of the Arab nation and mobilized Arabs against Israel. His leadership was relatively secure; he derived strength from that stance, which would be undermined in actively seeking a peaceful accommodation with Israel.

Israel continued to be governed by the Labor party, which was divided into major factions. That division inhibited taking bold de-escalation initiatives. Furthermore, there was widespread public consensus to maintain military strength and wait until the Arabs were ready to accept a Jewish state.

The international structure was still basically bipolar, ideologically and militarily. The United States continued to be the dominant economic power in a worldwide capitalist system. The ongoing U.S.-USSR cold war, however, was increasingly waged in competing for influence in several regions in the world, particularly the Middle East.

Under these circumstances, there were few major de-escalation efforts. Intermediaries from the United States made some attempts, but the efforts proved futile. Without achieving effective de-escalation agreements between Israel and any of its Arab neighbors, relations gradually deteriorated. In 1967, border fighting increased between Israeli and Syrian forces. A major escalation occurred in June when Nasser requested that UN forces stationed on Egyptian soil leave; the Israeli port of Elath was then cut off from the Red Sea by an Egyptian blockade at Sharm el Sheikh on the Gulf of Aqaba. Israel responded by attacking Egypt and Syria; Jordan joined the war alongside Egypt and Syria. In six days Israeli military forces had taken control of the Sinai, East Jerusalem, the west bank of the Jordan River, and the Golan Heights.[16]

1967–1973

The results of the sudden and immense Israeli victory transformed the conflict. Israel now possessed much land that could be traded for peace. The UN Security Council passed resolution 242, and special emissary Gunnar Jarring shuttled among the capitals of the major adversaries.[17] Although there were promises of a possible compromise, efforts at settlement failed. In 1969, other intermediary efforts were made by the U.S. government, undertaken shortly after Nixon became president.

In 1969, the War of Attrition was launched by Egypt against Israel, and intermediary efforts focused on ending that war. In August 1970, Secretary of State Rogers succeeded in achieving a cease-fire. The Egyptians, however, advanced their missile launchers, violating the cease-fire agreement, undermining the move as a possible step toward further accommodation. Furthermore, through a series of interrelated steps, the opposition of some Palestinian groups to the termination of Egypt's armed struggle led to an escalation of the conflict between the main units of the PLO in Jordan and the Jordanian government. After bloody fighting, the PLO armed units were driven from Jordan, settling mostly in Lebanon.

Following these events, the changes in Jordan and Egypt would seem to have made at least partial settlements with Israel more likely. The Jordanian government did not need to be as concerned about domestic Palestinian opposition to such moves. In Egypt, Nasser died after chairing a conference aimed at reunifying the Arab world. His successor, Anwar Sadat, began to orient Egyptian foreign policy slowly away from the Soviet Union and toward the United States.

Several de-escalation probes were made during this period by Sadat, by intermediaries between Israel and Egypt, and by Israelis seeking partial settlements with Egypt. None of these moves, however, resulted in an explicit agreement; the parties still seemed too far apart for a mutually acceptable accord. For Sadat, the alternative of using a limited war to force the start of negotiations that would yield minimally acceptable settlement terms took on increasing salience. In October 1973, Egyptian and Syrian armed forces launched a surprise attack on Israel.

1973–1982

The October war radically changed the structure of many components of the Arab-Israeli conflict, but this restructuring was not inherent to the war. The war aims of Arab adversaries were disparate, as is evident from a comparison of the Egyptian-Israeli and Syrian-Israeli conflicts.

Sadat's waging of the war was part of the movement, already under way, to work through the United States to reach a settlement with the State of Israel.[18] That settlement would not require Egyptian dominance or control, beyond the return of the Sinai. Syria, besides seeking to regain the Golan Heights, strove for greater influence in Palestine and continued to rely on the Soviets to counter U.S. influence in the region.

The war demonstrated the dependence of the primary antagonists on external powers—the United States and the Soviet Union—to continue fighting. It also demonstrated the limited goals that each could achieve by war, despite the immense punishment each could inflict on the other. In this context, major de-escalation efforts seemed possible, particularly since American-Soviet antagonism was muted by continuing détente. Nevertheless, the October war was a point of contention and mutual threat between the U.S. and Soviet governments. Moreover, the U.S. government quickly entered into mediation activities that effectively excluded the Soviet Union.

These mediation activities, conducted by Secretary of State Henry Kissinger, included two Egyptian-Israeli agreements and a Syrian-Israeli agreement and were limited to military stabilization and mutual security. No success was achieved in a mediation effort between Jordan and Israel, and by the mid-1970s U.S. efforts had slowed. The attention in Washington on Watergate, the resignation of Nixon, and the brief tenure of Ford inhibited America's taking major new approaches.

With Carter's assumption of office in January 1977, a new phase of peace efforts was begun. Initially, Carter and his advisers sought a comprehensive settlement through a peace conference on the Middle East, cochaired by the United States and the USSR. Doubting the success of such a venture, Sadat choose direct negotiations with Israel; his visit to Jerusalem further transformed the nature of the conflict. Israelis had already begun to believe that Egypt wanted to make peace from the experience of the Sinai I and Sinai II agreements.[19] The American public and leadership were enthralled by the prospect of an Egyptian-Israeli peace brokered by the United States. Resorting to a step-by-step policy and building on the developing trust between many Israelis and Egyptians, the U.S. government actively mediated the attainment of a peace treaty between Egypt and Israel. Sadat's breaking of Arab ranks and making peace with Israel made the Israeli-Palestinian conflict increasingly salient.[20] The "Palestinianization" of the conflict put more emphasis on the role of Jordan and Syria and especially the PLO.

Changes in Israel, the United States, and in the world context meant that in some regards the Palestinianization of the conflict made it less accessible to solution.[21] The Israeli election of May 1977 resulted in the Likud party, led by Menachem Begin, forming a new government with strong commitments to continued Israeli control over the West Bank and Gaza and expanded Jewish settlements in those territories. In 1980, Ronald Reagan was inaugurated as president, and the antagonism toward the Soviet Union greatly increased. Soviet influence was to be challenged everywhere, including in the Middle East. The PLO and Syria, because they were viewed as supported by the Soviets, were not to be regarded in Washington as parties whose interests should be served.

1982–1989

The provisions of the 1979 Egyptian-Israeli peace treaty included linking the withdrawal of Israel from the Sinai with the normalization of relations between the two countries. These and other steps in the implementation of the treaty were to be completed in three years. In June 1982, after the treaty was implemented, Israeli military forces invaded Lebanon to attack the PLO, which was based there.[22]

A framework for a comprehensive peace had been part of the Camp David accords; although Egyptian-Israeli negotiations were pursued on the status of the West Bank and Gaza Strip, they collapsed. The attack on the PLO in Lebanon promised a new solution for the Israeli government. It was believed the PLO could be eliminated as a major actor and Israel's northern borders made secure by a peace with Lebanon. The Palestinians on the West Bank and Gaza would then be obliged to reconcile themselves to having cultural and social autonomy, but not a state of their own.

Some steps in this direction were taken. The fighting forces of the PLO were withdrawn from Lebanon and dispersed in several Arab countries, and the United States mediated a peace agreement between Israel and Lebanon, although short-lived. Under pressure from Syria, the Lebanese government did not ratify the treaty. The U.S. military and other organizations were soon driven out of Lebanon. Furthermore, support for the PLO was enhanced among most Palestinians, notably those living in the territories occupied by Israel.

Meanwhile, in Israel, the consensus among Jews that had existed since the establishment of the State was shattered by the war in Lebanon. For the first time, profound divisions emerged over the possibility and desirability of making peace, on various terms, with the Palestinians and the Arab governments.[23] Some segments of the population were ready to trade land in the occupied territories for peace with the Arabs, even if this meant a Palestinian state led by the PLO. Other segments were unwilling to allow any Palestinian state to be established in any of the currently occupied territories. Many other "in-between" positions were held by even larger proportions of the Israeli population.

Without a dominant point of view in the electorate, Israel entered a phase of rule by broad coalition governments formed by the Labor and Likud parties. In the government so formed between 1984 and 1988, the prime minister was Shimon Peres for two years, and Yitzhak Shamir was foreign minister; they reversed roles for the second half of the four-year term of the so-called unity government. While Peres was prime minister, efforts to improve relations with Egypt and to negotiate a joint Jordanian-Palestinian delegation were made. There was progress toward a possible formula for negotiations, but they were not realized before Peres exchanged roles with Shamir under the terms of the coalition agreement.

The Iran-Iraq war preoccupied Arab governments and isolated Syria, the only Arab government supporting Iran. The United States, having failed grievously in Lebanon, was relatively inactive. In this context, mediation efforts were few and ineffective.

In December 1987 the popular Palestinian resistance in the occupied territories erupted into large-scale nonviolent action and violence, largely in the form of stone throwing.[24] A continuation of the status quo before the uprising appeared untenable to increasing numbers of both parties.

Intermediaries, official and nonofficial, became more active again. The key development was the shift in PLO positions at the end of 1988, which led to an opening of a dialogue with the United States. Even this breakthrough, however, did not lead to Israeli-Palestinian negotiations, which were delayed by Israeli government proposals for elections in the West Bank and Gaza Strip to select representatives. The U.S.-PLO dialogue was suspended by the U.S. in June 1990 after an attempted attack by PLO guerrillas.

In retrospect, it is easy to see the many times when greater perseverance, creativity, and willingness—by various adversaries and intermediaries—to take a risk toward de-escalation would have achieved results. For at least some of the adversaries, earlier partial settlements would have produced more benefits than the perpetuation of intense conflict. The persistence of a struggle creates additional obstacles to de-escalation and resolution, as mutual mistrust and hatred grow and as vested interests in fighting develop.

Generalizations

Major social forces within the countries of primary adversaries as well as the general international context constrain peacemaking efforts. They limit the initiatives taken and the possibility that initiatives will lead to de-escalation agreements. They also limit the chances that agreements will become steps toward peaceful relations. The nature of the conflict itself and the issues at stake also affect the possibilities of de-escalation and resolution. The United States and USSR did not directly threaten each other's existence the way the Jews of Israel and the Arabs of Palestine feel their collective existence has been threatened. The risk of mutual nuclear destruction in the U.S.-USSR conflict had different implications for those adversaries than did the experience of intense conventional wars and deadly attacks on civilians in the Middle East.

Within those constraints, and recognizing the particularities of each conflict, *how* initiatives are undertaken, the *way* in which negotiations are conducted, and the *terms* of agreements matter; they affect progress toward durable, integrated, secure relations among former adversaries. The review of specific conflicts indicates that peacemaking efforts have a cumulative effect. Cooperative relations do not suddenly arise between former enemies; they are gradually constructed, and setbacks are inevitable.

Partial settlements sometimes reduce the pressure for immediate, comprehensive settlements, and they may leave unsatisfied the needs of some groups among adversary coalitions. Often, however, partial settlements form building blocks in the construction of a stable, secure relationship insofar as they foster trust and confidence and create vested interests for further integration.

9
Inferences and
Policy Implications

In this final chapter, we can allow ourselves to be more speculative and more judgmental about the U.S.-USSR and Arab-Israeli conflicts than we have been. First, I consider the costs of the conflicts persisting as long and as intensely as they have; I then assess how well the conflict resolution perspective accounts for actual de-escalation and transformation; next, I discuss the policy making implications of the analyses; and, finally, drawing on the previous discussions, I consider applying conflict resolution methods to peacemaking efforts, speculating on attaining earlier de-escalations.

Although there is no universal peacemaking formula, we can study the components of effective de-escalation efforts generally to see which combination of elements more often result in reaching mutually accommodative agreements. If we can understand the reasons for the success and failure of de-escalation efforts, we might learn which application could lead to policies that reduce the chances of conflicts persisting at great risk.

The Costs of Waging Conflicts

The choice not to pursue de-escalation efforts often rests on a belief that continued struggle, and even escalation, will yield advantage. This assessment often underestimates the cost of not de-escalating a struggle. A context for assessing de-escalation efforts made versus those not made is the cost of having failed years ago to settle the conflicts under study. The cold war has ended, yet the burdens of waging it are often minimized or regarded as irrelevant now. But the costs of the cold war as well as the costs of the Arab-Israeli conflict are worth considering.

U.S.-USSR Conflict Costs

The costs of the cold war have been immense and ultimately are unknowable. Conceivably, all the problems in the world since 1948 could be attributed to it. While that is an exaggeration, the cold war has certainly exacerbated many of the world's problems. Here, I limit discussion to the Soviet Union and the United States and concentrate on relatively direct costs.

Social Costs The Soviet's burdens associated with Stalinism are not entirely attributable to the cold war or to capitalist encirclement after the October 1917 revolution. The totalitarian system had many domestic sources. The threat of foreign intervention, however, was used to justify internal control and gave plausibility to restrictions on freedom and the use of state terror as a defense against efforts at subversion. Indeed, domestic Soviet liberalization was associated with reduced hostility in American-Soviet relations. In the mid-1950s, for example, Khrushchev led a Soviet shift away from Stalinism in both foreign and domestic policies.

A similar, if less extreme, pattern can be seen in the United States. The threat of communism was used as a means of social control by dominant groups in the United States. Critics of U.S. official policies at home and abroad were attacked as Communists or Communist sympathizers. The intensity of such accusations was at its height in the period of McCarthyism in the mid-1950s. The careers and personal lives of people in the U.S. government, in education, and in the entertainment industry were badly damaged, and intellectual life stifled. Consequently, foreign policy alternatives narrowed and later problems exacerbated; for example, debates over U.S. Vietnam policy among Democrats in government were haunted by fearful memories of being charged with "losing" China.[1]

Economic Costs The economic drain on each economy of waging the cold war was great. For the Soviet Union, with its lower levels of production, the strain was greater than for the United States. It is impossible to know precisely what proportion of the Soviet economy has been devoted to the development and production of military equipment and to the maintenance of a large military force since some of those expenditures would have gone on even without a cold war, to maintain domestic order. In any case, the direct military expenditure probably ranged between 15 and 25 percent of the total domestic economy.[2] In addition, many of the most skilled persons were devoting their thoughts and energy to the enhancement of the armed forces and not to consumer products.

To rival and challenge the United States as a superpower, the leadership of the Communist party of the Soviet Union during the cold war extended its influence and control beyond the borders of the USSR. Cuba, Eastern Europe, North Korea, Vietnam, and several other countries in varying degrees and at various times were part of what some people in the West called the Soviet empire. Charles Wolfe, Jr., has estimated the costs of maintaining that dominion in terms of trade subsidies, trade credits, economic and military aid, and destabilization activities; at their peak in 1980, these costs constituted 7 percent of the ruble GNP and 3 percent of the dollar GNP.[3]

The burdens for the United States have also been immense in projecting military power throughout the world, threatening and waging war, and aiding allies and courting potential allies in the struggle to contain and defeat communism. Direct military expenditures have varied from highs of 9–10 percent of the GNP during the Korean and Vietnam wars to lows of 6–7 percent during the détente years.[4]

The cost of maintaining the American overseas domain of influence has been substantial, but according to Wolf they have been about half of the Soviet costs and only .3 percent of the much larger U.S. GNP. Other writers, however, have stressed the great drain that the channeling of research and development into military-related areas has been on the U.S. economy.[5] It has distorted that economy and greatly contributed to the trade deficit, to the budget deficit, and to the relative decline of the United States in the world economic system.

Human Costs Deaths from wars are the most immediate and severe costs of the U.S.-USSR conflict. Although the United States and the USSR did not wage war against each other directly, they have supported armed units fighting each other's military personnel, and each has ventured into wars and armed conflicts in part to counter the other. Those wars have resulted in many military and civilian deaths among many peoples.[6] In the Korean War (1950–53), the deaths have been estimated at 3 million, of which half were civilian; in the Vietnam War (1960–75), nearly two and a half million deaths have been estimated, of which half were civilian; and the war in Afghanistan (1978–89) caused an estimated three-quarters of a million deaths, of which 670,000 were civilians.

In addition to these direct war deaths, an undetermined number of deaths are attributable to increased exposure to radiation from nuclear weapon production and testing. Furthermore, the allocation of resources for military purposes reduced the funds that might have gone to health and welfare services, which would have enabled citizens to live longer. The decrease in life expectancy and increased infant mortality rates in the Soviet Union in the 1970s may be attributed in part to the military burdens carried by the USSR.

With these pressures in mind—whatever the benefits of waging the cold war may have been—the advantages of earlier de-escalation and settlement are obvious. An accommodation in the mid-1950s or even the early 1970s would have reduced the great burdens carried by the people in Eastern Europe, the USSR, and the United States. People in many parts of the world, including Eastern Europe, may have achieved more control over their destinies earlier.

Arab-Israeli Conflict Costs

The social, psychic, cultural, and economic costs of the Arab-Israeli conflict since 1948 have been immeasurable. There are, of course, many other conflicts in the Middle East involving great rivalries, and the cold war contributed to many of them. Nevertheless, the Arab-Israeli conflict has been primary and has added to the intensity and persistence of the other conflicts in the region. Some of the dimensions of the costs associated with these conflicts can be dealt with only briefly here.

Social Costs The Palestinians have borne and continue to bear great losses in the Arab-Israeli conflict. Their exodus from British-mandated Palestine began after the UN General Assembly passed the partition resolution in November 1947. By the time the mandate ended in May 1948, approximately 200,000 Palestinian Arabs had become refugees. By June 1949, the United Nations was caring for 940,000 refugees.[7] The 1967 war produced approximately another 300,000 refugees.

Many Palestinians have lived in refugee camps since the wars, mostly in Jordan and in Lebanon. The conditions of people raising their families in these camps have been difficult; even for those who have found employment and become members of other societies, the sense of collective loss is painful.

For those in other Arab societies directly engaged in the struggle against Israel, a sense of loss, intrusion, and humiliation is common. Attention to the conflict with Israel has meant a focus on external enemies rather than on internal social and economic development. The conflict has provided leaders with useful rallying cries to mobilize support for themselves.

Israeli society, too, has been greatly distorted by the ongoing struggle. Feeling embattled and surrounded by enemies, sacrifices for defense are readily made. Israeli citizens of Arab identity experience unequal treatment, justified by the external threat. Living as an occupying power in the West Bank and Gaza Strip and waging a struggle against terrorism and the intifada have limited the full democracy anticipated when Israel was established.

Economic Costs   The countries of the Middle East have spent extraordinary amounts of money on military weapons.[8] A great deal of the funds earned from exporting petroleum has been spent on arms; even relatively poor countries have devoted very large proportions of their resources to military uses. For example, the percentage of the GNP spent on the military in Israel was 3 percent in 1960 and 19 percent in 1986; in Syria the figures are 8 and 15 percent, respectively; in Jordan, 17 and 14 percent; in Iraq, 9 and 32 percent; in Egypt, 6 and 9 percent; and in Saudi Arabia, 6 and 23 percent.

Public expenditures for education and health have been much lower. In Israel, in 1986, public expenditures for education were 7.3 percent of the GNP and for health 2.1 percent. In Syria, the comparable percentages are 5.7 and .8 percent; in Jordan, the numbers are 5.1 and 1.9; in Iraq, 3.7 and .8 percent; in Egypt, 4.8 and 1.0 percent; and in Saudi Arabia, 10.6 and 4.0.

Human Costs   The frequent wars in the Arab-Israeli conflict and small-scale acts of violence have taken a heavy toll on human life.[9] Although the absolute number of deaths in the wars may seem small compared to the figures in the U.S.-USSR–supported regional wars, for the countries involved, those numbers are large. In the 1948 war, 8,000 military deaths were estimated; in the 1956 war, there were about 3,000 military and a thousand civilian deaths; in the 1967–70 fighting, military deaths were 25,000 and civilian deaths, another 50,000; in the 1973 war, 16,000 military personnel were killed; and in the 1982 war in Lebanon, 22,000 military personnel were killed and 40,000 civilians. Many persons were also killed in small-scale attacks—by Israeli military against guerrilla bases, by Palestinian armed units against Jews, and in the suppression of Palestinian groups by Arab governments.

Obviously, given these heavy costs, an earlier settlement would have been advantageous for most people in the region. It might well have enabled them to get on with their lives, building a life for their families and nations instead of holding out for better terms in the future.

Implications of Theoretical Perspectives

Throughout this book, I have interpreted the processes of de-escalation from the conflict resolution perspective and general international relations approaches. Let us see if it is possible to draw conclusions on the relative validity of these theoretical orientations.

Conflict Mitigation

The cases studied have illustrated the settlement of conflicts—though not necessarily their resolution in the sense of satisfying the basic needs of adversaries.[10] They might be taken as evidence of the importance of complete resolution to guard against conflicts flaring up again. They better support, however, the view that final resolutions are not achievable but that partial settlements are often steps toward later, fuller settlements, even if a comprehensive resolution is never attained.

The actual importance of settlements and of formally expressed agreements is consistent with prevailing ideas in the conflict resolution field. Agreements are rarely pieces of paper used to lure an adversary into a trap.[11] They generally provide the basis for settling particular issues and establishing mutual confidence for more comprehensive settlements. The process exposes the possibility of finding mutually beneficial solutions to a conflict. The frequent and significant contributions to conflict de-escalation made by formal mediators and others providing mediation services supports an emphasis on such roles and activities by conflict resolution analysts and practitioners.

There is further confirmation of the validity of the conflict resolution approach. Major de-escalation movements in each set of conflicts indicate the importance of reframing a conflict.[12] For example, the Egyptian government, under Sadat's leadership, narrowed the characterization of the conflict with Israel from a general Arab struggle against Israel and the imperialist West to a struggle between Egypt and Israel. Similarly, in the late 1980s,

Gorbachev and his associates reinterpreted the long ideological conflict between the socialist and imperialist camps, saying that government leaders of each country needed to focus on their many shared problems, adding that to solve their problems they would have to take the interests and concerns of each other into account.

We have also examined issues that generally are not adequately addressed in the conflict resolution field. The importance of the domestic and international context was noted again and again, because the choice of appropriate conflict resolution tactics and strategy is critical. Again, there are no all-purpose tools to mitigate the undesired aspects of conflicts; different methods are effective for different purposes at different times.

The timing of peacemaking efforts is important, but whether or not the time is right for a particular effort depends on the specific goals and the strategy chosen to reach them.[13] Thus, if the goal is to settle a peripheral issue, one without a long history of contention, the appropriate strategy is likely to include only major adversaries, treating the matter as an isolated dispute. Effectiveness in peacemaking efforts requires the selection of objectives and strategies that the party undertaking the effort can implement under prevailing conditions and in a particular time frame.

This formulation suggests another issue often ignored in the conflict resolution literature. Dispute settlement suggestions usually entail the adversaries' accepting the status quo, reconciling themselves to underlying realities. Those rejecting such suggestions base their rejection on a refusal to accept prevailing conditions, choosing to wait for better settlement terms in the future. In general, although some who advocate the conflict resolution approach stress its process nature as if independent of the outcome, they underestimate the extent to which the process affects the outcome and is therefore goal dependent.

Judgments about the right time for de-escalation, then, are not simple matters of beliefs about the nature of conflict conditions and the processes for changing them. They are also shaped by the values that would be advanced by one settlement rather than another. Time-frame judgments, then, are inseparable from conflict goals and moral concerns, discussed later in this chapter.

Statism

Most officials engaged in the conduct of international conflict use the language of the statist approach, emphasizing the role of coercion and military force. The Egyptian-Syrian attack on Israel in 1973, for example, and the oil embargo by OPEC were viewed by many Arabs as a necessary use of coercion to bring Israel to the negotiating table. Another example is the move toward accommodation by the Soviets in the mid-1980s, which Reagan administration officials credit to the U.S. military buildup and their vigorous efforts to counter Soviet influence in regional conflicts.

There is something self-fulfilling in this viewpoint, partly because officials seem to believe and act in those terms. Thus, if leaders believe that an adversary understands only force, then there is no point in seeking an accommodation until the other side can be forced to do so. Many Palestinian leaders, for example, have argued that a settlement with the Israeli government is not possible until the balance of forces has shifted enough to coerce Israelis to settle. They argue they will wait until power relations have changed, observing that the Crusaders were driven out of the Middle East only after two hundred years.

On the whole, however, the statist approach and its emphasis on coercion does not provide a comprehensive explanation of the changes described here. Israel has been the dominant military power for neighboring Arab governments and particularly for Arab Palestinians for the entire period examined here. Yet it has not been able to gain Arab acceptance of its permanence nor its control of the West Bank and Gaza Strip.

Our findings indicate that when accommodations have been made, they have come about through the discovery or creation of mutually acceptable terms of settlement. This was true for the long periods of tacit accommodation between Jordan and Israel and in the moves toward accommodation between Israel and Egypt, beginning with Sadat's presidency.

Similarly, the shift in Soviet policy toward Europe and the United States after 1985 cannot be explained simply by the great coercive strength of the United States. After all, for most of the 1950s and 1960s, the United States was militarily stronger than the USSR than it was in the 1980s. The change in Soviet policy was at least partly due to the achievements of previous steps toward mutual accommodation. New Soviet thinking may also reflect a recognition of a reality that had been hidden by a strict adherence to the traditional statist approach used even by Marxist Soviet leaders.

Populism

Since the populist approach emphasizes what might occur if people thought differently, it seems difficult to test by examining what happened in the past. It might, nevertheless, be assessed by considering what did not happen— why, in certain instances, de-escalation did not occur.[14] Some assessments can be made by considering effective steps toward mutual accommodations and the possible contribution of factors and processes regarded as important by adherents of this approach.

Some of the failures in progress toward a Palestinian-Israeli accommodation are at least partially explicable in terms of the populist approach. For example, the PLO cease-fire policy along Israel's northern border in 1981–82 might have been more effective as a step toward mutual accommodation if it were given enhanced symbolic salience and if a greater public commitment had been made by the PLO.

The increased mutual stereotyping and animosity between Jewish Israelis and Arab Palestinians and the contribution of those factors to the intractability of the Palestinian-Israeli conflict are also consistent with the populist approach. The lack of equalitarian interaction and personal bonds and the waging of a long-lasting struggle foster mistrust and dehumanized images, which certainly hamper de-escalation moves.

On the whole, this approach clarifies the continuance of exacerbating policies and relations. It appears less helpful, however, in explaining how adversarial relations eventually change. Appeals to justice and to the importance of human life as reasons for moving toward peace have often been made by official representatives of countries in their addresses to the UN General Assembly and in other forums, albeit with little impact.

Pluralism

The pluralist approach includes two emphases: the global system and the multiplicity of actors in international conflicts. From the cases examined here, much evidence can be cited that is consistent with the latter aspect. Certainly many actors, in addition to state representatives, have been key figures in de-escalation moves in both sets of conflicts. These nonstate actors significantly include transnational organizations, both governmental and nongovernmental. Organizations such as constituent organs of the United Nations, for example, have figured prominently in making suggestions for de-escalating conflicts and in mediating negotiations on peacemaking proposals. Nongovernmental organizations have been important in developing the preconditions for official moves and also for ensuring that the agreements reached endured and led to further accommodations.

Subnational actors are also critical in accounting for the de-escalation of the conflicts discussed. They include opposition parties and many other interest groups within adversary countries and affect the likelihood that initiatives will be undertaken, negotiations conducted, and agreements reached. Sometimes even factional disputes within a ruling government party or coalition can paralyze action. Disagreements, for example, within the Israeli Labor party in the early 1970s inhibited responsiveness to the explorative initiatives of Sadat.[15] An adversary may venture de-escalation efforts because its representatives believe they would be effective in reaching an opponent's constituency. At times, this has seemed to be the impetus for Soviet and PLO moves.

Subnational groups are also important in forming the transnational bridges that foster peace building. The multiplicity of such links in American-Soviet relations provides the basis for growing integration and cooperation. For example, in 1986 the Natural Resources Defense Council (NRDC), a private, U.S. organization, negotiated and signed an agreement with scientists from the Soviet Academy of Science jointly to staff three seismic monitoring stations in the United States and in the Soviet Union, testing verification possibilities for a very low-yield test ban treaty.[16] The relative paucity of nonofficial links between Egyptians and Israelis has limited the expansion of agreements and mutual integration between the two countries.

Useful as the insights from the pluralist approach are, they are often ad hoc and post hoc. They are not systematic and do not explain sources of effective pressure and the direction and strength of response.

Certain components of the conflict resolution approach are particularly useful in accounting for the effectiveness of various peacemaking efforts, including its emphasis on: the relevance of noncoercive inducements in effecting de-escalation movement; partial settlements as part of a longer chain of confidence-building agreements, perhaps leading to a comprehensive resolution; and the multiplicity of actors and issues and hence the multiplicity of conflicts and their interlocking character. At the same time, the limitations of the statist approach in accounting for de-escalation and conflict transformation have been made evident.

Implications of Policy Making

The de-escalation efforts examined and the comparative usefulness of different theoretical approaches in accounting for their successes suggest general guides for those parties wishing to pursue a de-escalation policy. These guides can be sharpened by considering in turn the analyses of conflicts, value issues, and choices of strategies.

Analyzing the Conflict

Those choosing a de-escalation strategy should carefully analyze the particular conflict in its global context, the relations between adversaries, and the domestic conditions that may impel or constrain the adversaries.

The global context includes an assessment of the course of the many other conflicts in which the primary adversaries in the focal conflict are engaged. Particularly pertinent are increases in the intensity of other disputes that could help to reduce the intensity of the focal conflict.

The availability of possible intermediaries is another important aspect of an international context. Which parties might serve as effective mediators depends on the nature of the conflict, its progress toward solution, and the global structure at a given historical point. For example, the United Nations has been able to play very different roles in peacemaking and peacekeeping in different periods. In its early years, the United States in many ways dominated the United Nations; with the entrance of dozens of newly independent countries, U.S. organizational dominance was considerably reduced, and the cold war further stalemated UN actions. With the end of the cold war, the United Nations is taking on a much more important role than it has played for decades.

Many domestic conditions are relevant in deciding when to initiate, pursue, terminate, or complete a de-escalation effort. An opportunity to initiate an accommodative move is the advent of new leadership in an adversary country. Initiatives are especially likely to be reciprocated insofar as they help a new leader to satisfy domestic challenges, which often include constituency weariness of a struggle and its burdens.

A comprehensive analysis by those undertaking de-escalation efforts should include consideration of the issues in contention, those diverse actors with a stake in the conflict, and the conflict's stage of development. Even those actors with a major stake in the conflict should be examined for their varying engagement in the fight. In the Arab-Israeli conflict, for example, the ruling family of Jordan has always had an important stake in the conflict but has varied from period to period in its degree of engagement. General relations between adversaries are multidimensional, so the issues are likewise manifold. Moreover, since conflicts are rarely fully resolved, past settlements leave legacies of contention to complicate conflict resolutions. Despite the multiplicity of issues in a conflict, each adversary is likely to select a few as central to the dispute; both may not agree, however, on which are primary issues.[17] Problems in contention vary in many other ways: they may be matters of greater or lesser salience, or they may involve material or value differences.

Finally, an analysis of a conflict should consider its stage of development at the time de-escalation is pursued. For example, a conflict, framed as it is by principal adversaries, may have only a brief history or may have gone on for years and appear intractable to many of its participants. During its life course, a conflict may be said to be escalating in extent and intensity, in a crisis stage, at a stalemate, or undergoing a kind of self-generating de-escalation.

Values

At the outset of the book, I pointed out that peacemaking may not always be valued highly, depending on other priorities. Moral concerns figure in peace making policies. The desirability of constructing peace according to a particular plan depends on who's values would be enhanced by de-escalation and who would benefit from a delay for a different outcome. The answers to such questions are likely to be debated by the partisans of every fight. The Arabs and particularly Palestinians continue to disagree among themselves about the advisability of having rejected settlement proposals, including the 1947 UN partition plan and accepting a transitional stage that would have provided for Palestinian autonomy for on the West Bank and Gaza during the 1980s.[18] I have not provided a hierarchy of values to guide decisions on morally right de-escalation and accommodation. I do offer four general considerations.

First, the history embodied in the U.S.-USSR and Arab-Israeli conflicts suggests that the cost of using organized violence is high. Partisans often discount costs because they believe that the threat of violence will make actual employment unnecessary. But even the burden of preparing to use a credible force is immense, evident for the USSR and the United States throughout the cold war. Moreover, once having threatened to use military force, employment sometimes seems inescapable, if only to maintain credibility. Having developed a capability to engage effectively in armed struggle, the use of military means is more likely, even in dubious circumstances.[19]

The lesson, it seems, is to develop nonviolent means of struggle as alternatives or supplements to war-making capabilities. These include the use of nonviolent coercion such as sanctions, boycotts, and civilian-based resistance. They also include making credible offers of benefits if agreements are reached. Nonviolent means include agreed-upon rules and procedures for dispute settlement and developing bonds of mutual dependence and networks of interpersonal relations.

Second, peacemaking efforts should be viewed comprehensively, even if only incremental steps seem advisable in the short term. Minimally, this means that the interests of all adversaries should be seriously considered. The dehumanization of an enemy, usually associated with the use of violence, certainly impedes such considerations.[20] Remembering the humanity of the enemy should effectively limit the worst aspects of the conflict. Had the demonization of the enemy in the Arab-Israeli conflict and in the cold war been avoided, the conflicts would probably have been resolved earlier.

The interests of all those with a stake in a conflict should be represented or at least acknowledged, including later generations and those segments of the contending populations not effectively part of the policy making elite groups. The settlement is then more likely to be enduring and mutually beneficial.

Third, given the inevitable uncertainty about the future and particularly the consequences of an armed struggle, possible future benefits should not be used to minimize contemporary costs. Asking the present generation to make great sacrifices for the good of future generations is almost certain to result in widespread pain and failure to win the desired peace in the future. These observations suggest that partial settlements reached relatively early in a fight are worth making. They reduce the pain of present-day hurts and are often the first steps to a more comprehensive settlement and peaceful relations.

Fourth, adversaries are well advised to avoid hubris. As the Greeks observed a long time ago, men who are successful may become so proud that they challenge the gods and then fall. The hubris that emboldens such men carries them to failure. Often, we can see it when international players with great power overreach as they seek to build on that power. It is advisable to be modest, even when current victories beckon us to further ones.

Choosing a Strategy

In constructing a strategy for de-escalating a conflict, the essential choices are what issues, parties, and inducements should be involved.

Issues The cases analyzed here indicate that particular kinds of issues are appropriate for effective de-escalation strategies under varying conditions. For example, relatively peripheral issues should be selected at the early stages of a de-escalation movement; minor issues should be framed separately and only later, when the conflict is de-escalating, linked to larger contentions. Attention to peripheral and discrete issues when conflicts are at an intense confrontational stage is useful for discovering whether an adversary is amenable to resolution.

Issues also vary in content and are differentially suitable for de-escalation movement, depending on the nature of the conflict and the relations among adversaries. For example, the attention to arms control in U.S.-USSR relations was often appropriate because the arms race was a shared problem and because there were many possibilities for settlements that had no substantive effect on the military strength of either side.[21]

To build peaceful relations between former adversaries, agreements should be sought on issues that can create vested interests in continuing cooperative interactions. Often peripheral and unlinked issues, although amenable to settlement, do not produce further de-escalation movement. They lack high drama and symbolic significance. For example, in U.S.-USSR relations, agreements on fishing rights have had little diffuse effect. A concerted campaign to endow them initially with symbolic importance could have been ventured; instead an opportunity to build popular good will was lost.

Parties   To choose parties for de-escalation effectively, two questions must be answered. First, among those with a major interest in a conflict, should only the most amenable to settlement be engaged, all major adversaries, or should only those who could prevent a settlement if excluded be part of the de-escalation effort? Second, should parties without a major interest in the conflict's outcome be included to play intermediary roles?

In answering the first question, considerations of fairness and justice cannot be avoided. If parties with important claims in a conflict are excluded from de-escalation moves, their interests are likely to be damaged. The German conquest of Czechoslovakia following the 1938 meetings in Munich among the heads of the British, French, German, and Italian governments is a classic case. Most Arab government heads said the same thing about the fate of the PLO in Lebanon, following the Egyptian-Israeli peace treaty mediated by the U.S. government.

Conversely, de-escalation often requires ignoring or minimizing the claims of parties with vital interests in a conflict. For example, the quick settlement of the Cuban missile crisis in 1962 required shunting aside Cuban assertions of its interests. Obviously, who is party to a de-escalation movement will shape the nature of the settlement. Hence, the choice of who to include in the efforts cannot be made without taking into account the kind of settlement one seeks, since it involves values as well as beliefs.

The inclusion of intermediaries, especially those assuming the role of mediator, often facilitates reaching and sustaining a de-escalation agreement and gives voice to interested parties not represented directly. This is often the case when the UN secretary general or the representative of another international organization participates in the de-escalation effort.

Aside from these normative considerations, my analysis suggests other guidelines for choosing parties. Intermediaries are particularly important in the early stages of the movement toward de-escalation; they may act as formal mediators, shuttling between parties not yet all willing to meet together. They may also informally provide mediation services in the course of their participation in multilateral conferences. Intermediaries can to some extent represent the interests of parties not directly engaged in a peacemaking effort. For example, the U.S. government, in its role as mediator during the Camp David negotiations between the Israeli and Egyptian delegations, to some degree represented the Palestinians. Its efforts to bring about a comprehensive peace were the manifestation of that representation.

A thorny issue in determining which party is to be represented in de-escalation efforts is the role of the many components of each major party. Judgments have to be made by each party at the negotiating table about the strength of the constituency support the representatives enjoy. Agreements reached that lack support from important constituency groups may never be ratified or implemented. For example, Arafat and the commitments of the PLO leadership have sometimes been undercut by elements of their constituency. External parties can also prevent agreements from being concluded or implemented. Often, especially in the Middle East, negotiations or pre-negotiations have been disrupted by violent acts directed at civilians. In many cases such actions, widely labeled as terrorism, were political acts intended to disrupt de-escalation movements.

These observations indicate a basic dilemma of peacemaking strategies. If only those willing to settle are involved in a de-escalation effort, the resulting agreement may never be realized. If, however, those who are intransigent but have power to prevent implementation are not involved in the effort, no agreement is likely to be reached or actualized.

To make wise choices of the actors to participate in a peacemaking effort, good information is needed about the capability various parties have to prevent the implementation of an agreement. Consideration should be given to including the most powerful of them in the negotiations, incorporating some of their interests in the de-escalation agreement, or isolating and constraining them from effectively interfering.

Inducements The three kinds of inducements used in waging a conflict—coercion, positive sanctions, and persuasion—are variously combined in every major international effort, often in social modes of interaction, such as wars, multilateral conferences, and bilateral aid programs.

Much attention has been given to the appropriate mixture of positive and negative sanctions, of carrots and sticks, for effective peacemaking. Simply being mean and tough or nice and conciliatory is not effective; these become postures, not policies. Policies should be reasonable, appropriate blends for particular goals. Mixing threats and promises, however, can sometimes undermine the credibility of each. For example, Khrushchev's policies in the 1950s sometimes suffered from this problem. Conciliation can be most effective after establishing an image of firmness.[22] The conciliation, then, must be sustained, particularly at the initial stage of de-escalation.

Persuasion in peacemaking policies is relatively neglected, except in terms of mobilizing constituency support. The mobilization of support, heard by the other side, often seems hostile and threatening. To be convincing, the messages to different audiences should not be too disparate. For example, contradictory signals have been a matter of concern for Israeli officials who have often dismissed PLO peace overtures, pointing out that PLO officials have made different statements in different places.

Persuasive efforts are important because whether an act is regarded as conciliatory or threatening is a matter of interpretation. In making a conciliatory gesture, the symbolic meaning given to it is critical. In Kennedy's American University speech, the recognition of Soviet suffering in World War II, its world power status, and a possible American contribution to maintaining the cold war were included to please the Soviets and to make proposals for a nuclear weapon test ban more credible.[23]

As part of the Soviet proposals in the late 1980s to restructure and reduce military forces in Europe, Soviet officials acknowledged that their past military strategy, designed to advance quickly into Western Europe if attacked, could be viewed in the West as threatening. That attached meaning to their proposals certainly made them more acceptable and serious. Although Western officials have often spoken understandingly of the Soviet fear of invasion, which arises from their history, the possible role of Western military strategy in evoking fears of attack has not been generally acknowledged.

The difficulties in making credible peacemaking overtures between enemies are great, since there are many grounds for misunderstanding.[24] For example, convinced of one's own peace-loving character, the other side's failure to recognize one's good intentions becomes evidence of its duplicity. Consistency between word and deed over an extended period and the use of many avenues of communication are important in penetrating the barriers of hatred and fear that a long-standing conflict engenders. This consistency was achieved by Egyptian leaders between the 1973 war and the 1979 peace treaty with Israel. It was not achieved, however, by either the PLO toward Israel or by Israel toward the PLO.

Persuasion also plays an important role in the long-term transformation of a conflict. A fundamental element in constructing peace is a conception of the relations between adversaries that include many cooperative strands.

This is likely to entail a reframing of the conflict so that shared interests and concerns take on greater prominence than when the conflict was intense.

Applying a Strategy

A peacemaking strategy embodies many stages, from preparing and undertaking initiatives and conducting negotiations to sustaining and enhancing accommodations. Those stages provide the framework for discussing the applications of a peacemaking strategy.

Preparing for Initiatives

Many actions that can be taken to make conditions ready for successful de-escalation efforts. One set of preparatory actions involves nonofficial actors that mobilize constituency support for de-escalation. This effort includes people-to-people diplomacy and informal meetings between individuals and groups from adversary countries. It includes the work of scholars, educators, and journalists who convey information about the parties to the conflict, explaining and interpreting their interests to each other. It includes ongoing transnational organizations in which persons from adversary countries meet and explore common ground.

The mobilization of support for de-escalation moves can also be fostered by constituency pressure. Social movements have helped to bring about such efforts in East–West arms control measures. If such efforts were larger in the United States in the later 1950s, the responsiveness to overtures by new Soviet leaders might have generated more substantial movement than actually occurred.

Another major way of preparing conditions is to involve or exclude certain parties so that primary adversaries will view themselves as relatively equal, or at least neither will expect to dictate the terms of settlement. In the Arab-Israeli conflict, once the United States and the Soviet Union had begun supporting opposing parties, de-escalation was difficult unless facilitated by cooperation between the U.S. and the Soviet governments. Achieving this cooperation was often a problem in Syrian-Israeli and PLO-Israeli de-escalation efforts. The Egyptian government moved toward peace with Israel as it moved out of the Soviet domain of influence.

Finally, another way to prepare for effective de-escalation is to reframe a conflict so that it will appear amenable to de-escalation, for example, by stressing dangers from a common enemy or shared problems. The reframing effort, however, should not be too distant from the reality experienced by principal adversaries. For example, early in the first term of Reagan's administration, Secretary of State Haig visited the major countries in the

Middle East and argued that the Soviet Union was the principal threat facing countries in the region.[25] Such a view could have made allies of the Israeli and conservative Arab governments. The argument, however, was so irrelevant to the reality of the Arab world generally that it failed to be convincing.

Other redefinitions have sometimes been effective. For example, in 1967, U.S. Secretary of Defense McNamara and President Johnson tried to convince Soviet Premier Kosygin, that the development of ABM systems was wasteful of resources as well as destabilizing and hence a burden and danger to both the United States and the USSR. Within a few years, the ABM systems were redefined as a common burden rather than a unilateral advantage.

Since the late 1980s, we have witnessed a radical redefinition of the American-Soviet conflict and of the role of armed forces in that conflict. Many peace movement organizations and research centers, particularly in the Federal Republic of Germany and the United Kingdom, argued that the military establishments in Europe and strategic nuclear weapon systems did not offer real security to anyone. Opposing sides threatened each other, feeding insecurity and a perceived need for more arms. These peace research organizations instead argued that neither side could be secure without the other side being secure, and that defense should not be provocative.[26] These and related ideas were articulated by Gorbachev and became the bases for a transformation of the arms control and arms reduction negotiations of the late 1980s.

Initiating De-escalation Moves

To break through long-standing mistrust, unilateral conciliatory gestures are often effective when nothing else will do. Such actions are unnecessary when there already has been considerable movement toward peacemaking. Nor are they necessary when there is a substantial convergence of forces supporting de-escalation; for example, as was the case in 1969 when the movement toward détente got under way.

An initiative is most likely to be effective if an adversary has prepared for it. A surprise may be easily misunderstood as a trick or as sign of weakness. Preparation may be informal and an unofficial sounding out of the other side.[27] It may be conducted by UN officials or by nonofficial mediators and include confidential exploratory discussions. For example, Kennedy's initiatives toward the Soviet Union in 1963 were preceded by official and unofficial discussions, as was Sadat's sudden visit to Jerusalem.

Having engaged in coercive actions against an adversary in the recent past does not bar effective de-escalation initiatives. Having a reputation for being strong is useful, particularly if it is presented in the context of being able to mobilize constituency support for peacemaking. Such a position formed the initial appeal of Nixon for the Soviets, of Kennedy after the Cuban missile crisis, of Begin for Sadat, and of Sadat for the Israeli government.[28]

The failure to exploit opportunities, however, is also notable. After the 1967 six-day triumph of the Israeli military forces, Israel "waited for a phone call" from its defeated foe. That time might have been right for an extended initiative by the Israelis, including explicit overtures, rather than a strategy of implicit understandings with the Kingdom of Jordan.

Reaching Agreements

A formal mediator can often provide vital services in facilitating negotiations and reaching an agreement—witness the contribution made by Carter at Camp David in 1978. Once negotiations are under way, mediation activities by unofficial mediators are generally less effective. The offering of benefits by one side to the other outside negotiations tends to improve the general climate of negotiations. Sometimes offers are clearly linked to progress in the negotiations, as was the case in those conducted in the early years of détente.[29] Likewise, strife between partners tends to hamper negotiations.[30]

Although controlling events outside of the negotiations is of course difficult, policy makers should keep in mind the importance of insulating the negotiations. Crises pose a special challenge; even carefully calibrated actions may unintentionally result in rapid escalations; Kennedy successfully prevented that from happening during the Cuban missile crises by closely monitoring the blockade of Cuba. Even if an untoward event occurs, its impact often can be contained. For example, the Soviets went ahead with the 1972 summit, despite the U.S. bombing of Hanoi. The shooting down of a U-2 espionage plane, however, led to the disruption of the Paris summit; if the U.S. and Soviet leaders had been able to work out a formula to limit the damage of the event, the summit could have proceeded.

To reach an agreement, negotiators must take into account the likelihood of support from their constituency. Sometimes, to ensure domestic support, commitments are made to compensate particular groups that believe they will bear too much of the costs of an agreement. This policy has often been pursued by government officials to gain support for arms control agreements, when commitments were made to domestic interest groups to modernize weapon systems.[31] Such commitments, however, may undermine the potential gains from an agreement and reduce the likelihood that they will constitute a step toward further accommodation.

The nature of constituency support for agreements, then, is often crucial. American public opposition to nuclear weapon testing was strong when the testing was done in the atmosphere, and an agreement to ban atmospheric testing was reached. Public support for a comprehensive test ban has not been as strong; if it had been forceful when an accord was close, for example, during Carter's term, agreement might have been reached, which would have had enduring consequences for limiting nuclear weapons.

Sustaining Agreements

Although certain domestic commitments may undermine an agreement's chances of survival and extension, an accord may help to create vested interests in its vitality. Thus, trade agreements are likely to create vested interests in those agreements among groups that will benefit from the trade. In U.S.-USSR relations during the early years of détente, many in the United States thought that the growth of American-Soviet trade would foster Soviet interest in maintaining good relations by sustaining and extending other agreements. Although it is doubtful that trading had much effect, the trade level was low and does not test the point. For American grain farmers, however, the Soviet export market was significant. Interestingly, Ronald Reagan campaigned for the presidency by attacking Carter for his interruption of grain sales in response to the Soviet invasion of Afghanistan. Consequently, in one of his first acts as president, Reagan sought to recapture a portion of the Soviet market for American farmers.

Agreements that reflect international reality so that signatories find compliance to be in their continuing interest are likely to be maintained. Some agreements restructure the international environment in ways that encourage compliance. For example, the Egyptian-Israeli peace treaty increased Egyptian reliance on the United States, which made Egyptian repudiation or major violations of the treaty appear costly and even dangerous.[32]

Effective peacemaking is an art, but it must rest on a knowledge of the particular conditions of a conflict and the general processes underlying the construction of peace. An abstract resolve to take a hard line or a soft line is not likely to be effective; the policies pursued must be appropriate to the specific conditions in which they are being undertaken.

In the cases examined, peace appears to be constructed incrementally, while efforts at a comprehensive resolution within a short time period are prone to failure. The good news is that even little steps can move parties toward peace. Peacemaking is a constant task, since new strife is likely to erupt even as an old fight is being settled. A consistent, long-term effort is needed.

Peace is not a condition to be achieved once and for all in which conflict ceases. We can try to develop processes that will mitigate the worst consequences of a conflict, which often means recognizing and accommodating an external reality—even if that requires settling for less. Conflicts become intractable and more and more difficult to resolve satisfactorily if the dominant party seeks to take advantage of its dominance and overreaches, or if the weaker party struggles on, expecting that someday its chances for victory will improve. Once a conflict has become subject to mutual partial accommodation, the groundwork for cooperative links has been constructed.

Finally, in many aspects of peacemaking, high officials are not the sole or even the fundamental actors. Large-scale social movements, opposition parties, transnational organizations, nonofficial intermediaries, and the electorate at large play significant roles. This is increasingly the case as the world undergoes fundamental democratization. Groups and categories of people that have participated little in policy making are increasingly seeking and gaining a share in making the policies that affect them. The result is often disorder but also greater justice than has prevailed in the past.

Epilogue:
The War in the Gulf

he war in the Persian Gulf and its aftermath provide a test for the ideas explored here. The Iraqi invasion and annexation of Kuwait in August 1990 and the expulsion of Iraq from Kuwait by military action in January and February of 1991 may seem to exemplify traditional power politics: A militarily strong state takes over a small country and then a much bigger power defeats the erstwhile conqueror and imposes its will. Supporters of the realist paradigm in international relations theory appear to be vindicated.

According to the analyses, I have presented in this book, however, that interpretation is at best oversimplified. I now discuss how alternative approaches explain the conflict in the Persian Gulf and the failure to de-escalate it before and after the invasion and during the postwar stages. I do not assume that de-escalation is always good; partisans and observers choose how far they think a conflict should escalate before de-escalation and settlement should be attempted.

Characterizing the Conflict

Responses to an international conflict are based on implicit or explicit theoretical interpretations of the nature of the conflict and its course of development. Adherents of different perspectives are likely to disagree over who the parties to a conflict really are, what the conflict is about, and how it is being waged.

From the realist point of view, the adversaries in the Persian Gulf conflict are states: Iraq, Kuwait, the United States, Saudi Arabia, and others in the region or those with major interests in the region. National interests are relatively clear and fixed. The leaders of each state advanced those interests as far as possible, relying largely on the use or threat of military force.

To some extent, the inadequacy of the statist approach explains the difficulty President George Bush had in articulating the nature of U.S. interest in the fight against Iraq. Bush acted and justified his actions only partly in terms of the realist perspective; he also presumed elements of other orientations. He often decried Iraq's violation of international norms and the tyranny of President Saddam Hussein to rally popular support and to undermine Saddam's claims; this conduct acknowledged the significance of popular opinion and shared understanding. Furthermore, the U.S. administration worked hard to build a coalition and gain UN legitimacy for the struggle against Iraq, again acknowledging the importance of nonstate actors in the conflict.

Bush and his small circle of advisers counted on the transformation in U.S.-USSR relations to make it possible for the United Nations to legitimate the use of force to drive Iraq out of Kuwait. Moreover, they recognized that the Arab-Israeli conflict was not so salient to Arab governments as to prevent them from joining forces with allies of Israel against another Arab government.

Like U.S. leaders, Saddam Hussein also based his strategy significantly on the importance of popular forces. He thought the Arab masses could be mobilized to undermine their governments and sought to bypass those governments by claiming to be the leader of the Arab people in their fight against "Western imperialists, Zionists, and their Arab lackeys." He believed that domestic opposition within the United States would limit George

Bush's willingness and ability to wage armed conflict. Finally, Hussein and his advisers apparently did not recognize the implications of the transformation in U.S.-USSR relations and overestimated the primacy of the Arab-Israeli conflict.

The protagonists in the conflict, then, were not simply states relying on coercive military strength. Government leaders acted as if they recognized that the norms, identities, and beliefs of people in each society were important; they exploited whatever international institutions and sentiments they thought would help their goals. The way these nonstate actors conducted themselves shaped the course of the conflict, including the war's aftermath.

The Conflict before Iraq Invaded Kuwait

To set the starting date of a conflict, or even of a crisis, is not an easy matter. Every partisan is likely to choose a starting time appropriate to its own purposes. In the United States there is a tendency to say that the crisis erupted on 2 August 1990. Iraqi officials and their supporters refer to prior difficulties with the Kuwaiti government. They sometimes refer to the end of World War I and the laying out of borders by the British. Although much is still in dispute about what happened during the several months preceding the Iraqi invasion, it is possible to examine alternative explanations for the conflict's escalation and speculate about what might have inhibited that escalation.

Even before the end of the Iraq-Iran war in August 1988, Iraqi officials made claims against Kuwait relating to the border between them and to access to the Gulf.[1] Shortly after the end of the war, Iraq's demands on Kuwait and other states in the Gulf increased: Iraq accused Kuwait and the United Arab Emirates of overproducing OPEC quotas, charged that Kuwait was drawing excess oil from the Rumaila field, which lies in Iraq and Kuwait, and demanded that Kuwait forgive the loans it made to support the Iraqi war effort against Iran.

Clear signs of an emerging Iraq-Kuwait crisis began to appear in February 1990, as Iraqi verbal attacks against the United States and Israel, as well as Kuwait, intensified. On 19 February, at the Arab Cooperation Council (ACC) meeting in Baghdad, Saddam demanded the withdrawal of U.S. ships from the Persian Gulf. At a subsequent summit meeting of the ACC on 24 February, he privately made it clear that he wanted more money from the Gulf States and would take it if it were not given to him.

In March, Iraq convicted and quickly executed a British journalist for spying. On 2 April, Saddam made a speech asserting that Iraq possessed binary chemical weapons and threatened, "We will make fire eat up half of Israel if it tries anything against Iraq." In late May, at the Arab League meeting in Baghdad, he called for the Arab liberation of Jerusalem and said he wanted $27 billion from Kuwait alone.

After an Iraqi official visited Kuwait and other sheikdoms, pressing them not to exceed their OPEC-determined production quotas, Gulf oil ministers met on 10 July in Jiddah, Saudi Arabia, to determine a response. Kuwait and the UAE, under pressure, agreed to adhere strictly to their quotas. It seemed to many observers that the crisis had been resolved with Iraq serving as the enforcer of OPEC rules. But Iraqi military forces near Kuwait were increased, not decreased.

The U.S. administration during and after the Iraqi war against Iran sought to improve relations with Iraq in spite of congressional debates about imposing sanctions against it because of its use of chemical weapons against its Kurdish citizens. Even amid growing Iraqi threats, U.S. government statements and actions were ambiguous.[2] For example, on 15 February, the Voice of America (VOA) editorialized in support of popular revolts against dictatorial regimes and was critical of secret police in several countries, including Iraq. In response to Hussein's protests, the U.S. State Department began to review all VOA editorials before they were broadcast.

There were signs of warnings to Iraq over its threats; for example, the U.S. government sold two KC-135 aerial-refueling tankers to Kuwait and on 24 July announced the sale and joint military maneuvers with the UAE in the Persian Gulf.[3] The next day, U.S. ambassador April Glaspie was called to meet with Hussein. What transpired at the meeting remains in dispute; certainly Hussein did not infer that the U.S. government would wage a devastating war against Iraq to protect Kuwaiti independence. On 31 July, U.S. Assistant Secretary of State John Kelly testified at a congressional hearing and affirmed that the U.S. position was to do "all we can to support our friends when they are threatened and to preserve stability."[4] In answer to a question, he agreed that the United States did not have any defense treaty with any Gulf country.

The Realist Interpretation

According to the statist view, the escalation that occurred was intentional. Saddam Hussein calculated that he could rapidly occupy Kuwait and create a new situation that would be difficult to change. The gains would be great: Iraqi debts to Kuwait would be eliminated, additional petroleum resources would be gained, the ability to affect oil prices would be greatly increased, and Iraqi influence in the region would be enhanced. The costs were not likely to be great since the risks of large-scale U.S. military intervention were small, since it necessarily depended on the cooperation of other Arab governments against a fellow Arab country.

The realist perspective would further explain the escalation as a result of the failure of Kuwait to build a counterforce to deter aggression and of the United States and other powers to present a credible deterrence. Escalation, then, was the result of inadequate information and understanding by all of the primary adversaries. Such miscalculation, however, by the principals raises doubt about the adequacy of the realist paradigm, which must explain the miscalculations in order to be adequate.

Admittedly, there is an alternative cynical interpretation: that the U.S. policy was successful, that it was intended to induce Saddam to attack, which would then be an excuse to destroy him. There are indications that the United States encouraged Kuwait to refuse Hussein's demands and hinted to him that the United States would not interfere with an Iraqi military action. It may well be that many U.S. officials expected Iraqi forces to take over small areas of Kuwait, perhaps the two unoccupied offshore islands and the land over the Rumaila oil field. The annexation of the whole of Kuwait apparently was not expected, as indicated by the lack of U.S. military readiness to counter the invasion and the absence of warning to the many U.S. and European citizens living and working in Kuwait.

According to this approach, escalation would have been slowed or stopped if Kuwait and the other Gulf States, in alliance with the United States, had taken steps to convince Hussein that any military action by his forces would be overwhelmingly thrown back. The failure of the efforts of the Arab governments in the Persian Gulf to prevent the escalation of an Iraqi attack, according to this perspective, was the result of placating and conciliatory actions.

The Pluralist and Populist Interpretations

According to the pluralist perspective, domestic factors in the societies of adversary countries constitute a major force in shaping foreign policy. The great Iraqi military capabilities and those controlling the military force provided a bureaucratic momentum to use military means to solve problems. According to the populist approach, a longer view is needed. The various cultures and social structures in Iraq, Kuwait, and other countries would have prevented the kind of escalation that occurred if they had been less supportive of authoritarian military regimes. More immediately, if Iraqi popular forces could have effectively reacted against mounting escalation, it might have been prevented.

In this view, the emergence of the crisis resulting in the Iraqi invasion of Kuwait would be explained in large part by the prevailing ways of thinking in the region and the social structures related to those ways of thinking. Thus, rulers can act without seeking public approval, and ruthless violence can exist without loss of legitimacy. In the United States, decisions about managing relations with countries in the Middle East at a pre-crisis stage can be made by a small circle of policy makers. Prevailing popular expectations include the propriety of using military force to conduct international affairs in that region.

Conflict escalation might have been averted if international conditions had been subject to change. For example, Iraqi actions might at least have been slowed if Hussein's appeals to rally support had been undermined, in part by making progress on issues relating to the Palestinians and to the great inequalities in wealth in the region.

The Conflict Resolution Interpretation

In this view, some would emphasize the failure of communication, particularly between the U.S. and Iraqi governments, in accounting for de-escalation failure. Cultural differences between Iraqi and American officials may have contributed to misunderstandings. (Admittedly, however, misunderstandings also occurred among Arab leaders.) In addition, a conflict resolution approach stressing strategic considerations would stress the balance of power among antagonists. In this case a strategic consideration would involve Kuwait's strengthening its coalition in order to negotiate a settlement. Negotiations between Iraq and Kuwait certainly did not follow recommended conflict resolution procedures. Negotiations were burdened by Iraq's threats that denied the vital interests of its opponents. De-escalation negotiations could probably not have been conducted on those terms at that time.

Supportive conditions should have been developed at a prenegotiation stage. Kuwait might have strengthened its bargaining position so that it would have been less vulnerable and tempting a target. Doing this would have meant improving relations with Jordan instead of estranging Jordan, which increased the likelihood of Jordan remaining neutral when Iraq attacked Kuwait. Kuwaiti rulers might also have enhanced Kuwait's legitimacy by giving greater political rights to its residents and citizens.

As an interested party, the U.S. government might also have encouraged Kuwait to be more forthcoming and yet also make clearer its support for the territorial integrity of the country. It might have acted to undercut Hussein's appeals by renewing the dialogue with the PLO, giving it a vested interest in relations with the United States and thus not let Hussein stand as an attractive alternative.

Conflict resolution methods might have been applied if all major actors had objectives that might be so served. Attention must be given to the development of objectives that could be advanced but that might entail consideration of the costs of failing to prevent further escalation of the conflict. Serious explorations regarding general negotiations, however, were lacking at this stage.

Escalation to War

The 2 August 1990 invasion of Kuwait by Iraq constituted a sharp intensification of the conflict, which unleashed further escalation despite peace efforts. The UN Security Council condemned the invasion on the same day. The Arab League, meeting in Cairo at the time of the invasion, debated what to do. King Hussein reported that in conversations with Saddam in Baghdad on 3 August, Saddam had made a commitment to withdraw from most of Kuwait and to discuss other grievances at a meeting in Jiddah on Sunday, 5 August, if the Arab League would agree not to condemn him.[5] Despite these assurances, the Arab League voted on the evening of 3 August to condemn the invasion. President Mubarak of Egypt gives a somewhat different account, reporting that he persuaded King Fahd of Saudi Arabia and others to delay the vote one day if Saddam would "whisper in our ears" that he was willing to withdraw from Kuwait and restore the ruling family. But he recalls that when King Hussein later called, after meeting with Saddam, no such commitment had been discussed.[6]

The U.S. position was initially uncertain, but by 5 August Bush heatedly declared that "this will not stand, this aggression against Kuwait."[7] On 6 August Secretary of Defense Dick Cheney and other U.S. officials presented the case to King Fahd for U.S. military deployment in his country to deter Iraqi aggression. To their surprise, the Saudis immediately invited the deployment. On the same day, the UN Security Council, with U.S. leadership, passed a resolution calling for economic sanctions against Iraq and on 25 August passed a resolution calling on member states to take measures to ensure compliance with the sanctions.

The determination of the U.S. government in its goals and the means needed to attain them quickly became focused. Getting Iraqi forces out of Kuwait and restoring the ruling family was clearly a U.S. and UN objective. In addition, not rewarding aggression was asserted to be an important component in any settlement to prevent Saddam from emerging strengthened in any way; indeed his humiliation and removal as head of the Iraqi government was sought.

The choice between using economic sanctions to contain and then strangulate the Iraqi regime and using military means to force the Iraqis out of Kuwait was discussed by some members of the U.S. administration, Congress, and the public. By October, without laying out the possible consequences of each course of action, Bush had decided that military force would be necessary. On 9 November he announced that a large increase in the U.S. military forces would be brought to the Gulf, signaling that the long stay necessary for the sanctions to work would not be part of U.S. policy. On 29 November, in resolution 678, the Security Council authorized member states cooperating with Kuwait to use all necessary means after 15 January 1991 to enforce previous Council resolutions.

Immediately after the 15 January deadline was passed, an intense air campaign was launched. Then, on 22 February, after a short burst of efforts at de-escalation negotiations, particularly by Gorbachev, Bush issued an ultimatum calling on the Iraqis to begin withdrawal from Kuwait within a day. When that deadline passed, the ground campaign was launched, quickly driving the Iraqi forces from Kuwait.

The Realist Interpretation

An explanation of the failure of de-escalation efforts frequently heard in the United States is that war was unavoidable since Saddam would not have left Kuwait unless forced out. A more sophisticated interpretation is that war was necessary because the U.S.-led coalition wanted to destroy the Iraqi military offensive capability and to humiliate Saddam so that he would be overthrown. War, then, was an appropriate instrument and conciliation was impossible. The U.S. government may have believed that other national interests would be served by taking military action, which would demonstrate resolve and overwhelming military capability.

An alternative interpretation is that it was the realist perspective that was followed by all the leaders of the principal adversaries but that the results were not what they intended. Each side had expected that it could force the other to yield; they were playing chicken, but neither side backed down. Everyone miscalculated.

The Pluralist and Populist Interpretations

Pluralists would stress bureaucratic rigidity within each society involved in the conflict. Policies, particularly military ones, once decided were not easily changed. The centralized nature of the Iraqi system made it particularly vulnerable to this failing. The Iraqi leadership did not take advantage of possible weaknesses in the coalition by making enough concessions credibly enough and early enough to disrupt the coalition. As it was, popular support for Hussein was significant in many Islamic countries, constraining the governments from actively supporting the coalition.

The U.S. government was sensitive to the possibility of divisive concessions and made it difficult for Hussein to offer any; it also moved quickly toward a military confrontation to preclude the weakening of the coalition. The views of vital coalition partners had to be given considerable weight, and the United States made compensatory commitments to keep the coalition together. Such considerations reduce the preeminence of a realist interpretation of escalating events.

Pluralists, giving relatively great weight to domestic forces and economic interests, would consider economic sanctions as potentially effective. They would have been more likely than traditional realist-based analysts to believe that an embargo against Iraq would, given time, have gained Iraqi withdrawal from Kuwait.

The end of the cold war was critical for combating the Iraqi invasion of Kuwait. With Soviet interest in cooperation with the West being great, the Security Council could act with little worry of vetoes; the large U.S. military forces in Europe were available and could be moved without exposing the United States or Europe to Soviet threat. Populist views add other insights. Personal factors contributed to the failure to limit or reverse escalation. Mubarak and Fahd had been personally assured by Saddam that Kuwait would not be invaded, so they felt deceived, as did Bush. Anger and resentment at the perceived duplicity of Saddam contributed to mistrusting any of his promises.

Certainly there was a great deal of popular attention to the crisis in the Gulf throughout the world. Large demonstrations were held in North Africa opposing the coalition. But within the coalition countries themselves, popular opposition was weak, except perhaps in Germany. Within the United States, public support for the president's policies was strong for economic sanctions and somewhat divided over the decision to begin military action. Once that decision was taken though, the mobilization of support was immense. Within Iraq, opposition to Iraqi policy was effectively suppressed and American appeals for Iraqis to overthrow Saddam were without effect.

The Conflict Resolution Interpretation

A negotiated settlement might well have been reached without waging a war. The question must be what would the terms of such a settlement likely have been and what would the consequences of a settlement so reached be compared to the results of a war. Many U.S. officials, in the administration and in the Congress, argued that continued sanctions would bring about an acceptable settlement, with less risk, lower costs, and better long-run consequences than would war.

The conflict resolution approach emphasizes considering the interests of all the adversaries and exploring the possibility of finding mutually acceptable settlements. Many suggestions were made by advocates of conflict resolution methods in the form of private and public communications. For example, many letters and op-ed articles were written and published in newspapers all over the United States; the suggestions generally included giving something, at least a face-saving option, to Saddam.[8]

Actually, mediation efforts themselves were limited. The UN secretary general, bound by Security Council resolutions, could not serve in a mediator role, nor did the U.S. government's stance allow any possibility for mediation or even negotiations. Saddam hinted at a possible negotiated settlement but did not offer them in a way that lent credibility, even to coalition members that might have been less adamant than the U.S. government.

If intermediaries had been allowed room for maneuver before the large augmentation of U.S. military forces in November 1990, before starting the air campaign in January 1991, or before launching the ground war in February 1991, those escalating moves might have been interrupted. Some of the adversaries' goals might have been so advanced, but for those goals that entailed the denial of vital matters to the opponent, the conflict resolution approach would not have been effective.

Conflict resolution advocates may have seemed unrealistic or even naive because primary adversaries were not seeking a settlement achievable by negotiation under the circumstances. The coalition leaders wanted to restore Kuwait's independence, but there were clear, if less openly expressed, additional goals: the destruction of Iraq's offensive military capability and the replacement of Hussein with a more compliant Iraqi leader. For the Iraqi government, these were clearly nonnegotiable issues.

From the conflict resolution perspective, considerable thought should have been given to the consequences of seeking goals that required such extreme means as war. Such attention would have indicated that government leaders of the principal adversaries were perhaps being unrealistic about what they could achieve in risking and then waging war. Enough people reaching this conclusion in any of the principal adversary countries might have changed the objectives, and the leaders would then seek instead what could be attained by acceptable means.

Postwar Peace Building

The war ended with what seemed a total victory, but it stopped short of militarily overthrowing Hussein or even completing the destruction of Iraqi military forces. Reverberations of the war will continue for years, but I will make an interim assessment in noting what the war has wrought and in speculating about the future.

Realist Interpretation

Most U.S. officials and politicians have argued that the war was vindicated. As difficulties in postwar Iraq and the Middle East mount, several critics argue that a less violent course would have been more successful. A negotiated withdrawal of Saddam's army from Kuwait, after a very long embargo, might have given time for other social processes to emerge within Iraq and would have been less convulsive for the region. Saddam Hussein may always believe that given the options he had in the fall of 1990, the course he chose was the best one for him. For the Iraqi people, of course, other options were preferable. Future arrangements in the region, according to the realist approach, will be based on military security and official relations. The major collective action will be to limit the military capability of Iraq.

Undoubtedly, the war has created some new conditions that provide new opportunities as well as constraints for taking steps toward peace in the Middle East. Following a realist approach, the victors will have considerable weight in the direction that any peacemaking moves take. Iraqi military strength will be limited and the role of the PLO more circumscribed as support for it is lessened. Nevertheless, even government officials assuming a statist approach adopt elements of other perspectives. Normative claims about international law and human rights, ethnic loyalties, and economic interests also influence policy making. Rhetoric aside, the peace that the U.S. government seeks in the region will not involve any fundamental changes; it will seek the reestablishment of conditions before the war, but with a nonthreatening Iraq.

Pluralist and Populist Interpretations

The pluralist and populist orientations attend to economic and social factors. The economic havoc resulting from the Iraqi invasion and the subsequent war have exacerbated already deteriorating economic conditions in the region.[9] The disruption of petroleum production affects not only Kuwait and Iraq but also the many countries whose citizens were employed there. It will take many years and immense sums of money to rebuild and restore the area. Deteriorating social conditions may well contribute to the destabilization of many of the regimes in region.

These approaches also focus on many nongovernmental actors. Despite realist orientations, officials will be obliged to consider nongovernmental parties seriously. Ethnic and religious identities are important bases for organization, as the persistent struggles by Palestinians, Kurds, and other peoples demonstrate.

Attention to these perspectives would foster societal changes, encouraging domestic movements toward democratization and increased ethnic autonomy. The multiple issues in contention in the region should become the basis for trade-offs in settlements. New social and political structures constitute, better than old forms, the complexity of reality in the Middle East. Thus, sovereignty may be divided in many ways, so that people may deal separately with national governments, regional authorities, and transnational organizations on such matters as military protection, water rights, and economic development.

Conflict Resolution Interpretation
A negotiated settlement, with the use of mediators and supplementary diplomacy, might have realized much of the same goals but at much less cost in human lives, environmental damage, and the standard of living for millions. The end of the cold war exemplifies these possibilities. The initially slow movement toward accommodation between the United States and the Soviet Union gradually gained momentum and, despite some regression, produced a full-scale transformation in the East and, with that, a dissolution of the conflict between the East and West.

The use of conflict resolution methods before the war would not have yielded the results that the war did. Insofar as major policy makers wanted the circumstances the war produced, they would regard the theories they applied as vindicated. What they wanted, however, had much to do with domestic matters and were not merely a means to achieve specific foreign policy goals. In the United States, for example, exorcising the ghost of Vietnam and justifying military expenditures (though explained on other grounds) were also important results. The goals that could have been attained by a greater reliance on conflict resolution methods might well have been the more desirable.

Such methods should be particularly relevant in the postwar stage. The application of a conflict resolution perspective would involve many parties—official and nonofficial—in preparing for negotiations. The great number of issues among the many parties in the region represent concurrent, interlocked conflicts. What may at first be seen as a gridlock may, upon analysis, be seen as an opportunity for trade-offs and maximizing mutual benefit.

National security is not defined only in terms of the military defense of borders. It must take into account economic inequalities among groups, cultural and social autonomy, personal safety, the general economic standard of living, and control over land, water, and petroleum resources.

It is important to be creative and innovative in discovering ways to construct elements of peace and mutually beneficial agreements that can then be built upon. One might envisage transnational water authorities helping to allocate water and increase the benefit for all. Peace building is a continuous process, not to be won by defeating an evil enemy in a single stroke. As war recedes into the past, the extent to which a region remains unchanged becomes manifest and the benefits of violence more illusory. So far there has been no transformation of any society nor of the relations between societies. Without such changes toward democratization and reconciliation, major moves toward mutual accommodation are unlikely to occur soon.

A few points emerge from this brief survey. First, the realist perspective is inadequate as an explanation of actual developments; as a policy guide, it is counterproductive. Military force produces large effects, but these effects are generally diffuse, often unintended, and in many regards disastrous. Even when used with overwhelming success, as in the war against Iraq, it does not achieve many goals. For the loser, obviously, the resort to armed force appears as a great error, though the pride in defeat by overwhelming force should not be underestimated. The destabilizing forces unleashed by war may also, in the longer run, produce the results the losers sought. Even when conflict is waged by immensely stronger parties assuming a realist perspective, the final outcome may not be much more to their liking than it would have been had they taken into account the interests of the adversaries and not resorted to violence.

Second, other approaches are not wholly adequate either. The conflict resolution approach adds important insights—and therefore provides useful guides for action—including that conflicts are resolved only over a long period of time, that mutually satisfactory outcomes are possible, that mediation can be facilitative, and that Track II and supplementary diplomacy can be useful. The conflict resolution approach, if narrowly conceived, limits applicability to only the escalation and crisis stages of conflicts. However, more broadly conceived, its ideas are relevant to prenegotiations, including fostering conditions that would make de-escalation efforts feasible.

Third, conflicts are messy. They do not have neat beginnings and endings, and rarely do any of the parties get what they originally wanted. In the long run, even clear victories turn out to have great costs for the victors. We lack good social theory and enough relevant information to form reasonably accurate expectations about the future.

Finally, values greatly affect policy choices. People may differ on something as basic as how much weight should be given to the number of humans killed in war, to the damage to environment, to the disruption of families, and to the continued oppression of one people by another. The values we hold even affect our agreement over various explanatory theories. For example, which actors should be included for explanatory purposes is not independent of who we think should be included for moral reasons. Moral judgments depend on the identity we assume—whether individual, group, party, nationality, or even those more inclusive.

From a broad human perspective, the escalation of the conflict in the Persian Gulf into a war was regrettable. The Iraqi government leaders and many others missed opportunities to prevent escalation and to satisfy the interests of many adversaries. The analysis undertaken in this book should serve to broaden the range of alternatives considered in waging struggles and to lengthen the time we take in seeking peace, justice, and freedom.

Notes

Chapter 1   The Quest for Peace

1. Richard E. Neustadt and Ernest R. May, *Thinking in Time: The Uses of History for Decision-Makers* (New York: Free Press, 1986); H. R. Alker, Jr., J. Bennett, and D. Meffer, "Generalized Precedent Logics for Resolving Insecurity Dilemmas," *International Interactions* 7 (1980): 165–200; Davis B. Bobrow, "Stories Remembered and Forgotten," *Journal of Conflict Resolution* 33 (June 1989): 187–209.

2. See, e.g., Joan V. Bondurant, *Conquest for Violence: The Gandhian Philosophy of Conflict*, rev. ed. (Berkeley: University of California Press, 1965); Birgit Brock-Utne, *Educating for Peace: A Feminist Perspective* (New York: Pergamon, 1985); K. J. Holsti, *International Politics*, 4th ed. (Englewood Cliffs, N.J.: Prentice Hall, 1983); Mark Macy, ed., *Solutions for a Troubled World*, vol. 1, Peace Series (Boulder, Colo.: Earthview); and Carolyn Stephenson, ed., *Alternative Methods for International Security* (Washington, D.C.: University Press of America, 1982).

3. Charles W. Kegley, Jr., and Eugene R. Wittkopf, eds., *The Nuclear Reader* (New York: St. Martin's, 1985), 47.

4. There are several works on war endings, e.g., Robert F. Randle, *The Origins of Peace: A Study of Peacemaking and the Structure of Peace Settlements* (New York: Free Press, 1973). There are also several works on preventing wars, e.g., Karl Deutsch et al., *Political Community and the North Atlantic Area* (Princeton: Princeton University Press, 1957); and Dietrich Fischer, *Preventing War in the Nuclear Age* (Totowa, N.J.: Rowman & Allanheld, 1984). Particularly lacking are systematic analyses of how international antagonisms are lessened and movement toward reduced tensions made.

5. Cyrus Vance, *Hard Choices* (New York: Simon and Schuster, 1983), 20.

6. Albert L. Weeks, *The Troubled Detente* (New York: New York University Press, 1976); and Richard Pipes, *U.S.-Soviet Relations in the Era of Détente* (Boulder, Colo.: Westview, 1981).

7. See Graham T. Allison, *Essence of Decision* (Boston: Little, Brown, 1971); Hans J. Morgenthau, *Politics among Nations* (New York: Knopf, 1962); and Edward Hallett Carr, *The Twenty Years' Crisis, 1919–1939,* 2d ed. (New York: St. Martin's, 1954).

8. See, e.g., C. Wright Mills, *The Causes of World War III* (New York: Simon and Schuster, 1958), 82.

9. Inis L. Claude, Jr., *Swords into Plowshares,* 4th ed. (New York: Random House, 1971); Ray Maghroori and Bennett Ramberg, eds., *Globalism Versus Realism: International Relations' Third Debate* (Boulder, Colo.: Westview, 1982); and John W. Burton, *World Society* (Cambridge: Cambridge University Press, 1972).

10. See, e.g., Stephenson, *International Security;* Robert C. Johanson, *The National Interest and the Human Interest* (Princeton: Princeton University Press, 1980); and Johann Galtung, *The True Worlds* (New York: Free Press, 1980).

11. Robert Jervis, *Perception and Misperception in International Relations* (Princeton: Princeton University Press, 1976); and Irving L. Janis, *Victims of Groupthink* (Boston: Houghton Mifflin, 1972).

12. Betty A. Reardon, *Sexism and the War System* (New York: Teachers College Press, 1985); Carol Cohn, "Slick'ems, Glick'ems, Christmas Trees, and Cookie Cutters: Nuclear Language and How We Learned to Pat the Bomb," *Bulletin of the Atomic Scientists* 43 (June 1987): 17–24; Diana E. H. Russell, ed., *Exposing Nuclear Phallacies* (Elmsford, N.Y.: Pergamon, 1989); Birgit Brock-Utne, *Educating for Peace: A Feminist Perspective;* and Terrell Northrup, "Women's and Men's Conceptualizations of War, Peace, and Security: Two Realities" (Program on the Analysis and Resolution of Conflicts, Syracuse, N.Y., April 1987, Working Paper 3, photocopied).

13. Immanuel Wallerstein, *The Modern World System II* (New York: Academic Press, 1980); Fernando Henrique Cardoso and Enzo Faletto *Dependency and Development in Latin America* (Los Angeles: University of California Press, 1979); Harry Magdoff, *The Age of Imperialism* (New York: Monthly Review Press, 1969); Robert O. Keohane and Joseph S. Nye, Jr., *Power and Interdependence: World Politics in Transition* (Cambridge: Harvard University Press, 1977).

14. Allison, *Essence of Decision;* and Morton H. Halperin, *Bureaucratic Politics and Foreign Policy* (Washington, D.C.: Brookings Institution, 1974).

15. D. Marie Provine, *Settlement Strategies for Federal District Judges* (Washington, D.C.: Federal Judicial Center, 1986); and Peter S. Adler, "Is ADR a Social Movement?" *Negotiation Journal* 3 (January 1987): 59–71.

16. Louis Kriesberg, "Interlocking Conflicts in the Middle East," *Research in Social Movements, Conflicts and Change* 3 (1980): 99–119.

17. John W. Burton, *Conflict: Resolution and Provention* (New York: St. Martin's, 1990).

18. Arnold Lewis, "The Peace Ritual and Israeli Images of Social Order," *Journal of Conflict Resolution* 23 (1979): 688.

19. Oran Young, "International Regimes: Problems of Concept Formation," *World Politics* (April 1980): 331–36; and Obert O. Keohane and Joseph S. Nye, Jr., "Complex

Interdependence, Transnational Relations, and Realism: Alternative Perspectives on World Politics," in *The Global Agenda*, ed. Charles W. Kegley, Jr., and Eugene R. Wittkopf (New York: Random House, 1988), 257–71.

20. For example, see Joshua S. Goldstein and John R. Freeman, *Three-Way Street: Strategic Reciprocity in World Politics* (Chicago: University of Chicago Press, 1990).

21. Louis Kriesberg, *Social Conflicts*, 2d ed. (Englewood Cliffs, N.J.: Prentice Hall, 1982); also see Morton Deutsch, *The Resolution of Conflict: Constructive and Destructive Processes* (New Haven, Conn.: Yale University Press, 1973); William A. Gamson, *Power and Discontent* (Homewood, Ill.: Dorsey Press, 1968; and Ralph H. Turner, "Determinants of Social Movement Strategies," in *Human Nature and Collective Behavior: Papers in Honor of Herbert Blumer*, ed. Tamotsu Shibutani (Englewood Cliffs, N.J.: Prentice Hall, 1970).

22. Louis Kriesberg, "Social Theory and the De-Escalation of International Conflicts," *Sociological Review* 32 (August 1984): 471–91.

23. Kriesberg, "Interlocking Conflicts"; Yair Evron and Yaacov Bar Simantov, "Coalitions in the Arab World," *The Jerusalem Journal of International Relations* 1 (2) (Winter 1975).

24. The argument about falling dominos was made about Southeast Asia and the importance of keeping South Vietnam from "falling to the Communists." See, e.g., David Halberstam, *The Best and the Brightest* (Greenwich, Conn.: Fawcett Publications, 1972). The argument was used more recently in regard to Central America. See, e.g., the testimony of Lt. Col. Oliver L. North at the Iran-contra hearings.

25. Kriesberg, "Interlocking Conflicts."

26. See David J. Singer, "Inter-Nation Influence: A Formal Model," *American Political Science Review* 17 (June 1963): 420–30, and David A. Baldwin, "The Power of Positive Sanctions," *World Politics* 24 (October 1971): 19–38.

27. Jeremy J. Stone, *Strategic Persuasion: Arms Limitation through Dialogue* (New York: Columbia University Press, 1967).

28. *New York Times*, 21 Nov. 1981.

29. The use of carrots as well as sticks is exemplified in many accounts of diplomacy: e.g., Henry Kissinger, *The White House Years* (Boston: Little, Brown, 1979), 1135–36, discusses that on his visit to Moscow, before the 1972 summit meeting, he wanted to gain Soviet help in dealing with the North Vietnamese government. He did not bring rewards to the Soviet government in order to gain that help, but he held out the prospect of a broad improvement in relations with the U.S.

30. Goldstein and Freeman, *Three-Way Street*.

31. See, e.g., Charles E. Osgood, *An Alternative to War or Surrender* (Urbana: University of Illinois Press, 1962); Richard Smoke and Willis Harmon, *Paths to Peace: Exploring the Feasibility of Sustainable Peace*, Institute of Noetic Sciences (Boulder, Colo.: Westview, 1987); and Mark Sommer, *Beyond the Bomb* (Chestnut Hill, Mass.: Expro Press, 1985).

Chapter 2   The U.S.-USSR and Middle East Cases

1. Anwar el-Sadat, *In Search of Identity: An Autobiography* (New York: Harper & Row, 1978), 15.

2. Irving Louis Horowitz, *Three Worlds of Development: The Theory and Practice of*

International Stratification (New York: Oxford University Press, 1966); and V. Kubalkova and A. A. Cruickshank, *International Inequality* (London: Croom Helm, 1981).

3. Wallace E. Lambert and Otto Klineberg, *Children's Views of Foreign Peoples: A Cross-National Study,* Century Psychology Series (New York: Meredith, 1967); and Howard Tolley, *Children and War: Political Socialization to International Conflict* (New York: Teachers Colleges Press, Columbia University, 1973).

4. It has been estimated that only 9 percent of the contemporary states are ethnically homogeneous. For nearly one-third, the largest ethnic group makes up less than half population. See Walker Connor, "Nation-Building or Nation-Destroying?" *World Politics* 24 (April 1972): 319–55.

5. Soviet charges of subversion were made, e.g., by Andrei Gromyko, first vice-chairman of the Council of Ministers of the USSR and Soviet minister of foreign affairs. He said in his report at the 16 June 1983 sessions of the USSR Supreme Soviet: "Hostile actions of a political and economic nature are being taken against the countries of socialism. Ideological subversion is being carried out against them and resort is being made to subversive actions and other actions that are impermissible in the practice of interstate relations. This is seen with particular clarity in the policies of the West in respect to the Polish People's Republic" (Moscow: Novosti Press Agency Publishing House, 1983), 8.

6. Robert O. Keohane and Joseph S. Nye Jr., eds. *Transnational Relations and World Politics* (Cambridge: Harvard University Press, 1972); Raymond Vernon, *Sovreignty at Bay: The Multinational Spread of U.S. Enterprise* (New York: Basic Books, 1971); William M. Evan, *Knowledge and Power in a Global Society* (Beverly Hills, Calif.: Sage, 1981); and Robert C. Angell, *Peace on the March: Transnational Participation* (New York: Van Nostrand Reinhold, 1969). See also, David E. Apter and Louis Wolf Goodman, eds., *The Multinational Corporation and Social Change* (New York: Praeger, 1976); and Louis Kriesberg, "International Nongovernmental Organizations and Transnational Integration," *International Associations* 24 (11) (1972): 520–25.

7. Peter Wolf, "International Social Structure and Resolution of the International Conflicts, 1920–1965," *Research in Social Movements: Conflicts and Change* 1 (Greenwich, Conn.: JAI Press, 1978), 35–60; and Ernst B. Haas, *The United Nations and Collective Management of International Conflict* (New York: United Nations Institute for Training and Research, 1986).

8. Michael J. Pentz and Gillian Stovo, "The Political Significance of Pugwash," in *Knowledge and Power in a Global Society,* ed. William M. Evan (Beverly Hills, Calif.: Sage, 1981), 199. See also, M. S. Voslensky, "The Pugwash Movement," in *Problems of War and Peace,* Academy of Sciences of the USSR, Institute of Philosophy (Moscow: Progress Publishers, 1972), 351–58.

The International Conferences on Science and World Affairs are known as the Pugwash conferences, named for the place in Nova Scotia where the first meeting was held. At the first meeting, in July 1957, the twenty-two participants were nearly all natural scientists; gradually, more social scientists also joined the conferences. Leading scientists from the United States, the Soviet Union, Japan, Great Britain, and other countries now attend. Their combined expertise and stature enable them to discuss many issues—e.g., how to control nuclear weapons and convey information to high government officials.

9. Dan Morgan, *Merchants of Grain* (New York: Viking, 1979).

10. The proportions were calculated based on data from *The World Almanac and Book of Facts 1986*, ed. Harry Hansen (New York: Newspaper Enterprise Association, 1986), 103, 142; and Mark S. Hoffman, ed., *The World Almanac and Book of Facts 1990* (New York: Newspaper Enterprise Association, 1990), 77, 79.

11. Georgi Arbatov, *The War of Ideas in Contemporary International Relations* (Moscow: Progress Publishers, 1973), 10.

12. Ibid., 14.

13. Barry Hughes, *The Domestic Context of American Foreign Policy* (San Francisco: W. H. Freeman, 1978).

14. For example, see the discussions of the military-industrial-political complexes in the United States and USSR: Dieter Senghaas, *Rüstung und Militarismus*, (Frankfurt a.M.: Suhrkamp, 1972); Steven Rosen, ed., *Testing the Theory of the Military-Industrial Complex* (Lexington, Mass.: D. C. Heath, 1973); Egbert Jahn, "Armaments and Bureaucracy in Soviet Society," *Bulletin of Peace Proposals* 10 (1) (1979): 108–15.

15. Quoted in Richard M. Nixon, *Six Crises* (New York: Doubleday, 1963), 62; and Ralph K. White, *Fearful Warriors: A Psychological Profile of U.S.-Soviet Relations* (New York: Free Press).

16. John W. McDonald, Jr., and Diane B. Bendahmane, eds., *Conflict Resolution: Track Two Diplomacy*, U.S. Department of State, Foreign Service Institute (Washington, D.C.: GPO, 1987).

17. *New York Times*, 1 June 1986, sec. A, p. 1. See also John P. Windmuller, *American Labor Movement, 1940–1953* (Ithaca, N.Y.: Institute of International and Labor Relations, 1954); and Jeffrey Harrod, *Trade Union Foreign Policy* (Garden City, N.Y.: Doubleday, 1972).

18. George F. Kennan, *Russia and the West under Lenin and Stalin* (Boston: Little, Brown, 1961), 391.

19. There are many accounts of McCarthyism, e.g., Edward A. Shils, *The Torment of Secrecy* (Glencoe: Free Press, 1956).

20. Joan Peters, *Time Immemorial* (New York: Harper & Row, 1984), 79; and see David Shipler, *Arab and Jew* (New York: Doubleday, 1956).

21. Saul H. Mendlovitz and R. B. J. Walker, eds., *Towards a Just World Peace* (Boston: Butterworths, 1987); Charles Chatfield, *Peace Movements in America* (New York: Schocken Books, 1972); and Malcolm Saunders and Ralph Summy, "One Hundred Years of Australian Peace Movement, 1885–1984," *Peace and Change* 10 (Fall–Winter 1984): 39–75.

22. Morton H. Halperin, "Arms Control: A Twenty-Five Year Perspective," *Journal of the Federation of American Scientists* 36 (June 1983).

23. Samuel Lubell, *The Future of American Politics* (New York: Doubleday, 1956).

24. See Seymour Melman, *The Permanent War Economy: American Capitalism in Decline*, (New York: Simon and Schuster, 1974); and Paul Blumberg, *Inequality in an Age of Decline* (New York: Oxford University Press, 1980).

25. For general accounts of the U.S.-USSR conflict, see Joseph L. Nogee and Robert H. Donaldson, *Soviet Foreign Policy since World War II*, 3d ed. (Elmsford: Pergamon, 1988), 95–96; Raymond L. Garthoff, *Detente and Confrontation* (Washington, D.C.: Brookings Institution, 1985); Walter LeFeber, *America, Russia, and the Cold War, 1945–*

1984 (New York: Knopf, 1985); Nikolai V. Sivachev and Nikolai N. Yakovlev, *Russia and the United States* (Chicago: University of Chicago Press, 1979); and Adam B. Ulam, *The Rivals: America and Russia since World War II* (New York: Viking, 1971). For the Arab-Israeli conflict, see Fred J. Khouri, *The Arab-Israeli Dilemma,* 3d ed. (Syracuse, N.Y.: Syracuse University Press, 1985); Amos Elon, *The Israelis: Founders and Sons* (New York: Holt Rinehart, 1971); Edward Said, *The Question of Palestine* (New York: Vintage, 1980); Charles D. Smith, *Palestine and the Arab-Israeli Conflict* (New York: St. Martin's, 1988).

26. O. Edmund Clubb, *China and Russia* (New York: Columbia University Press, 1971).

27. Glenn H. Snyder and Paul Diesing, *Conflict among Nationals: Bargaining, Decision Making and System Structure in International Crises* (Princeton: Princeton University Press, 1977).

28. *New York Times,* 16 June 1983.

29. The quotations are from a speech to the American Society of Newspaper Editors, *New York Times,* 25 April 1981.

30. Since the Soviet emphasis on peaceful coexistence in relations between socialist and capitalist countries began in the 1950s, references to the struggle between socialism and imperialism and the inevitable triumph of socialism have been muted, but references to the ideological struggle continued into the early 1980s: "And this period is marked by a confrontation of an intensity and acuteness unprecedented in the whole of the post-war period, of two diametrically opposite world outlooks, two political courses—socialism and imperialism. A struggle is in the process for the minds and hearts of billions of people in the world. And the future of mankind depends to no small degree on the outcome of this ideological struggle"—General Secretary Andropov of the Central Committee of the CPSU, 15 June 1983, at a plenary meeting (Yuri V. Andropov, "Analysis of Existing Situations and Landmarks for the Future" [Moscow: Novosti Press Agency Publishing House, 1983], 5–6.) Later in the speech, Andropov restated a long-standing assertion: "Communists are convinced that the future belongs to socialism. Such is the march of history. But this does not mean at all that we are going to engage in the 'Export of Revolution' in interference in the affairs of other countries. . . . We firmly believe that socialism will ultimately prove its advantages precisely in conditions of peaceful competition with capitalism" (p. 29).

31. William A. Gamson and Andre Modigliani, *Untangling the Cold War: A Strategy for Testing Rival Theories* (Boston: Little, Brown, 1971).

32. Mary Kaldor, *The Baroque Arsenal* (New York: Hill and Wang, 1981); Fred Kaplan, *The Wizards of Armageddon* (New York: Simon and Schuster, 1983); and Senghaas, *Rüstung und Militarismus.*

33. Khouri, *Arab-Israeli Dilemma*; Nadav Safran, *From War to War* (New York: Pegasus, 1969); and Charles D. Smith, *Palestine and the Arab-Israeli Conflict* (New York: St. Martin's, 1988).

34. Helena Cobban, *The Palestinian Liberation Organization: People, Power, and Politics* (Cambridge: Cambridge University Press, 1984); William B. Quandt, Fuad Jabber, and Ann Mosely Lesch, *The Politics of Palestine Nationalism* (Los Angeles: University of California Press, 1973).

35. David Hirst and Irene Beeson, *Sadat* (London: Faber and Faber, 1981); and el-Sadat, *In Search of Identity*.

36. Clinton Bailey, *Jordan's Palestinian Challenge, 1948–1983: A Political History* (Boulder, Colo.: Westview, 1984); Arthur R. Day, *East Bank/West Bank: Jordan and the Prospects for Peace* (New York: Council on Foreign Relations, 1986).

Chapter 3   Taking Initiatives

1. In recent years, more attention has been directed to getting parties to the negotiating stage. See, e.g., Janice Gross Stein, *Getting to the Table* (Baltimore: Johns Hopkins University Press, 1989); Harold H. Saunders, *The Other Walls: The Politics of the Arab-Israeli Peace Process* (Washington, D.C.: American Enterprise Institute, 1985); and I. William Zartman, *Ripe for Resolution: Conflict and Intervention in Africa* (New York: Oxford University Press, 1985).

2. Louis Kriesberg, "Peace Movements and Government Efforts," *Research in Social Movements, Conflicts and Change* 10 (Greenwich, Conn.: JAI Press, 1988):57–75; and Charles Chatfield, *Peace Movements in America* (New York: Schocken, 1972).

3. Snyder and Diesing, *Conflict among Nations*.

4. This seems to be particularly true in war ending. There is considerable writing on what finally brings one side to the conclusion that it is defeated—not a simple matter. See, e.g., Frank L. Klingberg, "Predicting the Termination of War: Battle Casualties and Population Losses," *Journal of Conflict Resolution* 10 (June 1966): 129–71.

5. Snyder and Diesing, *Conflict among Nations*.

6. Jacob Berkovitch, *Social Conflicts and Third Parties: Strategies for Conflict Resolution* (Boulder, Colo.: Westview, 1984).

7. See the discussion in *Resolving Disputes between Nations: Coercion or Conciliation*, by Martin Patchen (Durham, N.C.: Duke University Press, 1988); Henry Kissinger, *Years of Upheaval* (Boston: Little, Brown, 1982); and Robert Einhorn, *Negotiating from Strength: Leverage in U.S. Arms Negotiation* (New York: Praeger, 1986).

8. Ralf Dahrendorf, *Class and Class Conflict in Industrial Society* (Stanford, Calif.: Stanford University Press, 1959).

9. Nikolai Lebedev, *The USSR in World Politics* (Moscow: Progress Publishers, 1980); John Lenczowski, *Soviet Perceptions of U.S. Foreign Policy* (Ithaca, N.Y.: Cornell University Press, 1982); and Peter M. E. Volten, *Brezhnev's Peace Program* (Boulder, Colo., 1982).

10. Snyder and Diesing, *Conflict among Nations*.

11. *New York Times*, 18 Sept. 1981, A3; and I. William Zartman and Maureen R. Berman, *The Practical Negotiator* (New Haven: Yale University Press, 1982).

12. Cited in Williams B. Bader, *Austria between East and West, 1945–1955* (Stanford, Calif.: Stanford University Press, 1966), 186–87.

13. Uri Avnery, *My Friend, The Enemy* (Westport, Conn.: Lawrence Hill, 1986), 74; Yehuda Lukacs and Abdalla M. Battah, eds. *The Arab-Israeli Conflict* (Boulder, Colo.: Westview, 1988).

14. Louis Kriesberg, "Strategies of Negotiating Agreements: U.S.-Soviet and Arab-Israeli Cases," *Negotiation Journal* (January 1988): 19–29.

15. Stuart Thorson, "Conceptual Issues," in *Intractable Conflicts and Their Trans-*

formation, ed. Louis Kriesberg, Terrell A. Northrup, and Stuart J. Thorson (Syracuse, N.Y.: Syracuse University Press, 1989).

16. Kriesberg, "Interlocking Conflicts," 99–118.

17. Kriesberg, *Social Conflicts.*

18. Yale Richmond, *U.S.-Soviet Cultural Exchanges, 1958–1986* (Boulder, Colo.: Westview, 1987), 138.

19. Ibid., 135.

20. Jimmy Carter, *Keeping Faith* (New York: Bantam, 1982).

21. Adam Ulam, *Expansion and Coexistence: Soviet Foreign Policy, 1917–73,* 2d ed. (New York: Praeger, 1974); Gordon R. Weihmiller and Dusko Doder, *U.S.-Soviet Summits* (Boston: University Press of America, 1986); Khouri, *Arab-Israeli Dilemma*; and Garthoff, *Detente and Confrontation.*

22. Garthoff, *Detente and Confrontation.*

Chapter 4   Accounting for the Initiatives

1. Barry Hughes, *The Domestic Context of American Foreign Policy* (San Francisco: W. H. Freeman, 1978).

2. Joseph R. Gusfield, "Social Movements and Social Change: Perspectives of Linearity and Fluidity," in *Research in Social Movements, Conflict and Change* 4 (Greenwich, Conn.: JAI Press, 1981): 317–39.

3. Louis Kriesberg, "Peace Movements and Government Efforts," *Research in Social Movements, Conflicts and Change,* 10 (Greenwich, Conn.: JAI Press, 1988): 57–75; and Jo Husbands, "Domestic Factors and De-Escalation Initiatives: Boundaries, Process, and Timing," in *Timing the De-escalation of International Conflicts,* ed. Louis Kriesberg and Stuart Thorson (Syracuse, N.Y.: Syracuse University Press, 1991).

4. Louis Kriesberg and Abdul Quader, "L'Opinion publique americaine et l'U.R.S.S.: Les annees 70," *Etudes Polemologiques,* 2 (1984): 5–36.

5. Glenn T. Seaborg, *Kennedy, Khrushchev and the Test Ban* (Berkeley: University of California Press, 1981), 8.

6. John P. Robinson and Robert Meadows, *Polls Apart* (Cabin John, Md.: Seven Locks Press, 1982); and Hazel Erskine, "The Polls: Atomic Weapons and Nuclear Energy," *Public Opinion Quarterly* 27 (Summer 1963): 155–90.

7. Seaborg, *Kennedy, Khrushchev and the Test Ban,* 122.

8. Kissinger, *White House Years.*

9. Hazel Erskine, "The Polls: Is War a Mistake?" *Public Opinion Quarterly* 34 (Spring 1970): 134–50.

10. Kriesberg and Quader, "L'Opinion publique"; and Louis Kriesberg, Harry Murray, and Ross A. Klein, "Elites and Increased Support for U.S. Military Spending," *Journal of Political and Military Sociology* 10 (Fall 1982): 275–97.

11. Strobe Talbott, *Deadly Gambits* (New York: Knopf, 1984).

12. David Caute, *The Great Fear: The Anti-Communist Purge under Truman and Eisenhower* (New York: Simon and Schuster, 1978); and Fred J. Cook, *The Nightmare Decade: The Life and Times of Senator Joe McCarthy* (New York: Random House, 1971).

13. Ole R. Holsti and James Rosenau, *American Leadership in World Affairs* (Boston: Allen & Unwin, 1984).

14. Nikita Khrushchev, *Khrushchev Remembers,* trans. and ed. Strobe Talbott (New York: Bantam, 1976), 251.

15. CIA, "USSR: Measures of Economic Growth and Development, 1950–80," prepared for the U.S. Congress Joint Economic Committee (Washington, D.C.: GPO, 1982); and CIA, "Allocation of Resources in the Soviet Union and China, 1983," *Hearings Held before the Subcommittee on International Trade, Finance, and Security Economics of the Joint Economic Committee, United States Congress* (14 September 1983).

16. Mikhail Gorbachev, "October and Perestroika: The Revolution Continues," report marking the seventieth anniversary of the Great October Socialist Revolution, 2 November 1987 (Moscow: Novosti Press Agency, 1987).

17. Lenczowski, *Soviet Perceptions of U.S. Foreign Policy.*

18. El-Sadat, *In Search of Identity,* 208.

19. David Hirst and Irene Beeson, *Sadat* (London: Faber and Faber, 1981), 242–46.

20. Personal interviews with Saad Eddin Ibrahim, Abdul Monem al-Mashat, and Sayed Yassim, Cairo, June 1985.

21. Mohamed Sid-Ahmed, "Egypt: The Islamic Issue," *Foreign Policy* 69 (Winter 1987–88): 22–39.

22. Raymond William Baker, *Egypt's Uncertain Revolution under Nasser and Sadat* (Cambridge: Harvard University Press, 1978); and John Waterbury, *The Egypt of Nasser and Sadat* (Princeton: Princeton University Press, 1983).

23. Day, *East Bank/West Bank.*

24. Ann Mosely Lesch, *Political Perceptions of the Palestinians on the West Bank and the Gaza Strip: Special Study 3* (Washington, D.C.: Middle East Institute, 1980); Michael Curtis et al., *The Palestinians* (Transaction Books: New Jersey, 1975); and Ali E. Hillal Dessouki and Bahgat Korany, *The Foreign Policies of Arab States* (Boulder, Colo.: Westview, 1984).

25. Cobban, *The Palestinian Liberation Organization*; Quandt, Jabber, and Mosely Lesch, *Palestinian Nationalism.*

26. Michael Brecher, *The Foreign Policy Systems of Israel: Setting, Images, Process* (Oxford: Clarendon Press, 1972).

27. Personal interviews with Meir Paeli, Jerusalem, June 1986.

28. Yoram Peri, *Between Battles and Ballots: Israeli Military in Politics* (Cambridge: Cambridge University Press, 1983).

29. Walter Laqueur, *The Struggle for the Middle East* (New York: Macmillan, 1969); and Safran, *From War to War.*

30. Thomas M. Franck, *Nation against Nation* (New York: Oxford University Press, 1985); David A. Kay, *The Changing United Nations* (New York: Academy of Political Science, 1977).

31. Yair Evron and Yaacov Bar Simantov, "Coalitions in the Arab World," *Jerusalem Journal of International Relations* 1(2) (Winter 1975).

32. Richard Lowenthal, *Model of Ally? The Communist Powers and the Developing Countries* (New York: Oxford University Press, 1976); and Roger Kanet, *The Soviet Union and the Developing Nations* (Baltimore, Md.: Johns Hopkins Press, 1974); W. W. Rostow, *The World Economy: History and Prospect* (Austin: University of Texas Press, 1980); Walter Goldfrank, *The World System of Capitalism: Past and Present* (Beverly

Hills, Calif.: Sage, 1979); Harry Magdoff, *The Age of Imperialism: The Economics of U.S. Foreign Policy* (New York: Monthly Review, 1969); and Victor V. Rymalov, *The World Capitalist Economy: Structural Changes, Trends, and Problems*, trans. H. Campbell Creighton (Moscow: Progress Publishers, 1982).

33. Quandt, Jabber, and Mosely Lesch, *Palestinian Nationalism*.

34. Ze'ev Schiff and Ehud Ya'ari, *Israel's Lebanon War*, trans. Ina Friedman (New York: Simon and Schuster, 1984); and Richard A. Gabriel, *Operation Peace for Galilee: The Israeli-PLO War in Lebanon* (New York: Hill and Wang, 1984).

35. William B. Quandt, *Camp David* (Washington, D.C.: Brookings Institution, 1986).

36. Avnery, *My Friend, The Enemy*, 292.

Chapter 5 Starting Negotiations

1. Currently, research and writing on this matter are being conducted. See, e.g., Stein, *Getting to the Table*.

2. Fred C. Ikle, *How Nations Negotiate* (New York: Harper & Row, 1964).

3. Baldwin, "The Power of Positive Sanctions," 19–38; and Kriesberg, *Social Conflicts*.

4. Osgood, *An Alternative to War*.

5. Snyder and Diesing, *Conflict among Nations*. A few empirical analyses of the GRIT approach have been made, and they lend support to the idea; see Amitai Etzioni, "The Kennedy Experiment," *Western Political Quarterly* 20 (June 1967): 361–80; Deborah Larson, "Crisis Prevention and the Austrian State Treaty," *International Organization* 41 (Winter 1987): 27–60; and Goldstein and Freeman, *Three-Way Street*.

6. Robert Axelrod, *The Evolution of Cooperation* (New York: Basic, 1984).

7. In the many interviews I had with government officials and former officials from the U.S., the USSR, Egypt, Israel, and other countries, I asked about efforts to use persuasion in international negotiations. Although many respondents told about their efforts and what they believed was successful in influencing negotiation partners, none admitted having been persuaded by the efforts of their counterparts.

8. Arthur M. Schlesinger, Jr., *A Thousand Days: John F. Kennedy in the White House* (Boston: Houghton Mifflin, 1965), 906.

9. Ismail Fahmy, *Negotiating for Peace in the Middle East* (Baltimore, Md.: Johns Hopkins University Press, 1983).

10. Arkady N. Shevchenko, *Breaking with Moscow* (New York: Ballantine, 1985), 226–27.

11. McDonald and Bendahmane, *Conflict Resolution*; Ralph Earle II, "Private Intervention in Public Controversy: Pros and Cons," in *Timing De-escalation*; and John McDonald, "Further Explorations of Track Two Diplomacy," in *Timing the De-escalation of International Conflicts*, ed. Louis Kriesberg and Stuart Thorson (Syracuse, N.Y.: Syracuse University Press, 1991).

12. Roger Fisher, "Fractionating Conflict," in *International Conflict and Behavioral Sciences: The Craigville Papers*, ed. Roger Fisher (New York: Basic, 1964): 90–110; and Kissinger, *White House Years* and *Years of Upheaval*.

13. Robin Ranger, *Arms and Politics, 1958–1978* (Toronto: Macmillan, 1979).

14. Khouri, *Arab-Israeli Dilemma*.

15. Kissinger, *White House Years*; Gerard Smith, *Double Talk: The Story of the First Strategic Arms Limitation Talks* (N.Y.: Doubleday, 1960); and John Newhouse, *Cold Dawn: The Story of SALT* (New York: Holt, Rinehart and Winston, 1973).

16. William B. Quandt, *Camp David* (Washington, D.C.: Brookings Institution, 1986); and Carter, *Keeping Faith*.

17. Avnery, *My Friend, The Enemy*.

18. Asher Susser, "Double Jeopardy: PLO Strategy toward Israel and Jordan," Policy Paper 8 (Washington, D.C.: Washington Institute for Near East Policy, 1987).

19. *New York Times*, 17 Nov. 1988; 7, 8, and 15 Dec. 1988.

20. I. William Zartman, "Negotiations as a Joint Decision-Making Process," in *The Negotiation Process*, ed. I. William Zartman (Beverly Hills, Calif.: Sage, 1977), 67–86.

21. Raymond Cohen, *Culture and Conflict in Egyptian-Israeli Relations* (Bloomington: Indiana University Press, 1990).

22. Ibid., 129–32.

23. Louis Kriesberg, "Assessing Positive Inducements in U.S.-Soviet Relations: Report of a Pilot Study," Syracuse University Program on the Analysis and Resolution of Conflicts, 1988.

24. Herbert C. Kelman, "Overcoming the Psychological Barrier: An Analysis of the Egyptian-Israeli Peace Process," *Negotiation Journal* (July 1985): 213–34.

25. Personal interviews with Theodore Sorenson, 20 March 1979, and Arthur Schlesinger, 9 October 1978; Etzioni, "The Kennedy Experiment," 361–80; and Louis Kriesberg, "Noncoercive Inducements in U.S.-Soviet Conflicts: Ending the Occupation of Austria and Nuclear Weapons Test," *Journal of Political and Military Sociology* 9 (Spring 1981): 1–16.

26. Schlesinger, *A Thousand Days*, 900–902.

27. Lyndon Baines Johnson, *The Vantage Point: Perspectives of the Presidency, 1963–1969* (New York: Holt, Rinehart and Winston, 1971), 465.

28. Abba Eban, ed., "The Nine-Point Peace Plan," in *Israel's Foreign Relations: Selected Documents, 1947–1974*, ed. Meron Medzini, vol. 2 (Jerusalem: Ministry for Foreign Affairs, 1976), 856.

29. Based on a personal interview with Paul Warnke in Syracuse, N.Y., 11 July 1983; see also, Strobe Talbott, *Endgame: The Inside Story of SALT II* (New York: Harper & Row, 1979), 10; and Garthoff, *Detente and Confrontation*. Perhaps Carter did not want to appear weak and was uncertain that a comparable concession would be quickly won from the Soviets.

30. Moshe Zak, "Talking to Hussein," *The Jerusalem Post International Edition* (4 May 1985): 10–12; Steve Posner, *Israel Undercover* (Syracuse, N.Y.: Syracuse University Press, 1987).

31. Ulam, *Expansion and Coexistence*.

32. Walter Laqueur and Barry Rubin, eds., *The Israel-Arab Reader*, rev. and updated ed. (New York: Penguin, 1984), 518.

33. Khouri, *Arab-Israeli Dilemma*.

34. Zak, "Talking to Hussein," and Posner, *Israel Undercover*.

35. Landrum Bolling, "Strengths and Weaknesses of Track Two: A Personal Account," in *Conflict Resolution: Track Two Diplomacy*, ed. John W. McDonald, Jr., and

Diane B. Bendahmane, U.S. Department of State, Foreign Service Institute (Washington, D.C.: GPO, 1987), 53–64; Maureen R. Berman and Joseph E. Johnson, eds., *Unofficial Diplomats* (New York: Columbia University Press, 1977); Pentz and Stovo, "The Political Significance of Pugwash"; and Joseph Rotblat, *Pugwash: The First Ten Years* (New York: Humanities Press, 1968).

36. Susan Borker, Louis Kriesberg, and Abu Abdul-Quader, "Conciliation, Confrontation, and Approval of the President," *Peace and Change* 2 (Spring 1985): 31–48.

37. Larson, "Crisis Prevention and the Austrian State Treaty."

38. Ole R. Holsti, "Cognitive Dynamics and Images of the Enemy: Dulles and Russia," in *Enemies in Politics,* ed. David J. Finley et al. (Chicago: Rand McNally, 1967), 25–96.

39. Kriesberg and Quader, "L'Opinion publique," 5–36.

40. Eytan Gilboa, *American Public Opinion toward Israel and the Arab-Israeli Conflict* (Lexington, Mass.: Lexington Books), table 3–3. The question was "Do you feel that Egypt really wants just peace in the Middle East, only reluctantly wants just peace, or really does not want peace?"

41. Landrum R. Bolling, "Quaker Work in the Middle East following the June 1967 War," in *Unofficial Diplomats,* Berman and Johnson; and interview with John Mroz in New York, 21 May 1979.

42. Norman Cousins, *The Improbable Triumvirate* (New York: Norton, 1972).

43. Ibid., 116.

44. Moshe Dayan, *Breakthrough: A Personal Account of the Egypt-Israel Peace Negotiations* (New York: Knopf, 1981); and interview with Dan Pattir in Washington, D.C., 17 June 1982.

45. Kriesberg, "Assessing Positive Inducements."

46. Kriesberg, "Social Theory," 471–91; Kriesberg, "Transforming Conflicts in the Middle East and Central Europe," in *Intractable Conflicts and Their Transformation,* ed. Louis Kriesberg, Terrell A. Northrup, and Stuart J. Thorson (Syracuse, N.Y.: Syracuse University Press, 1989), 109–31.

47. James R. Ozinga, *The Rapacki Plan* (Jefferson, N.C.: McFarland, 1989).

48. Louis Kriesberg, "Noncoercive Inducements in U.S.-Soviet Conflicts: Ending the Occupation of Austria and Nuclear Weapons Tests," *Journal of Political and Military Sociology* 9 (Spring 1981): 1–16.

49. David P. Forsythe, *United Nations Peacemaking* (Baltimore, Md.: Johns Hopkins University Press, 1972).

50. Louis Kriesberg and Stuart J. Thorson, eds., *Timing the De-Escalation of International Conflicts* (Syracuse, N.Y.: Syracuse University Press, 1991).

51. El-Sadat, *In Search of Identity,* 306.

52. Frances B. McCrea and Gerald E. Markle, *Minutes to Midnight* (Newbury Park, Calif.: Sage, 1989).

Chapter 6   The Negotiation of Agreements

1. Alex Glicksman, "The Other Side of Negotiations," in *Conflict Management and Problem Solving: Interpersonal to International Applications* (New York: New York University Press, 1987), 210–14.

2. Alva Myrdal, *The Game of Disarmament* (New York: Pantheon, 1976).

3. Otomar J. Bartos, "Simple Model of Negotiations," in *The Negotiation Process* (Beverly Hills, Calif.: Sage, 1977), 13–27; Zartman, *Ripe for Resolution*; Louis Kriesberg, "Carrots, Sticks, and De-escalation: U.S.-Soviet and Arab-Israeli Relations," *Armed Forces and Society* 13 (Spring 1987): 403–23; and Louis Kriesberg, "Timing and the Initiation of De-escalation Moves," *Negotiation Journal* 3 (October 1987): 375–84.

4. Garthoff, *Detente and Confrontation*; Kriesberg, "Social Theory," 471–91.

5. Ronald J. Young, *Missed Opportunities for Peace: U.S. Middle East Policy, 1981–1986* (Philadelphia: American Friends Service Committee, 1987).

6. Roger Fisher and William Ury, *Getting to YES* (Boston: Houghton Mifflin, 1981); Howard Raiffa, *The Art and Science of Negotiation* (Cambridge: Harvard University Press, 1982); Jeffrey Z. Rubin and Bert R. Brown, *Social Psychology of Bargaining and Negotiation* (New York: Academic Press, 1975); and Ikle, *How Nations Negotiate*.

7. Sometimes international meetings occur without careful advance planning, and new options sometimes result; e.g., consider the summit meeting at Reykjavik; Brent Scowcroft, John Deutch, and R. James Woolsey, "A Way Out of Reykjavik," *New York Times Magazine* (25 Jan. 1987): 40–42, 78–84; and Weihmiller and Doder, *U.S.-Soviet Summits*.

8. Kissinger, *White House Years*; and Fisher and Ury, *Getting to Yes*.

9. Zartman, "Negotiations as a Joint Decision-Making Process."

10. Charles E. Osgood, *An Alternative to War*.

11. Axelrod, *Evolution of Cooperation*.

12. Bartos, "Model of Negotiations."

13. Johnson, *Vantage Point*.

14. Kriesberg, "Noncoercive Inducements," 1–16.

15. Johnson, *Vantage Point*.

16. Garthoff, *Detente and Confrontation*.

17. Talbott, *Deadly Gambits*.

18. Richard Haass, "Ripeness, De-escalation, and Arms Control: The Case of INF," in *Timing the De-Escalation of International Conflicts*, ed. Kriesberg and Thorson (Syracuse, N.Y.: Syracuse University Press, 1991); Talbott, *Deadly Gambits*.

19. Earl Berger, *The Covenant and the Sword: Arab-Israeli Relations, 1948–1956* (London: Routledge & Kegan Paul, 1965).

20. Saadia Touval, *The Peace Brokers* (Princeton: Princeton University Press, 1982); and Elmore Jackson, *Middle East Mission* (New York: W. W. Norton, 1983).

21. Berger, *The Covenant and the Sword*; and Khouri, *Arab-Israeli Dilemma*.

22. Khouri, *Arab-Israeli Dilemma*.

23. Young, *Missed Opportunities for Peace*.

24. Ulam, *Expansion and Coexistence*; Khrushchev, *Khrushchev Remembers*.

25. Kriesberg, "Interlocking Conflicts," 99–118.

26. Etzioni, "The Kennedy Experiment," 361–80; and Kriesberg, "Noncoercive Inducements," 1–16.

27. Seaborg, *Kennedy, Khrushchev and the Test Ban*, 178–81.

28. Schlesinger, *A Thousand Days*, 906.

29. See Kissinger, *White House Years*; John Newhouse, *Cold Dawn*.

30. Ranger, *Arms and Politics*.

31. Bennett Ramberg, *The Seabed Arms Control Negotiations: A Study of Multilateral Arms Control Conference Diplomacy,* monograph series in World Affairs, vol. 15 (Denver: University of Denver, 1978).

32. Vance, *Hard Choices*; and Neustadt and May, *Thinking in Time*.

33. Talbott, *Deadly Gambits*.

34. The 1979 announcement of the "discovery" of a Soviet military brigade in Cuba is an example; see Neustadt and May, *Thinking in Time*.

35. Lothar Ruehl, *MBFR: Lessons and Problems,* Adelphi Papers, no. 126 (London: International Institute for Strategic Studies, 1982); and Talbott, *Deadly Gambits*.

36. Garthoff, *Detente and Confrontation*.

37. Ibid., 767.

38. Talbott, *Deadly Gambits*.

39. Ibid.; and Garthoff, *Detente and Confrontation*.

40. Berger, *The Covenant and the Sword*; Barry Rubin, *Arab States and the Palestine Conflict* (Syracuse, N.Y.: Syracuse University Press, 1981); and Avi Shlaim, *Collusion across the Jordan* (New York: Oxford University Press, 1988).

41. Khouri, *Arab-Israeli Dilemma*.

42. Nadav Safran, *Israel: The Embattled Ally* (Cambridge: Harvard University Press, 1978).

43. Mordechai Gazit, "The Peace Process, 1969–1973: Efforts and Contacts," *Jerusalem Papers on Peace Problems* 35 (Jerusalem: Magnes Press, 1983); and Forsythe, *United Nations Peacemaking*.

44. Berger, *The Covenant and the Sword*; and Rubin, *Arab States*.

45. Touval, *Peace Brokers*; and Gazit, *Peace Process*.

46. Gazit, *Peace Process*; and Berger, *The Covenant and the Sword*.

47. Khouri, *Arab-Israeli Dilemma*.

48. UN Security Council Resolution 242 (1967), in Khouri, *Arab-Israeli Dilemma*, 541–42.

49. Gazit, *Peace Process*; Touval, *Peace Brokers*; and Kissinger, *White House Years*.

50. Interview with Joseph Sisco, 26 June 1979, Washington, D.C. In his statement of 9 December 1969, Secretary of State Rogers outlined U.S. policy regarding the establishment of peace in the Middle East, which included the establishment of recognized political borders, "confined to insubstantial alterations" from the 1949 armistice agreements; a just settlement of the problem of Palestinians made homeless in the wars of 1948 and 1967; the unification of Jerusalem and "roles for both Israel and Jordan in the civic, economic and religious life of the city"—Meron Medzini, ed., *Israel's Foreign Relations Selected Documents, 1947–1974* (Jerusalem: Ministry for Foreign Affairs, 1976), 878; for background, see Safran, *Israel*, 432–35.

51. Bailey, *Jordan's Palestinian Challenge,* 54–62.

52. Mohamed Heikal, *The Road to Ramadan* (New York: Quadrangle, 1975).

53. Touval, *Peace Brokers*.

54. Kissinger, *White House Years*.

55. Ibid.; Touval, *Peace Brokers*; and Yitzhak Rabin, *The Rabin Memoirs* (Boston: Little, Brown, 1979).

56. Touval, *Peace Brokers,* 269.

57. Based on interviews with Israeli foreign ministry officials, 29 December 1977, who pointed out that they had made an offer and expected a response in the form of a counteroffer but felt none had come.

58. Touval, *Peace Brokers*; Carter, *Keeping Faith*; and Dayan, *Breakthrough*.

59. Quandt, *Camp David*, 224. In other words, both delegations had hard-and soft-liners. Israeli Defense Minister Ezer Weizman served as a quasi-mediator in these negotiations; see Louis Kriesberg, "Formal and Quasi-Mediators in International Disputes," *Journal of Peace Research* 28 (February 1991): 19–27; and Ezer Weizman, *The Battle for Peace* (New York: Bantam, 1981).

60. *New York Times*, 27 March 1979.

61. Geoffrey Aronson, *Creating Facts: Israel, Palestinians and the West Bank* (Washington, D.C.: Institute for Palestine Studies, 1987); Quandt, *Camp David*; and Khouri, *Arab-Israeli Dilemma*.

62. Saunders, *The Other Walls*.

63. Borker, Kriesberg, and Abdul-Quader, "Conciliation, Confrontation," 31–48.

64. El-Sadat, *In Search of Identity*, 208.

65. Saadia Touval and I. William Zartman, eds.,*International Mediation in Theory and Practice* (Boulder, Colo.: Westview, 1985).

66. Officially, "Basic Principles of Relations between the United States of America and the Union of Soviet Socialist Republics."

67. Carter, *Keeping Faith*; and Ramberg, *Seabed Arms Control Negotiations*.

68. Fisher and Ury, *Getting to YES*.

69. Touval, *Peace Brokers*, 158–59; and Gazit, *Peace Process*.

70. In fall 1954, the Egyptians tried several persons, mostly Jews, for sabotage. Two were executed—to Israel's outrage. The defendants were guilty, however, and Israelis later struggled over who had ordered the sabotage. Dinhas Lavon was the minister of defense at the time, hence the "Lavon affair." Lavon, however, was probably innocent. Berger, *The Covenant and the Sword*, 181.

71. Louis Kriesberg, "Policy Continuity and Change," *Social Problems* 32 (December 1984): 89–102.

Chapter 7 The Consequences of Agreements

1. John W. Burton, *Conflict and Communication: The Use of Controlled Communication in International Relations* (London: Macmillan, 1969); and Raiffa, *Art and Science of Negotiation*.

2. Kriesberg, *Social Conflicts*.

3. Morton H. Halperin, *Bureaucratic Politics and Foreign Policy* (Washington, D.C.: Brookings Institution, 1974); and Kriesberg, "Policy Continuity and Change," 89–102.

4. David Mitrany, *A Working Peace System* (Chicago: Quadrangle, 1966).

5. Ernst B. Haas, *The Uniting of Europe* (Stanford, Calif.: Stanford University Press, 1958); Louis Kriesberg, "German Evaluations of the European Coal and Steel Community, 1950–1956" (in German), *Kölner Zeitschrift für Soziologie und Sozialpsychologie* (1959) 11 (3): 496–516; Louis Kriesberg, "German Leaders and the Schuman Plan," *Social Science*, 35 (April): 114–21; and Amitai Etzioni, *Political Unification* (New York: Holt, Rinehart and Winston, 1965).

6. Kriesberg, "Policy Continuity and Change," 89–102; Harold L. Wilensky, *The*

Welfare State and Equality (Berkeley: University of California Press, 1975); and Nathaniel S. Keith, *Politics and the Housing Crisis since 1930* (New York: Universe, 1973).

7. Garthoff, *Detente and Confrontation;* Pipes, *U.S.-Soviet Relations;* Weeks, *The Troubled Détente;* and R. J. Rummel, *Peace Endangered: The Reality of Détente* (Beverly Hills, Calif.: Sage, 1976).

8. For the ways agreements may be reached that take into account parties' different valuations of time, see Raiffa, *Art and Science of Negotiation.*

9. Stanley Lieberson, "An Empirical Study of Military-Industrial Linkages," *American Journal of Sociology* 76 (January 1971): 562–84.

10. Young, *Missed Opportunities for Peace.*

11. See discussion in Kriesberg, Northrup, and Thorson, *Intractable Conflicts*; and Kriesberg and Thorson, *Timing De-escalation.*

12. For example, see Jerry W. Sanders, *Peddlers of Crisis* (Boston: South End Press, 1983).

13. Morgenthau, *Politics among Nations.*

14. William Korey, "The Story of the Jackson Amendment, 1973–75," *Midstream* 21 (March 1975): 7–36; and Kissinger, *Years of Upheaval.*

15. Ibid.

16. Sen. Adlai Stevenson III sponsored an amendment with even greater effect on possible Soviet imports from the United States. The Stevenson amendment limited credit to the USSR to $300 million over a four-year period, unless emigration restrictions were lessened and the Soviets were more forthcoming in arms control negotiations. It was passed by Congress together with the Jackson-Vanik amendment.

17. *New York Times,* 29 Nov. 1986.

18. *New York Times,* 24 Oct. 1989.

19. G. W. Rathjens, Abram Chayes, and J. P. Ruina, *Nuclear Arms Control Agreements: Process and Impact* (Washington, D.C.: Carnegie Endowment for International Peace, 1974).

20. Ranger, *Arms and Politics.*

21. Kissinger, *White House Years*; and Robert J. Pranger, ed., *Detente and Defense: A Reader* (Washington, D.C.: American Enterprise Institute for Public Policy Research, 1976); Alexander L. George, *Managing U.S.-Soviet Rivalry: Problems of Crisis Prevention* (Boulder, Colo.: Westview, 1983).

22. Kriesberg and Quader, "L'Opinion Publique Americaine et l'U.R.S.S.," 5–36; Tom W. Smith, "General Liberalism and Social Change in Post World War II America: A Summary of Trends," in *Social Indicators Research* 10 (January 1982): 11–28; Tom W. Smith "The Polls: American Attitudes toward the Soviet Union and Communism," *Public Opinion Quarterly* 47 (Summer 1983): 277–92.

23. Kriesberg and Quader, "L'Opinion publique."

24. National Opinion Research Center (NORC) *General Social Survey.*

25. *New York Times,* 3 Dec. 1989.

26. Louis Kriesberg and Ross A. Klein, "Changes in Public Support for U.S. Military Spending," *Journal of Conflict Resolution* 24 (March 1980): 79–111; and NORC *General Social Survey.*

27. Sanders, *Peddlers of Crisis*; Clarence Y. Lo, "Theories of the State and Business

Opposition to Increased Military Spending," *Social Problems* 29 (April 1982): 424–38; and NORC General Social Survey.

28. Allen H. Barton, "Consequences and Conflict among American Leaders," *Public Opinion Quarterly* 38 (Winter 1974/75): 507–30.

29. Kriesberg, Murray, and Klein, "Elites and Increased Support," 275–97; and Charles W. Kegley, Jr., and Eugene R. Wittkopf, *American Foreign Policy: Pattern and Process* (New York: St. Martin's, 1982); and Holsti and Rosenau, *American Leadership in World Affairs*.

30. Paul Marantz, "Peaceful Coexistence: From Heresy to Orthodoxy," in *The Dynamics of Soviet Politics*, ed. P. Cooks, R. V. Daniels, and N. W. Heer (Cambridge: Harvard University Press, 1976), 293–308.

31. Egbert Jahn and Jutta Tiedtke, "Politische Stromungen in der sowjetischen Entspannungspolitik," in *Friedensanalysen Fur Theorie und Praxis*, vol. 9, ed. Reiner Steinweg (Frankfurt a.M.: Suhrkamp, 1979), 50–80; and Oded Eran, *Mezhdunarodniki: An Assessment of Professional Expertise in the Making of Soviet Foreign Policy* (Ramat Gan, Israel: Turtodove Publishing, 1979).

32. Personal interview with Carl Kaysen, Boston, 30 August 1979.

33. Terry L. Heyns, *American and Soviet Relations since Detente* (Washington, D.C.: National Defense University Press, 1987).

34. *New York Times*, 25 May 1984, sec. D, p. 1.

35. Heyns, *American and Soviet Relations*, 119. The numbers refer to scholars exchanged through IREX, CIES, and NAS.

36. James Cracraft, "Unofficial Thaw in the Cold War," *Bulletin of Atomic Scientists* 42 (May 1986): 20–22.

37. SIPRI, *World Armaments and Disarmament: SIPRI Yearbooks 1958, 1968, 1983* (London: Taylor & Francis); International Institute for Strategic Studies, *The Military Balance, 1987–1988* (London, 1987); Abraham S. Becker, *Sitting on Bayonets: The Soviet Defense Burden and the Slowdown of Soviet Defense Spending*, Center for the Study of Soviet International Behavior, RAND/UCLA (December 1985); and Thomas R. Cusack and Michael Don Ward, "Military Spending in the United States, Soviet Union, and the People's Republic of China," *Journal of Conflict Resolution* 25 (September 1981): 429–69. See also Louis Kriesberg, "Consequences of Efforts at De-escalating the American-Soviet Conflict," *Journal of Political and Military Sociology* 14 (Fall 1986): 215–34.

38. *New York Times*, 8 Dec. 1988.

39. Davis B. Bobrow, "Uncoordinated Giants," in *Foreign Policy USA/USSR*, ed. Charles W. Kegley, Jr., and Pat McGowan (Beverly Hills, Calif.: Sage, 1982).

40. Alan Wolfe, *The Rise and Fall of the "Soviet Threat": Domestic Sources of the Cold War Consensus* (Washington, D.C.: Institute for Policy Studies, 1979).

41. Miroslav Nincic, "Fluctuations in Soviet Defense Spending: A Research Note," *Journal of Conflict Resolution* 27 (December 1983): 648–60.

42. Sanders, *Peddlers of Crisis*.

43. Nogee and Donaldson, *Soviet Foreign Policy*, 114–16.

44. Bader, *Austria between East and West*, 186–87.

45. Newhouse, *Cold Dawn*; and Michael J. Pentz and Gillian Slovo, "The Political

Significance of Pugwash," in *Knowledge and Power in a Global Society*, ed. William M. Evan (Beverly Hills, Calif.: Sage, 1981), 175–203.

46. Talbott, *Endgame*.

47. Goldstein and Freeman, *Three-Way Street*. The authors have extended and adapted the WEIS and COPDAB data in several ways: They present WEIS data provided by Charles McClelland for the years after 1979, which were not yet publicly available; and they used the weighting scheme developed by Jack Vincent to translate the WEIS data into a cooperation-conflict continuum compatible with the COPDAB data.

48. George, *Managing U.S.-Soviet Rivalry*.

49. Garthoff, *Detente and Confrontation*, 609–12, 1123–24.

50. John L. Scherer, ed., *USSR Facts and Figures Annual*, vol. 6 (New York: Academic International Press, 1982); and the Soviet Jewry Research Bureau of the National Conference on Soviet Jewry, Washington, D.C., through personal letters and telephone calls.

51. *Moscow News* 50 (3350), 11 Dec. 1988, p. 5.

52. Heikal, *The Road to Ramadan*.

53. Khouri, *Arab-Israeli Dilemma*; and Carter, *Keeping Faith*.

54. Day, *East Bank/West Bank*.

55. On 31 July 1988, King Hussein announced that Jordan would cut all legal and administrative ties to Israeli-occupied territory, surrendering Jordan's claims to the West Bank in favor of the PLO. On 4 August 1988, King Hussein said Jordan would stop paying the salaries of twenty-one thousand Palestinian civil servants on the West Bank. See Council on Foreign Relations, *Foreign Affairs Chronology, 1978–1989* (New York, 1990.)

56. Russel A. Stone, *Social Change in Israel: Attitudes and Events, 1967–1979* (New York: Praeger, 1982).

57. Ibid.

58. SIPRI Yearbook, 1976, table 6A.13.

59. SIPRI Yearbook, 1976, 1984, 1989.

60. Zak, "Talking to Hussein," 10–12; and Posner, *Israel Undercover*.

61. Ann Mosely Lesch, "Egyptian-Israeli Relations: Normalization or Special Ties?" in *Israel, Egypt and the Palestinians*, ed. Ann Mosely Lesch and Mark Tessler (Bloomington: Indiana University Press, 1989), 65–81; and Joel Bainerman, "Cold Peace Chills Trade with Egypt," *Jerusalem Post International* (5 May 1990).

62. Ann Mosely Lesch, "Egyptian-Israeli Boundry Disputes: The Problem of Taba," in *Israel, Egypt and the Palestinians*, ed. Ann Mosely and Mark Tessler (Bloomington: Indiana University, 1989), 43–60.

63. Evron and Simantov, "Coalitions in the Arab World"; see also Anne Sinai and Allen Pollack, *The Syrian Arab Republic* (New York: American Academic Association for Peace in the Middle East, 1976).

64. Rivka Yadlin, *An Arrogant, Oppressive Spirit: Anti-Zionism as Anti-Judaism in Egypt* (Oxford: Pergamon, 1989).

65. Kriesberg, Northrup, and Thorson, *Intractable Conflicts and Their Transformation*.

66. Nogee and Donaldson, *Soviet Foreign Policy.*

67. William B. Quandt, *Camp David* (Washington, D.C.: Brookings Institution, 1986).

68. Kriesberg and Quader, "L'Opinion publique."

69. Garthoff, *Detente and Confrontation*; Khrushchev, *Khrushchev Remembers.*

70. Senghaas, *Rüstung und Militarismus*; and David Holloway, *War, Militarism and the Soviet State* (New York: Institute for World Order, 1981).

71. Mark Gasiorowski and Solomon W. Polachek, "Conflict and Interdependence: East–West Trade and Linkages in the Era of Detente," *Journal of Conflict Resolution* 26 (December 1982): 709–29.

Chapter 8   Transformations and Continuities

1. Kriesberg, "Transforming Conflicts."

2. LeFeber, *America, Russia, and the Cold War.*

3. Seaborg, *Kennedy, Khrushchev and the Test Ban.*

4. Khrushchev, *Khrushchev Remembers,* 420–21, 460–61.

5. Raymond L. Garthoff, "Cuban Missile Crisis: The Soviet Story," *Foreign Policy* 72 (Fall 1988): 61–80; and Thorson, "Conceptual Issues."

6. Sivachev and Yakovlev, *Russia and the United States.*

7. Pipes, *U.S.-Soviet Relations*; and Rummel, *Peace Endangered.*

8. Louis Kriesberg, "Explaining the End of the Cold War," Program on the Analysis and Resolution of Conflicts, Syracuse University Occasional Paper, 1990.

9. Nish Jamgotch, Jr., ed., *Sectors of Mutual Benefit in U.S.-Soviet Relations* (Durham, N.C.: Duke University Press, 1985); and Richmond, *U.S.-Soviet Cultural Exchanges.*

10. Jorgen Dragsdahl, "How Peace Research Has Reshaped the European Arms Dialogue," *Annual Review of Peace Activism, 1989* (Boston: Winston Foundation for World Peace, 1989), 39–45.

11. Gale Warner and Michael Shuman, *Citizen Diplomats* (Cabin John, Md.: Sevenlocks, 1987)

12. Forsythe, *United Nations Peacemaking.*

13. Bailey, *Jordan's Palestinian Challenge*; Anne Sinai and Allen Pollack, eds., *The Hashemite Kingdom of Jordan and the West Bank* (New York: American Academic Association for Peace in the Middle East, 1977).

14. El-Sadat, *In Search of Identity.*

15. Laqueur, *The Struggle for the Middle East.*

16. Safran, *From War to War.*

17. Touval, *Peace Brokers.*

18. El-Sadat, *In Search of Identity.*

19. Stone, *Social Change in Israel.*

20. Herbert C. Kelman, "The Palestinianization of the Arab-Israeli Conflict," *Jerusalem Quarterly* 46 (Spring 1988).

21. Interview with Moshe Shamir, of Likud, in Jerusalem, 16 June 1977, and with Hatem Husseini, Palestine Information Center, Washington, D.C., 30 April 1979.

22. Khouri, *Arab-Israeli Dilemma*.

23. Shipler, *Arab and Jew*; Yael Yishai, "Dissent in Israel: Opinions on the Lebanon War," *Middle East Review* 16 (Winter 1983/84): 38–44; and Yoram Peri, "The Rise and Fall of Israel's National Consensus," *New Outlook* 26 (May 1983): 28–31, and 26 (August–September 1983): 26–32.

24. Edy Kaufman, "The *Intifadah* and the Peace Camp in Israel," *Journal of Palestine Studies* 68 (Summer 1988): 66–80; Don Peretz, *Intifada* (Boulder, Colo.: Westview, 1990).

Chapter 9   Inferences and Policy Implications

1. Halberstam, *Best and the Brightest*.

2. See Carl G. Jacobsen, *The Soviet Defence Enigma* (Oxford: Oxford University Press, 1987); Dmitri Steinberg, "Trends in Soviet Military Expenditures," *Soviet Studies* 42 (October 1990).

3. Charles Wolf, Jr., "The Costs and Benefits of the Soviet Empire," in *The Future of the Soviet Empire,* ed. Henry S. Rowen and Charles Wolf, Jr. (New York: St. Martin's, 1988), 135.

4. SIPRI, *World Armaments and Disarmament: SIPRI Yearbooks 1958, 1968, 1983* (London: Taylor & Francis); and International Institute for Strategic Studies, *The Military Balance, 1987–1988* (London, 1987).

5. Melman, *Permanent War Economy*; and Lloyd J. Dumas, *The Overburdened Economy* (Berkeley: University of California Press, 1986).

6. The data on deaths are from Ruth Leger Sivard, *World Military and Social Expenditures, 1989,* 13th ed. (Washington, D.C.: World Priorities, 1989).

7. Richard Allen, *Imperialism and Nationalism in the Fertile Crescent* (New York: Oxford University Press, 1974), 417 n. 25; see also Khouri, *Arab-Israeli Dilemma*; and Edward W. Said et al., *A Profile of the Palestinian People* (Chicago: Palestine Human Rights Campaign, 1983).

8. Sivard, *World Military*.

9. Ibid.

10. John W. Burton, *Resolving Deep-Rooted Conflict: A Handbook* (Lanham, Md.: University Press of America, 1987).

11. As Leon Festinger writes (agreeing with Kurt Lewin), making a decision gives dominance to that alternative; people tend to "stick to a decision." Festinger, *A Theory of Cognitive Dissonance* (Stanford, Calif.: Stanford University Press, 1957), 33–36.

12. Kriesberg, Northrup, and Thorson, *Intractable Conflicts*.

13. Kriesberg, "Timing and the Initiation of De-Escalation Moves."

14. Harry B. Hollins, Averill L. Powers, and Mark Sommer, eds., *The Conquest of War: Alternative Strategies for Global Security* (Boulder, Colo.: Westview, 1989); and Norman V. Walbek, *Saving the Planet: The Politics of Hope* (Winona, Minn.: Northland, 1985.

15. Interview with Yossi Beilin in Jerusalem, 19 June 1985; and Peri, *Between Battles and Ballots*.

16. John W. McDonald, "Further Explorations of Track Two Diplomacy," in *Timing*

the De-escalation of International Conflicts, ed. L. Kriesberg and S. Thorson (Syracuse, N.Y.: Syracuse University Press, 1991).

17. The disagreement over the nature of the struggles contributes to its intractability but also to its potential for transformation; see Kriesberg, Northrup, and Thorson, *Intractable Conflicts.*

18. Interview with Mayor Elias Freij, Bethlehem, 24 November 1983.

19. For example, creating an expanded special-forces capability in the Kennedy administration facilitated the initial deployment of U.S. military forces in the Vietnam War. See Halberstam, *Best and the Brightest.*

20. Genocide is the most extreme example of violence. See, e.g., Isador Walliman and M. N. Dobkowski, *Genocide and the Modern Age: Etiology and Case Studies of Mass Deaths* (New York: Greenwood, 1977); and John L. P. Thompson and Gail A. Quets, "Genocide and Social Conflicts," in *Research in Social Movements, Conflicts and Change,* ed. Louis Kriesberg, vol. 12 (Greenwich, Conn.: JAI Press), 245–66.

21. Myrdal, *Game of Disarmament.*

22. Snyder and Diesing, *Conflict among Nations,* 248; Alexander George, David K. Hall, and William E. Simons, *Limits of Coercive Diplomacy* (Boston: Little, Brown, 1971), 238–45.

23. Interviews in New York with Sorenson, 20 March 1979, and Schlesinger, 9 October 1978; Schlesinger, *A Thousand Days.*

24. White, *Fearful Warriors.*

25. Young, *Missed Opportunities for Peace.*

26. Dragsdahl, "Peace Research," 39–45.

27. MacDonald, "Further Explorations."

28. El-Sadat, *In Search of Identity.*

29. Garthoff, *Detente and Confrontation*; and Kissinger, *White House Years.*

30. P. Terrence Hopmann, "The Changing International Environment and the Resolution of International Conflicts: Negotiations on Security and Arms Control in Europe," in *Timing the De-escalation of International Conflicts,* ed. L. Kriesberg and S. Thorson (Syracuse, N.Y.: Syracuse University Press, 1991)

31. Rathjens, Chayes, and Ruina, *Nuclear Arms Control Agreements.*

32. Interview in Cairo with Muhamed Sayed Said, 11 June 1985; see also Rivka Yadlin, "Egyptian Perceptions of the Camp David Process," *Middle East Review* 18 (Fall 1985): 45–50.

Epilogue   The War in the Gulf

1. Walid Khalidi, "The Gulf Crisis: Origins and Consequences," *Journal of Palestine Studies* 20 (2) (Winter 1991): 5–28; Judith Miller and Laurie Mylroie, *Saddam Hussein and the Crisis in the Gulf* (New York: Times Books, 1990); and Bob Woodward, *The Commanders* (New York: Simon and Schuster, 1991).

2. Paul A. Gigot, "A Great American Screw-Up: The U.S. and Iraq," *Wall Street Journal,* 18 Dec. 1990.

3. Woodward, *Commanders,* 210.

4. Miller and Mylroie, *Saddam Hussein,* 19.

5. *New York Times,* 16 Oct. 1990.

6. *New York Times,* 8 Nov. 1990.

7. Woodward, *Commanders,* 260.

8. Louis Kriesberg, "Forcing Iraq's Withdrawal," *Post-Standard,* Syracuse, N.Y., 10 Oct. 1990, sec. A, p. 13; Roger Fisher, "Winning without War," *Boston Globe,* 4 Nov. 1990, sec. A, p. 17; Roger Fisher, Andrea Kupfer, and Douglas Stone, "How Do You End a War?" *Boston Globe,* 8 Feb. 1991; and Howard Raiffa, Jeffrey Z. Rubin, and Jeswald W. Salacuse, "Mideast Peace Can Be Negotiated," *Newsday,* 14 Dec. 1990, p. VI.

9. Joe Stork, "The Gulf War and the Arab World," *World Policy Journal* 2 (Spring 1991): 365–74.

Index

Abdullah, King of Jordan, 105, 131, 137
ABM treaty, 130, 134, 145, 158, 181, 219
ACC. *See* Arab Cooperation Council
Adler, Peter S., 238*n*15
Adversary relations: integration and, 2, 9;
 in U.S.-USSR conflict, 26–30; in Arab-
 Israeli conflict, 30–33; undertaking of
 initiatives and, 37–40; variation in initiatives and, 71–75; in compared conflicts, 76; initiation of negotiations and,
 89–90, 118–19; negotiation of agreements and, 145; consequences of agreements and, 155, 167–72; Persian Gulf
 conflict and, 224, 225, 234. *See also*
 Consequences of agreements; Legitimacy; Power relations; U.S.-USSR relations
Afghanistan, Soviet invasion of, 73, 158,
 159, 162, 205, 221
Agreements: survival of, 4, 178, 183;
 terms of, 120, 126; integrative, 152;
 undermining of, 154, 155, 180; effec-

tiveness of, 158; violations of, 158;
 nonmajor, 167, 169, 214. *See also*
 Consequences of agreements; Negotia-
 tion of agreements
Ahmed, Mohamed Sid-, 245*n*21
Al Fatah, 67
Alker, H. R., Jr., 237*n*1
Allen, Richard, 256*n*7
Allies, 36–37, 172
Allison, Graham T., 238*nn*7, 14
Ametistov, Ernest, 173
Anderson, Robert B., 131, 138
Andropov, Yuri V., 242*n*30
Angell, Robert C., 240*n*6
Antarctica treaty, 106, 124, 129, 135, 148
Anti-Communist sentiment, 61, 62, 160,
 186, 203–4
Appeasement, 2
Apter, David E., 240*n*6
Arab Cooperation Council (ACC), 225
Arab countries: goals of, 32, 198–99;
 public pressure and, 65–68; partition-

tions by, 21, 27, 28; socialization of hostility and, 23–24; changes in leadership and, 27, 36, 40, 77; identification of initiatives by, 40–42; strategic choices and, 79, 111; conciliatory gestures and, 83, 111; constituency support and, 111, 117. *See also* Constituency pressures

Gradualist strategy, 141

Graduated Reciprocation in Tension-Reduction (GRIT) strategy, 83, 112

GRIT strategy. *See* Graduated Reciprocation in Tension-Reduction strategy

Gromyko, Andrei, 240*n*5

Gusfield, Joseph R., 244*n*2

Haas, Ernst B., 240*n*7, 251*n*5

Haass, Richard, 249*n*18

Haig, Alexander, 28, 218

Halberstam, David, 239*n*24, 256*nn*1, 19

Hall, David K., 257*n*22

Halperin, Morton H., 238*n*14, 241*n*22, 251*n*3

Hammani, Said, 88

Hammer, Armand, 86

Hansen, Harry, 241*n*10

Harmon, Willis, 239*n*31

Harriman, Averell, 134

Harrod, Jeffrey, 241*n*17

Heer, N. W., 253*n*30

Heikal, Mohamed, 250*n*52, 254*n*52

Helsinki accords, 145, 192

Heyns, Terry L., 253*nn*33, 35

Hirst, David, 243*n*35, 245*n*19

Historical context, 13–15, 17–24. *See also* Domestic conditions; Global context

Hoffman, Mark S., 241*n*10

Hollins, Harry B., 256*n*14

Holloway, David, 255*n*70

Holsti, K. J., 237*n*2

Holsti, Ole R., 244*n*13, 248*n*38, 253*n*29

Hopmann, P. Terrence, 257*n*30

Horowitz, Irving Louis, 239*n*2

Hubris, 214

Hughes, Barry, 241*n*13, 244*n*1

Human rights, 27, 172–73, 193

Husbands, Jo, 244*n*3

Hussein, Saddam, 224–36

Husseini, Hatem, 255*n*21

Hussein I, King of Jordan, 32, 66, 67, 116, 132, 141, 143, 229

Ibrahim, Saad Eddin, 245*n*20

Idealist approach, 6–7. *See also* Populist approach

Ideological struggle, 23, 74; U.S.-USSR conflict and, 20, 27–28, 29, 72, 186, 242*n*30

Ikle, Fred C., 246*n*2, 249*n*6

Implementation of agreements: U.S.-USSR relations and, 157–58; Arab-Israeli relations and, 173–75; peacemaking policies and, 216

Indirect confrontation, 172

Indirect negotiations, 108, 131, 132, 144, 148

Inducements: pluralist approach and, 8; in conflict resolution approach, 10; increasing importance of, 12–13; initiation of negotiations and, 83–84, 91, 102–6, 111–15; types of, 83–84; patterns in, 91, 102–6, 111–15; negotiations without, 102, 104–5, 114; effectiveness of, 111–15; negotiation of agreements and, 125–26, 134, 149–50; survival of agreements and, 180–82; peacemaking policies and, 213, 216–18. *See also* Coercion; Persuasion; Positive sanctions

Infallah policy, 66

INF treaty, 130, 136–37, 159

Initiation of negotiations, 81–120; as phase of de-escalation, 4; ideas important to, 82–90; centrality of issues and, 86–87, 110; patterns of, 90–110, 110–17; account of patterns in, 110–17

Initiatives, 4, 34–57; domestic conditions and, 35–36, 58–69; adversary relations and, 37–40; identification of, 40–42;

Initiatives (*continued*)
    expected rejection of, 41; extended
    campaigns and, 42; in U.S.-USSR con-
    flict since *1948*, 42, 43–49, 56; vari-
    eties of, 42, 56; in Arab-Israeli conflict
    since *1948*, 50–55; multiplicity of,
    56, 76; minor, 56, 104, 113; patterns
    among, 56–57, 75–79; preconditions
    for, 58–75; theoretical perspectives on,
    75–79; frequency of, 76–78; strategic
    implications and, 79–80, 218–20; not
    leading to negotiations, 91; means of
    communication of, 102; peacemaking
    policies and, 218–20. *See also* Induce-
    ments
Institute for U.S. and Canada Studies, 20
Institutionalization of conflict, 21, 23–24,
    36, 37, 193–94
Integration, 2, 9, 18
Interconnected conflicts, 11–12, 30, 31–
    32, 71
Interest groups, 24
Intermediaries: initiatives and, 35, 36–37,
    56–57, 79–80; private individuals as,
    42; U.S.-USSR conflict and, 57, 70, 148;
    would-be, 75; in compared conflicts,
    76, 132–33; in Arab-Israeli conflict,
    104, 105, 108, 115, 131, 138, 139–42,
    148, 195, 198; as parties to negotia-
    tions, 115–16, 215–16; in negotiation
    of agreements, 128, 148, 220; conflict
    analysis and, 212; Persian Gulf conflict
    and, 232
International functionalism, 153–54
International governmental organizations,
    19, 37, 70, 108–9, 153–54, 210. *See
    also* United Nations
International Institute for Strategic Stud-
    ies, 256n4
Interpersonal approach, 6, 7. *See also*
    Populist approach
Intersocietal interaction, 13. *See also*
    Government interaction
Intifada, 89
Intransigent parties, 154, 155, 180, 216

Iran-Iraq war, 67, 200
Iraq. *See* Iran-Iraq war; Persian Gulf con-
    flict
Israel, State of: use of military force by,
    23, 196; goals of, 32; political parties
    in, 32, 68–69, 142, 143, 196, 200; le-
    gitimacy issue and, 33, 39, 76, 87; pub-
    lic pressure and, 68–69; invasion of
    Lebanon and, 75, 199–200; views of
    Arab countries in, 175; military spend-
    ing in, 175–76, 183, 206; patterns of
    conflictful and cooperative actions and,
    176–77; law of return in, 178; social
    costs of conflict and, 206. *See also*
    Arab-Israeli conflict; Israeli occupied
    territories
Israeli-Egyptian peace treaty. *See*
    Egyptian-Israeli peace treaty of *1979*
Israeli occupied territories, 30–32, 66,
    132, 142–43; Palestinian uprising in,
    67–68, 69, 79, 89, 175
Issues: multiplicity of, 11–12, 212;
    shared view of, among adversaries, 39–
    40, 119–20; centrality of, 86–87, 109–
    10, 116–17, 125; linkage of, 87–88,
    110, 125, 134, 174, 181, 183, 199; ne-
    gotiation of agreements and, 135, 149;
    conflict analysis and, 212; peacemaking
    policies and, 214–18. *See also* Goals
Issue salience: focal conflict and, 12; U.S.-
    USSR conflict and, 29; Arab-Israeli con-
    flict and, 30; initiatives and, 36, 40, 78;
    negotiation of agreements and, 135;
    Persian Gulf conflict and, 224, 228. *See
    also* Linkage

Jabber, Fuad, 242n34, 245n25, 246n33
Jackson, Elmore, 249n20
Jackson, Henry, 157
Jackson-Vanik amendment, 157, 162
Jacobsen, Carl G., 256n2
Jahn, Egbert, 241n14, 253n31
Jamgotch, Nish, Jr., 255n9
Janis, Irving L., 238n11

Parties to conflict (*continued*)
36–37, 210, 212; conflict analysis and,
212; interests of, and peacemaking policies, 213–14; in Persian Gulf conflict,
225, 231. *See also* Allies; Intermediaries

Parties to negotiation: strategic choice
and, 84–86, 115–16, 125; excluded
parties and, 86, 180, 218; types of combinations of, 106–9; intermediaries
and, 115–16; negotiation of agreements
and, 148–49; peacemaking policies
and, 215–16. *See also* Bilateral negotiation; Multilateral negotiation; Negotiation involving intermediaries;
Signatories

Patchen, Martin, 243*n*7

Pattir, Dan, 248*n*44

PDFLP. *See* Popular Democratic Front for
the Liberation of Palestine

Peace, conceptions of, 2–3, 38

Peacemaking methods, 14

Peacemaking policy: conflict analysis and,
211–12; values and, 213–14; strategic
choices and, 214–18; application of
strategies, 218–22; Persian Gulf conflict and, 228

Peace movement, 24, 40, 60, 68, 77, 118

Peace research, 192–93, 219

Pentz, Michael J., 240*n*8, 248*n*35,
253*n*45

People's Republic of China (PRC), 36, 40,
70

Peres, Shimon, 69, 132, 143, 176, 200

Peretz, Don, 256*n*24

Peri, Yoram, 245*n*28, 255*n*23, 256*n*15

Peripheral issues, 110, 116–17, 125, 128,
149, 214–15. *See also* Issue salience;
Linkage

Pershing II missiles, 38, 130, 137

Persian Gulf conflict, 223–36; transition
to de-escalation and, 2; theoretical approaches and, 224–25, 226–29; historical context and, 225–29; negotiations
in, 228, 231–32; escalation to war in,

229–32; postwar assessment of, 232–
35; postwar peace building in, 232–35

Persuasion, 12, 84, 217–18, 246*n*7

Peters, Joan, 241*n*20

PFLP. *See* Popular Front for the Liberation
of Palestine

Pipes, Richard, 238*n*6, 252*n*7, 255*n*7

PLO. *See* Palestine Liberation Organization

Pluralist approach, 7–8; initiatives and,
35–36, 37, 39, 76; domestic conditions
and, 58–59; initiation of negotiations
and, 82, 83, 84; consequences of agreements and, 153, 178–79; validity of,
210–11; Persian Gulf conflict and,
227–28, 230–31, 233–34

Polachek, Solomon W., 255*n*71

Political boundaries: ethnic groups and,
18; U.S.-USSR conflict and, 29; Arab-
Israeli conflict and, 30–32, 138, 141,
194; Persian Gulf conflict and, 225. *See
also* Israeli occupied territories

Political parties: in Israel, 32, 68–69,
142, 143, 196, 200; votes for opposition and, 59, 62. *See also* Constituency
pressures

Political recognition. *See* Legitimacy

Pollack, Allen, 254*n*63

Popular Democratic Front for the Liberation of Palestine (PDFLP), 140

Popular Front for the Liberation of Palestine (PFLP), 140

Populist approach, 6–7, 10; initiatives
and, 35, 38, 39, 76, 78; power relations
and, 38; domestic conditions and, 58–
59; initiation of negotiations and, 82,
83; consequences of agreements and,
155, 179; validity of, 209–10; Persian
Gulf conflict and, 227–28, 230–31,
233–34

Positive sanctions, 12, 83–84, 104, 148,
150

Posner, Steve, 247*nn*30, 34, 254*n*60

Power relations: global inequity in, 17;
between U.S. and USSR, 28–29, 72–73;

United Nations: role in de-escalation, 19, 212; Arab-Israeli conflict and, 56–57, 105, 108–9, 131, 139; U.S.-USSR conflict and, 70–71, 107; peacekeeping forces (UNEF), 74; Security Council resolution *242,* 89, 90, 139, 197; initiation of negotiations and, 90, 108–9; Eighteen-Nation Disarmament Committee (ENDC), 107, 129, 135; Conciliation Commission for Palestine (CCP), 108; Persian Gulf conflict and, 229, 232. *See also* Intermediaries; International governmental organizations

United States: goals in U.S.-USSR conflict, 27–28; mediation in Arab-Israeli conflict, 57, 104, 105, 108, 115, 139–41, 142–42; relation between public pressure and government action in, 59–62, 78; conciliatory gestures by, 103; trade relations with USSR, 161–63; military spending in, 164, 166–67, 182, 204; hostile and cooperative conduct toward USSR, 169, 171, 172; developments in, and accommodation, 193; PLO and, 200; role as intermediary, 228. *See also* Superpowers; U.S.-USSR conflict; U.S.-USSR relations

U.S. cruise missiles, 38, 130, 137, 158
United States Information Agency (USIA), 22
U.S. National Council of Catholic Bishops, 3
U.S.-USSR conflict: phases of de-escalation and, 4–10; conflict resolution approach to, 9; role of UN in, 19; major escalations in, 25; de-escalation initiatives in, 26–30, 42, 43–49, 56, 58–64, 69–70; adversary relations in, 26–30, 72–73, 76; changes in, 28–30, 72–73; common interests and, 30; compared with Arab-Israeli conflict, 33, 56, 76; power relations and, 38, 39; intermediaries in, 57, 70, 148; domestic conditions and, 58–64; global context, 69–70; issue linkage and, 87; major negotiations in,

92–98; initiatives by outside parties and, 105; combinations of parties to negotiation and, 107; major agreements in, 127–30; negotiation of agreements and, 133–37, 149; consequences of agreements and, 156–73; bilateral agreements, by year, 168; costs of, 203–5; U.S. goals in, 229–30
U.S.-USSR fishing agreements, 167, 179, 215
U.S.-USSR relations: Arab-Israeli conflict and, 36, 70, 71; transformation of, 103, 153, 190–91, 234; consequences of agreements and, 156–73; net cooperation score for, 169–72; cumulative movement in, 182, 183–84, 186–93; late *1970*s deterioration in, 189–90; Persian Gulf conflict and, 224, 225, 231, 234
U.S.-USSR Trade and Economic Council, 162
Ury, William, 249n6, 251n68
USSR. *See* Union of Soviet Socialist Republics (USSR)

Values, 213–14, 236
Vance, Cyrus, 238n5, 250n32
Vanik, Charles, 157
Verity, C. William, 162
Vernon, Raymond, 240n6
Vietnam War, 60–61, 62, 73, 188, 205, 234
Voice of America (VOA), 226
Volten, Peter M. E., 243n9
Voslensky, M. S., 240n8

Walbek, Norman V., 256n14
Walker, R. B. J., 241n21
Wallerstein, Immanuel, 238n13
Walliman, Isador, 257n20
Ward, Michael Don, 253n37
War deaths, 204–5, 206–7
Warner, Gale, 255n11
Warnke, Paul, 247n29